Sheltering Women

Sheltering Women

Negotiating Gender and Violence
in Northern Italy

SONJA PLESSET

STANFORD UNIVERSITY PRESS

STANFORD, CALIFORNIA 2006

Stanford University Press
Stanford, California

Printed in the United States of America on acid-free, archival-quality paper

Library of Congress Cataloging-in-Publication Data
Plesset, Sonja.
Sheltering women : negotiating gender and violence in northern Italy / Sonja Plesset.
p. cm.
Includes bibliographical references and index.
ISBN-13: 978-0-8047-5301-2 (cloth : alk. paper)
ISBN-10: 0-8047-5301-6 (cloth : alk. paper)
1. Women—Italy—Parma—Social conditions. 2. Sex role—Italy—Parma. 3. Wife abuse—Italy—Parma. 4. Abused wives—Italy—Parma. 5. Abused women—Italy—Parma. I. Title.
HQ1645.P37P44 2006
362.82′92094544—dc22

2006005164

Typeset by Bruce Lundquist in 10/12.5 Palatino

Contents

Acknowledgments

ABOVE ALL, I thank my friends and colleagues in Parma who welcomed me and enfolded me in the fabric of their lives. Without their kindness and generosity, this study would never have been possible. I am indebted to them for feeding me delicious food, teaching me phrases of *dialetto*, showing me the beautiful historic sites of Parma, taking me to the opera, inviting me for holiday meals, and caring for me in countless ways. To protect their privacy, I will not mention them by name, but I am forever grateful.

During graduate school, my thinking was shaped by the wisdom and guidance of my committee members, Michael Herzfeld, Mary Steedly, and Kay B. Warren. I want to thank them for their critical engagement with this project from the very beginning. At each stage our discussions challenged, broadened, and sharpened my thinking. These conversations stand out as the highlight of my graduate experience. I am especially indebted to my advisor, Michael Herzfeld, for his ability to provide a rare blend of guidance, critical insight, and constant encouragement by being a teacher, mentor, and friend. Michael and Nea also kept me well fed throughout my time in Cambridge with their delicious Chinese and Italian dinners. It's always a treat to spend an evening in their company.

I am also grateful to scholars in Italy who helped me think through many of my findings. Maria Minicuci has been a dear friend and mentor since the very beginning of my fieldwork. Her insightful feedback on the manuscript helped me fine-tune many aspects of my analysis. Anna Paini is a friend and colleague I met in Parma. It was a delight to have an anthropologist so close by. I greatly enjoyed her company while conducting fieldwork, and her insights into local life and the history of Italian feminism have been invaluable.

My research in Italy also benefited from many years of advice and encouragement from Davydd Greenwood, whose mentoring helped shape my early work at Cornell and motivated me to pursue graduate studies, and from David Kertzer, whose experience, insight, and deep understanding of Italian social life helped me throughout my time in the field. At Harvard, I have benefited from an unusually close cohort of peers and friends. I thank the members of my writing group, Manduhai Buyandelgeriyn, Vanessa Fong, Erica James, and Nicole Newendorp, for their critical and engaged feedback throughout the dissertation and book-writing process. Their wisdom and friendship sustained me and this project in innumerable ways. A special thanks to Kristin Gilbert, as well, whom I met at the final stages of this project. It was her patience and expertise that guided me through my final set of revisions.

As a postdoctoral fellow at the Center for Interdisciplinary Research on AIDS, Yale School of Medicine, I had the opportunity to begin a new research project while continuing with the revisions on this book. During my time at CIRA I received helpful feedback on various chapters from my mentor Kim Blankenship, as well as from Jeannette Ickovicks and my postdoctoral colleagues Joseph Hellweg, Nalini Tarakeshwar, Stephanie Milan, Yasmina Katsulis, and Kavita Misra. Participating in our interdisciplinary seminars, and listening to the insights of my colleagues from other fields, inspired new and exciting ways of thinking about my material.

There are numerous friends and colleagues who generously reviewed and re-reviewed my manuscript. I am particularly grateful to Nicole Newendorp, Vanessa Fong, Kimberley Reilly, Novita Amadei, and Mónica Renta. I am also very thankful for the helpful feedback provided by the reviewers chosen by Stanford University Press. David Sutton went above and beyond with his extremely thoughtful comments and criticisms. I also would like to thank the editors at Stanford University Press: Patricia Katayama, who first expressed interest in my project, and Kate Wahl, who helped facilitate the publication process and provided advice and encouragement throughout. I was fortunate to have Anna Eberhard Friedlander shepherd me through the final stages of production with her expert editorial advice and wisdom.

Many thanks to my friends and family—the Bergerson, Berkowitz, and Plesset families, and dear friends from Chappaqua, Ithaca, Cambridge, New York, and New Haven—who supported me in incalculable ways. Laurel Spindel, Erin McMonigal, and Cynthia Miller Idriss visited at various points during my years of frequent trips to Italy, at times even participating in fieldwork. At all stages of this project they provided sustenance and the gift of enduring friendship. I am also grateful to friends and colleagues from the Yale School of Forestry, the Harvard Expository Writing Program, and Mather House for their encouragement. Finally, my deepest gratitude goes to my sister Annie and my parents, Maxwell and Tina, who began feeding me books at a very young age. Their faith, love, and support are with me always.

Financial support for my dissertation research and writing were generously provided by a Mellon Language Training grant administered by the Department of Anthropology at Harvard University, a NIMH predoctoral fellowship administered by the Department of Social Medicine at Harvard University, a dissertation research grant from the Minda de Gunzburg Center for European Studies, a dissertation completion grant from the Josephine de Kármán Fellowship Trust, and a writing grant from the Cora Du Bois Charitable Trust. I also thank Harvard University's Expository Writing Program for a Gordon Gray Writing Grant, which supported the final phase of manuscript revisions.

Sheltering Women

Introduction

THE IDEA FOR THIS PROJECT began in 1997, when I visited the city of Bologna and noticed a large billboard in the main piazza. On the sign I saw a cartoonlike stick figure with curly hair and a long outstretched arm intended to signify resistance. Beside the figure were the words *Zero tolerance contro la violenza sulle donne* (Zero tolerance against violence against women).[1] I was immediately intrigued by this very public display of protest. Though I had come to Bologna to study an entirely different topic,[2] I decided to call the number listed on the billboard in order to find out more about the "Zero Tolerance" campaign. I had a long-standing interest in gender and women's lives, and decided to investigate what the campaign was all about. My curiosity led me to Bologna's Casa delle Donne (Women's House) and to the regional and national network of women's organizations that exist throughout Italy. I soon discovered that Bologna was one of many cities in Emilia-Romagna with an active domestic violence program. After several weeks of travel throughout the region, I eventually settled in Parma, a historically leftist city[3] with just the right population size, history, and layout for an ethnographic study of community reactions to intimate-partner violence.

Parma is small, but not too small, with just enough people (approximately 170,000) to qualify as an urban setting and yet retain the intimate feeling of a town where people know one another and serendipitous meetings can occur on a regular basis. With its historic *piazza del duomo*, open-air market, and numerous parks and gathering spots within walking distance of each other, the city makes it easy to meet up with people and move among various locations on a daily basis.

Parma is known throughout Italy and the world for its wealth and sophistication.[4] Residents of Parma pride themselves on their high quality of life, their passion for opera, and their gastronomical delicacies.[5] As I continued to spend time in Parma, I realized that my project would entail studying intimate-partner violence in precisely the place where it supposedly does not occur—a wealthy city that prides itself on being modern, socially progressive, and quintessentially European. Although most people I spoke with recognized violence against women to be an important social issue, many told me it was a problem that primarily existed in the southern regions of Italy. Quite a few, in fact, suggested I change my field site to a town in Calabria or Sicily in order to get a sense of "real" gender inequality and oppression. Such essentialist rhetoric is widespread throughout the Italian peninsula and has been used by academics and politicians alike to account for socioeconomic, political, and social differences between northern and southern Italy (Schneider 1998).

After two months of preliminary research conducted in November and December of 1998, I returned to Parma in August of 1999 and began what I thought would be a year of fieldwork focused on community responses to heterosexual intimate-partner violence.[6] Soon after arriving, I became a volunteer with Parma's two main service providers for battered women: the leftist or communist organization known as Women United and the Catholic organization known as Family Aid. In addition to supplying food, housing, and counseling, these two organizations gave women an opportunity to explore their own histories and chart new trajectories for the future. Although clients were ostensibly free to make their own decisions about their lives, the particular choices they made were routinely criticized, often in sharply opposing ways, by caseworkers, board members, and volunteers. I soon discovered that the ideological vision of what it means—or *should* mean—to be a woman in Italian society, as elsewhere, was highly contested ground. For the women working within Women United, the feminist movement had opened the door for women to exist independently of men. Motherhood and marriage were seen as choices and not necessities. For the women working within Family Aid, motherhood was a woman's most important duty. Although self-sufficiency was important, especially in cases of partner violence, ultimate success lay in finding a new male mate and perpetuating the nuclear family.

My project began to take shape around what mattered most to the people I was working with. I began to draw links between the contrasting visions of gender, family, and hierarchy that I was observing within Women United and Family Aid, and the ambivalence about gender relations that I was noting in the larger society. What was originally a project focused on intimate-partner violence expanded to encompass questions about gender relations, Italian feminism, and the laws that govern marriage and family. Rather than soften the focus on violence, this expansion served to provide a more nuanced setting and allowed me to contextualize violence as one part of a continuum of hierarchy and subordination.

Violence means different things in different parts of the world (Riches 1986; Gilsenan 2002), but violence also means different things when examined from different vantage points within a particular cultural context. According to David Riches, "Anglo-Saxon understandings indicate that 'physical hurt done to others' counts as violence only in certain social contexts," meaning that when the physical hurt is considered illegitimate, only then is it understood as violence (1986:3). In many cases, the state may determine a boundary between what is considered merely force or physical hurt (legitimate) and what is considered violence (illegitimate) that is at odds with individual experience. In Italy, the legal system recognizes violence within the home only when the physical hurt is repetitive and intentional. At the same time there are women's centers that determine a broad range of unacceptable and hence illegitimate acts. In her work on domestic violence in nineteenth- and twentieth-century Hawaii, Sally Engle Merry suggests that "a continuing tension is created by the disjunction between legal processes that attempt to define the legal meaning of wife battering solely in physical terms and the experiential meaning of violence that is rooted in conceptions of masculinity, femininity, and the family" (1994:970).

Just as there may be a divergence between law and individual experience, there may also be divergences among individuals living within a particular cultural context. There are some women who accept the blows they receive as part of the "sacrifice" they must make in order to keep their family intact. There are others who live with violence for long periods of time before recognizing their experiences as unacceptable and deciding to request a separation. And there are still others who immediately interpret physical hurt inflicted by a husband or partner as illegitimate violence. There is, of course, an even fuller range of understandings among men and women who have been performers, observers, and non-observers of physical acts of harm. As Michael Gilsenan suggests, the study of violence can "tell us much about the ways in which groups and persons organize and imagine themselves, constitute relations of power and hierarchy, and create social identities and meanings" (2002:99).

Violence itself, however, can be difficult to study and even more difficult to write about (Daniel 1996; Gilsenan 2002). This book is not an "ethnography of violence"; nor is it an "anthropography of violence" along the lines of what Daniel (1996) produced from his work on collective violence in Sri Lanka. Instead, it attempts to study violence as one aspect of a larger system of hierarchy and power that exists in a particular form in Italy, but also exists in many different forms in many different parts of the world. Violence against women that occurs within the home and is performed by intimates is an act that takes place in villages, towns, and cities around the globe. By situating my study in Italy, I do not wish to suggest it is any more or less pervasive in Italy than it is in the United States, Europe, South America, Asia, or anywhere else. Statistics on intimate-partner violence are notoriously difficult to compile, and attempts to pinpoint locations where such violence might be more severe risk falling into the trap of what Daniel suggests an ethnography of violence might produce. As he suggests about his own research,

> To see the ultimate significant effects of this work as ethnographic would exculpate other peoples in other places whose participation in collective violence is of the same sort; even more dangerously, it could tranquilize those of us who live self-congratulatory lives in times and countries apparently free of the kind of violence that has seized Sri Lanka recently, could lull us into believing that we or our country or our people were above such brutalities. (Daniel 1996:7)

When I tell people in the United States that my work focuses on intimate-partner violence in Italy, many are anxious to know what I "discovered" through my research. "Is it a big problem in Italy?" some inquire. Others suggest, "It's much worse over there, isn't it?" Some are even hopeful I may have discovered a solution, and ask, "Did you find out why it happens?" I find such questions uncomfortable, but I do my best to explain that violence against intimates is a problem in many places, no more and no less significant in Italy than in our own backyards. Although violence itself, whether collective or personal, is "in many ways incoherent, nondescribable, defiant of sense-making" (Merry 1994:970–971), I hope that by situating violence within one particular cultural context, and underscoring the importance of recognizing intimate-partner violence as a nearly ubiquitous phenomenon whose meaning is shaped in local cultural realities, we can learn how

individuals negotiate, question, resist, and cope with behaviors that often defy explanation. At the same time, I am hopeful that we can understand some of the larger social processes that intersect with the shaping
of individual subjectivities and move toward creating locally relevant
systems and avenues of support.

In his discussion of how anthropologists can approach the study of
violence, Michael Gilsenan aptly notes that "our own anthropological
listening leads us to examine in great detail people's own narratives of
violence within and among communities and persons," and while "we
try to elicit the images and memories of those who do not necessarily
have a public voice," at the same time "such inquiries run the risk of
voyeurism and a kind of pornography, of probing acute personal and
collective traumas only to write in a way that appeals to a reader's un-
easy sense of exploitation" (2002:109–110). Gilsenan is right to remind
us of this risk, but we must also respect the agency of the individuals
we work with and allow their own theoretical musings to structure our
retelling of their lives. Rather than fit the narratives I was privy to into
some preexisting theoretical framework, I found that each narrative
contained its own theories—about violence, about gender, and about
making sense of daily life.

In this book, I provide the political, cultural, historical, and legal
contexts for understanding two indigenous explanations for intimate-
partner violence: first, that violence against women reflects the cultural
and historical gender inequalities embedded in Italian society, including what some termed "old-fashioned" or "traditional" understandings of masculinity; and second, that violence against women reflects
confusion and ambivalence about "new" or "modern" forms of gender
relations. The first explanation places the blame on tradition; the second
cites the transition to modernity as the culprit. Both emphasize societal
understandings of gender and emphasize collective, rather than individual, responsibility.

It is now widely accepted that modernity encompasses gendered processes, and that conceptions of gender are often used by state and local
actors to symbolize and make sense of modernity. Lisa Rofel, among
others, has demonstrated that "gender differentiation—the knowl-
edges, relations, meanings, and identities of masculinity and femininity—operates at the heart of modernity's power" (1999:19). But just as
understandings of gender can be used to lay claim to particular visions
of modernity, so can understandings of modernity be used to lay claim
to particular visions of gender. In this book, I am primarily interested

in the latter approach, specifically how local agents use the categories of tradition and modernity as rhetorical strategies to negotiate gender relations and gender change. Rather than presuppose any characteristic that is common to "modernity" or "tradition," I take these categories as ways of thinking about time, change, identity, and subjectivity.

As categories that are filled with meaning by both state and local actors, tradition and modernity are often used in strategic ways to help make sense of daily social life. Although this book is about the *uses* of tradition and modernity, and engages many of the oppositions within Parma and Italian society at large, through my fieldwork I realized that it was the overlap of these oppositions that would provide the most insight into the realities of everyday life. I could have written about modernity and tradition, or communism and Catholicism, or Women United and Family Aid (indeed such oppositions appear again and again in the pages that follow), but such a book would not have accurately represented my experience in the field. Although these oppositions clearly existed, and were referenced repeatedly by friends and colleagues, I also observed many moments of overlap in which the oppositions became flexible tools for individuals on the ground. This volume focuses on the moments of overlap, the gray areas where oppositions that were once distinct no longer appeared as orderly, and the boundaries between seemingly rigid categories actually became quite permeable. Ultimately, this book is about gender change in Parma and the challenges, frustrations, and successes people experienced as they negotiated such change in their daily lives.

Structure of the Book

Chapter 1 first sets the stage with an introduction to the daily rhythms of Parma, an overview of my fieldwork methodology (what I've termed "fieldwork through networks"), and a discussion of the theoretical frameworks within which I situate my research.

The book continues, in Chapter 2, with a history of the "postfeminist" period of Italian society. Through the narratives of former feminist activists living in Parma, I explain my use of this term, trace a broad sketch of Italian feminism, and outline the key political opposition (communist vs. Catholic) that divided Italian society for close to half a century. In Chapter 3, I move to a discussion of the ideologies of gender and family that informed daily practice within Women United and Family Aid. A detailed look at the methodologies of these organizations and at the services they provide offers vivid examples of the negotiation of gender proficiency that was underway in the 1990s. Women United was founded by women with political roots in the Italian Communist Party who endeavored to recognize gender difference and build solidarity among women. Family Aid, on the other hand, was founded by women with strong connections to Catholicism who anchored their mission in the preservation of life and the production of "good" mothers.

In chapters 4 and 5, I turn to the layers of shame many women experience when faced with a violent husband or partner. Shaped by the confluence of, on the one hand, local Catholic norms that allow a husband to hit his wife for purposes of "education," and, on the other, feminist ideals that proclaim women's independence from men, the shame many feel is complex, difficult to displace, and only compounded by the inconsistencies of the Italian legal system.

In the final chapter, I consider the sites of resistance I discovered through my participation in daily life at Women United and Family Aid. As microcosms of society at large, the two organizations revealed the rigidity and malleability of gender relations in Italian society.

Although the chapters in this book are largely ethnographic, the theoretical subtext reveals how ordinary Italians used the categories of tradition and modernity as organizing tropes to talk about gender, hierarchy, and violence during a time of significant social and political change. As the people of Parma dealt with declining birthrates, the fall of Italy's dominant postwar political parties, new economic realities, and the legal and social victories of the feminist movement, gender became a site for the articulation of difference on political, regional, and local levels. This book examines such articulations as they played out in women's organizations, marriages, heterosexual partnerships, families, and courtrooms.

Though I have not attempted to disguise the name of the city, all names and locations of individuals and institutions have been changed in order to protect the identities of the people who so generously opened their lives to me. On occasion, I have created composite identities or disguised certain biographical facts in order to further protect the identities of my friends and colleagues. All my research was conducted in standard Italian with occasional phrases of dialect (most people in Parma use standard Italian), and all translations of conversations, interviews, and Italian publications (unless otherwise indicated) are my own.

Engaging the Field

A PARMA SI VA IN BICI (in Parma you bike) was a phrase I heard over and over during my fourteen months of fieldwork. When I arrived for the very first time in Parma, I was struck by the sight of so many people on bicycles. Cyclists took their place as part of traffic and were not afraid to ride directly beside buses and cars, in the streets of the historic city center as well as on major roads leading out of town. During other trips to Italy, I had grown accustomed to the constant whir of *motorini* (scooters) and *moto* (motorcycles), but Parma was the first city I visited where an ordinary one-speed bicycle seemed to be the dominant mode of transportation. I saw parents riding with children in child seats (at times with one child in front and another in back), men and women biking to work in suits and dresses, elderly ladies on bicycles bundled up in fur coats and hats, and nuns riding with their black dresses and habits flowing behind them in the wind. Although I first found the city's emphasis on its wealth and sophistication incongruous with the widespread practice of bicycle riding, as I learned more about daily life in Parma—the importance of keeping up appearances and reproducing centuries-old "traditions"—I came to understand bicycle riding as one of many aspects of local life that illustrate the ongoing construction of personhood and identity.

The daily *passeggiata* or stroll through the streets of the city center is another example of how residents of Parma fill the categories of modernity and tradition with locally informed symbols and meanings. Except for Sunday mornings, when the streets possess an eerie calm, Parma is often full of people doing errands, walking to work, meeting friends and family, and going shopping. During the week the pulse of the city changes throughout the day. The streets are bustling throughout the early hours, especially just before 1:00 PM when people hurry to get home in time for the midday meal. Then there is a two-hour lull in the afternoon when shops and offices close for the *pausa pranzo* (lunch break) and many people are home eating and relaxing. By 3:00 or 3:30 the streets are busy again with people returning to work or continuing with the day's errands. In the early evening, the streets again fill with people, but this time people walk at a more leisurely pace as they engage in the daily *passeggiata* and stroll through the city with family and friends.[1]

Although for many residents an evening *passeggiata* is a part of the week's daily rhythm, Saturdays are special. Children are in school and many businesses are open on Saturday mornings, but by Saturday afternoon the weekend has officially begun. The sidewalks fill with couples, families, and groups of friends. As people stroll up and down Via Cavour and the uppermost section of Strada della Repubblica, they frequently stop to chat with a friend or acquaintance or to look inside a shop window.[2]

Some call the weekend *passeggiata* the fashion show of Parma, as people often dress in fashionable, name-brand clothing in order to *fare bella figura* as they stroll through the city streets.[3] *Fare bella figura*, which literally translates as "to make a beautiful figure," is an expression used commonly throughout Italy. According to Sydel Silverman, "The concern with one's *bella figura*, or 'good face,' is ever-present as a quite self-conscious guide to behavior. The concept is a measure of personal integrity, but it has little to do with one's essence, character, intention, or other inner condition; rather it centers upon public appearances. To acquire and preserve *bella figura* requires being impeccable before the eyes of others" (Silverman 1975:40).

Whereas in English one might use the expression "to look good" or "to make a good impression," there is no direct equivalent for *fare bella figura*, which connotes the performative aspect of putting on a good display for neighbors, colleagues, friends, and anyone who happens to notice. The expression also can be used with respect to cities, countries, and institutions. For instance, Italy may *fare bella figura* by performing in a certain way to a worldwide audience. In Parma, when people spoke to me about the way they acted in a particular situation they might say, *ho fatto bella figura* (I cut a fine figure). Use of *bella figura* can also refer to a more generic mode of acting or behaving, as in *quando fai bella figura* (when you cut a fine figure, or, when you make a good showing). The same is true for *brutta figura*, to cut a poor figure. An individual or an institution may *fare brutta figura*, and an individual can also *fare brutta figura* for a larger entity by behaving in a particular way.[4] For example, when the president of the multinational Parmalat was arrested on fraud charges, he cut a bad figure not only for himself and his family, but also for Parma and the rest of Italy.

Although residents frequently emphasize Parma's status as a "modern" European city, at the same time they also draw links to particular notions of the past. In Parma, *bella figura* involves the strategic performance of modernity as well as of tradition. While it is imperative to be well versed in certain aspects of "tradition," it is also important to demonstrate particular aspects of a "modern" lifestyle. For example, one must speak the local dialect of Parma, but one must know when, how, and with whom to use it. And not only is it important to engage in the traditional *passeggiata*, but one must also display a mastery of the latest fashions and styles while participating in the *passeggiata*.

The importance of *bella figura* may be particularly significant in Parma not only because of the city's history but also because of its wealth and reputation in international markets.[5] When I spoke with Parmigiani about the city of Parma, they often told me, at times apologetically, that Parma is a city that "puts on airs" and "looks down" on other nearby cities. Many explained that residents of the neighboring city Reggio Emilia come from a "farming culture," whereas Parma has an aristocratic history that makes its citizens feel as if they are better than everyone else.[6] Parma was a capital city during the reign of Maria Luigia (Empress Marie Louise), and this feeling of superiority has been reproduced in the contemporary era with the growth of several of Parma's small, family-run firms, such as Barilla and Parmalat, into global enterprises.

In Gloria Nardini's exploration of the significance of *bella figura* in Italy, she defines *bella figura* as "a construct that refers to face, looking good, putting on the dog, style, appearance, flair, showing off, ornamentation, etiquette, keeping up with the Joneses, image, illusion, esteem, social status, reputation—in short, self-presentation and identity, performance and display" (Nardini 1999:7). Although Nardini's definition of *bella figura* may sound like an essentializing depiction of Italians as being overly concerned with self display, it is important to note that although the phrase itself is used by Italians in towns and cities throughout the peninsula, the actions associated with making a *bella* or *brutta figura* shift according to place and context as well as by gender, age, and class (11).[7]

Much as the concept of "taste" is discussed by Bourdieu (1986) as a way in which individuals produce and maintain class boundaries, *bella figura* may be viewed as part of a system of class distinction and hierarchy. *Bella figura*, however, encompasses far more than habits, attitudes, tastes, and preferences in food, leisure activities, reading material, fashion, and so on, for it is intricately tied to performance and the way tastes and preferences are enacted and displayed. It is not enough to simply enjoy opera; one must attend the performances at Parma's Teatro Reggio in fashionable attire and spend time during intermissions mingling in the entrance area in order to cut a *bella figura*.

For the upper classes in Parma, cutting a *bella figura* means wearing the right brand-name clothing, going on a *settimana bianca* (ski vacation, literally "white week") in the winter, going to a beach house in Liguria in the summer, belonging to the right tennis and swim club, and frequenting particular circles of people. For people of almost all social classes, particularly women, cutting a *bella figura* means serving an abundant meal when company is over and maintaining an immaculate household. For many teenagers, it means riding a scooter, owning a particular type of cell phone, and frequenting particular bars and clubs. For practicing Catholics, it means going to church on Sunday and engaging in volunteer activities through the church or other religious organizations. And for former communists, it means being politically active and volunteering for cooperatives and other leftist volunteer associations. As one of Nardini's informants explained, *bella figura* "is like a Sunday dress almost, something you put on to masquerade what you actually are; you try to be part of the group that already has the social status that you are looking for" (Nardini 1999:10). In her work on the wealthy central-Italian town of Prato, Elizabeth Krause notes a similar attention to display and performance. Krause points to "acquiring appliances, designing and caring for the home, displaying taste through clothing, and participating in leisure activities" (2005:74) as particularly important.

Bella figura has much to do with class, but it is also highly gendered. For women, maintaining a *bella figura* can mean making sure one's children are dressed in clean, pressed clothes, taking good care of parents and in-laws, and keeping a clean and orderly home. Carole Counihan

(2004) details the many ways that Florentine women struggled to meet exacting standards for household chores throughout the 1980s and into the twenty-first century. There are also numerous ways that *bella figura* can affect women living with partner or spousal abuse.

During my volunteer work at Women United, caseworkers told me how difficult it can be for women to come forward and admit the violence of their husbands or partners. They explained that many women are reluctant to seek help from friends, relatives, or local agencies out of fear that it will cast a negative light on their families. Although it is difficult for women of all social classes to ask for help, the caseworkers speculated that it may be particularly difficult for upper-class women and those who have participated in the feminist movement. Coming forward with a story of violence means asking for help from a stranger, admitting a period of acquiescence or acceptance of violence, and acknowledging a failure to anticipate a man's violence before falling in love or getting married. Many women endure the violence silently rather than admit that for years they remained quiet and hoped their husbands would change.

Although the movement against intimate-partner violence is relatively new to Italy, within the region of Emilia-Romagna there have been numerous publicity campaigns, such as Bologna's Zero Tolerance initiative, that have raised awareness about the presence of violence in women's daily lives. Such campaigns have helped encourage women to seek help, but, ironically, the more "modern" a woman thinks she is, the more difficult she might find it to ask for assistance.

Intimate-Partner Violence

Despite the ubiquity of domestic violence and the plethora of publications on it by social workers, psychologists, lawyers, sociologists, and others, anthropologists have only slowly begun to consider the issue an important area of research. Dorothy Ayers Counts, Judith K. Brown, and Jacquelyn C. Campbell (1992) put together one of the first anthropological volumes devoted to cultural perspectives on wife beating; Matthew Gutmann (1996, 1997a, 1997b) addresses the issue in his work on gender and masculinity; and Laura McClusky (2001) wrote one of the first full-length ethnographies of intimate-partner violence that contextualizes narratives of violence within a larger cultural framework. Aside from these pioneering works, few anthropologists have placed intimate-partner violence at the center of their ethnographic studies.

In her work on domestic violence in a Mayan village in Belize, Mc-Clusky (2001) suggests several reasons for the dearth of anthropological work on intimate-partner violence. One potential explanation she raises centers on ethics and whether studies of unpleasant aspects of a particular culture might conflict with anthropologists' mission to protect and support the people they study. McClusky finds such an explanation difficult to accept, as anthropologists have addressed many distasteful aspects of local cultures, including war, mutilation, and many other forms of violence. Instead, McClusky suggests that "perhaps domestic violence is not exotic enough. Unlike foot binding, unlike suttee, unlike cannibalism, we ourselves perform this ugliness, just like 'exotic' cultures" (2001:7). It is an intriguing suggestion, but I find that this explanation also falls short, as there are many "ugly" aspects of our own culture that we have no problem studying in others. What about racism? What about class oppression? Clearly such topics have received ample attention from anthropologists working in areas throughout the world, including the United States.

The puzzle of why anthropologists have largely avoided the topic of intimate-partner violence may have something to do with the discipline's long history of subordinating topics central to women's lives, but I find that it also has much to do with the following factors. First, intimate-partner violence is extremely difficult to study. As Sarah Hautzinger (2003) points out in her review of McClusky's book, such acts often take place in very private temporal and physical spaces. Unless one is actually working at a women's shelter, it is difficult to obtain narratives of abuse. Even when one does gain access to women experiencing violence, it is difficult to record the narratives of women who are in the midst of such tremendous crisis and upheaval. I myself found it morally unsavory to ask women to tell me their life histories at the precise moment in which they had left their partners and uprooted their lives. Some women went into hiding, deathly afraid that their partners would somehow track them down, while others continued with their jobs but were unable to return home to visit friends, family members, and neighbors. I felt that even broaching the topic of a life-history interview could put these women in a bind, given my dual role as a shelter volunteer and anthropological researcher.

Second, anthropologists' preferred method of data collection is engaged observation of the micro-level details of daily life. It is difficult to correlate such an approach with the realities of intimate-partner violence. Where does an anthropologist situate herself? How can she participate in daily life? Some social workers, sociologists, and others focus on decontextualized case studies, with the goal of producing explanatory models; such an approach is indeed possible in the shelter environment, but clearly this will not work for anthropologists hoping to gain access to the mundane but intimate spaces of everyday life. In order to engage in participant observation, and situate narratives of violence in a larger cultural field, we must devise ways of doing so without placing ourselves or our informants in danger.

Third, and perhaps most vexing, intimate-partner violence is nearly universal in that it takes place on a regular basis in places throughout the world (Desjarlais et al. 1995), yet it clearly operates in diverse ways and within diverse cultural logics. Similar to the conundrum of gender itself, intimate-partner violence raises a question many feminist scholars have grappled with: how do we make sense of this violence as both a locally constructed issue and a phenomenon with universal significance?

As Harriet Lyons explains in her foreword to the second edition of the volume edited by Counts, Brown, and Campbell, "anthropologists who wish to study maltreatment of women cross-culturally are stuck between the proverbial rock and its corresponding hard place" (Lyons 1999:vii). On the one hand, declaring the abuse of women to be a universal problem clashes with anthropology's focus on the particularities of moral worlds. On the other hand, refusing to define violence against women as a problem of pandemic proportions masks the pain and suffering of millions of women. Clearly the solution is not for anthropologists to become involved in the search for universal causality and predictive models. Such an approach goes against much of what the discipline has endeavored to accomplish over the past century. Instead, it seems that what anthropology can offer is an in-depth look at how people talk about and make sense of violence in everyday life. Just as anthropologists study the violence of war, poverty, and the state and ask "how subjectivity—the felt interior experience of the person that includes his or her positions in a field of relational power—is produced through the experience of violence and the manner in which global flows involving images, capital, and people become entangled with local logics in identity formation" (Das and Kleinman 2000:1), so must we study and question the violence that occurs in the home. Our mandate, it seems, is twofold: first, we must endeavor to subject violence among intimates to the same theoretical and methodological rigor we use to assess other forms of global violence, and second, we must make our studies accessible to people who can apply the knowledge to locally formed and informed interventions.

When I asked people in Parma why a husband or a boyfriend might hit, slap, kick, threaten, or berate his female partner, the explanations I heard often focused on ideas of tradition and modernity. Some spoke harshly against "traditional" gender norms that approved of male violence for purposes of "education," while others expressed hesitation about a shift to "modernity" that has left men confused and in search of an identity. Images of tradition and modernity thus emerged as prominent themes in the everyday logics of individuals experiencing, committing, and observing gendered violence. It is for this reason that I situate my work on intimate-partner violence in Parma within the larger context of the critique and counter-critique of modernization theory and build on the work of David Sutton (1996, 1998), Vassos Argyrou (1996), Deniz Kandiyoti (1997, 2002), Jane Collier (1997), and others who see "tradition" and "modernity" as categories used by local actors to negotiate political, economic, and social change.

Intimate-Partner Violence in Italy

As Linda Gordon (1988) suggests, family violence is both historically and politically constructed. Definitions of family violence—what is and is not acceptable—as well as explanations, excuses, and responses, vary through both time and space. In her work, Gordon calls attention to what she terms the "depoliticization of family-violence scholarship"— namely, the failure to examine family violence within a particular political and social context. As Gordon points out, the "discovery" of child abuse in the United States in the 1960s and the public discussion surrounding family violence assumed that the problem was a new one. Many examined family violence as if it "were a social problem above politics, upon which 'objective' scientific expertise could be brought to bear" (Gordon 1988:4). As Elizabeth Pleck (1987) illustrates, there were actually two other points in American history when family violence was highlighted as a social ill.

During the period from 1640 to 1680, Puritans passed laws against wife and child abuse, and the period between 1874 and 1890 saw the creation of societies for the prevention of cruelty to children (SPCC's) as well as outreach efforts to women suffering domestic violence (Pleck 1987:4). Pleck suggests that the reason for increased attention to violence within the home during particular historical periods may have something to do with an increase in rates of prevalence, but advises that this explanation is not always empirically supportable. Instead, she suggests that it may have more to do with the presence (or absence) of a particular social and political atmosphere. For example, the Puritans of Massachusetts Bay had certain religious and moral principles that gave rise to laws aimed at curbing family violence, even though the rate of household murder in the community was quite low. Pleck notes that regardless of whether domestic crime rates were high or low, "in all the reform periods, small organizations and dedicated individuals . . . made family violence a social issue that demanded public attention" (1987:5). By considering the political and historical construction of family violence, as well as the "ebb-and-flow pattern of concern about family violence over the last century" (Gordon 1988:2), scholars such as Gordon and Pleck demonstrate the importance of situating studies of family violence within the overall political and social climate of a given society.

In Italy, the most recent movement against intimate-partner violence began in the second half of the 1980s, when groups of women previously involved in the Italian women's movement began to set up local *telefoni rosa* (telephone hotlines), *centri anti-violenza* (antiviolence centers), and *case delle donne e rifugi* (drop-in centers and shelters) (Terragni 1997b; Romito 2000). By the 1990s there were more than eighty centers located in various cities and towns throughout the peninsula, roughly one-quarter of which offered housing in *case rifugio*, or apartments with secret addresses (Romito 2000:109). Many of the centers collaborated with local public and private entities such as the police force, emergency-room personnel, social workers, and, at times, Catholic shelters and family support agencies.

Despite the growth of the movement against violence against women in Italy, statistics that document the prevalence of intimate-partner violence are still very difficult to locate. Aside from the publications of local *centri anti-violenza* and *case delle donne*, only a handful of researchers have focused their attention on gathering quantitative or qualitative data on the violence against women that takes place within families and households. Carmine Ventimiglia (1988, 1996, 2002), who was a sociologist at the University of Parma for many years, stands out as one of the most influential among the scholars who first brought the topic of family violence to national attention. Other important Italian scholars include Tina Bassi (1993, 1997), Patrizia Romito (2000), and Laura Terragni (1997a, 1997b), who are working to expand the field of study.

There are a number of reasons for the dearth of data on intimate-partner violence in Italy. For one, it is a problem that only began to be recognized in the country in the late 1980s. In Italy, as in many other parts of the world, violence against women was (and is) an accepted part of daily life for many people. In addition, nearly all the work that has been done to raise awareness and help women living with violence has been done by independent, nonprofit women's groups that work with very limited funding. Although most, if not all, of these groups keep detailed records on the numbers of women they see on a daily basis, few centers have the time or money to devote to research and analysis. Their first concern, and rightly so, is the women coming to the centers in need of help. And, of course, it is widely known that intimate-partner violence is underreported throughout the world; while some women press charges against their husbands and/or seek assistance from local agencies, many others continue living with the violence or leave their partners without ever reporting their experiences.

In Italy, the documentation problem may be particularly difficult because of the structure of the legal system. Although there are specific and serious crimes that men (and women) who abuse their partners can be accused of, such crimes are categorically broad and difficult to track. One such category is the crime of *maltrattamenti in famiglia* (mistreatments within the family), which is often used in cases of intimate-partner violence but is extremely difficult to prove and requires that the accuser demonstrate a prolonged climate of intentional violence. Patrizia Romito, a researcher from the University of Trieste who has focused much of her work on sexual and domestic violence in Italy, explains that although the crime is considered serious, and its prosecution can proceed *d'ufficio* (with or without an individual pressing charges), in reality this rarely occurs (Romito 2000:81). The police are reluctant to intervene in family situations and rarely keep accurate records that could be used to prove continuous and intentional violence. According to research conducted in 1991, between 1981 and 1987 there were 20,007 *denuncie* (charges) of *maltrattamenti in famiglia* in the entire country and only 2,773 convictions. This amounts to roughly a 14 percent conviction rate in cases of intimate-partner violence (Terragni 1997b:187).

The official numbers represent only a very small fraction of the violence that women experience on a daily basis. As Terragni points out, from 1984 to 1994 there were an average of 2,184 official reports per year of *maltrattamenti in famiglia* recorded for all of Italy (1997b:188). However, data for the year 1995 from two organizations—the Casa delle donne maltrattate di Milano and the Casa delle donne di Bologna—reveal that in just these two cities a combined total of more than 1,200 women sought help in one year alone. Such figures indicate that many women who experience violence and seek help from women's centers do not press charges with the police. As with most places in the world, we have no reliable way of estimating the prevalence of intimate-partner violence in Italy, but even if we measured just the numbers of women seeking help from the *centri anti-violenza* and *case delle donne* that exist in various cities throughout the peninsula, we could easily come up with numbers that exceed 8,000 or 10,000 per year.[8]

Despite the growth of *centri anti-violenza* and *case delle donne* and the work they do to help women and raise awareness, there are still many stories of women who turn to family members, emergency rooms, police stations, or local parishes and are told to endure for the sake of the family. Patrizia Romito recorded numerous narratives of violence during her research in Trieste. One woman explained, "He bit me terribly, I was afraid and took off. I went to my father's house. I wanted to stay there but he told me not to put him in the middle. He told me I should go back home because he's my husband." Another mentioned that her mother-in-law "knew what happened at our house but she stayed quiet because she was scared her son would return home. She told me that he has a difficult personality and that she knows because he used to hit her for many years but at the end of the conversation, her final comment was: If you two split up, I'll die of a broken heart." Still another described her experience at the hospital: "One evening I went to the emergency room beaten all over and the doctor told me: 'Signora, don't press charges, he's your husband.' Exact words. At that point I felt like a worm, I got up and went back home" (all quotes from Romito 2000:74–75).

Of course, not all family members and public agencies respond in this way. According to Romito, between 70 and 90 percent of the women she interviewed who had experienced violence spoke with someone about their experiences—family members, friends, police and hospital personnel, teachers, and other public officials—and about one-quarter received helpful support (Romito 2000:77).

Modernity and *Mentalità*

When I questioned women and shelter workers about the tremendous variation in the way institutions and individuals responded to intimate-partner violence, their answers invariably invoked the idea of *mentalità,* or mentality.[9] Although the Italians I worked with rarely spoke about a national Italian mentality, I repeatedly heard people in Parma cast class differences, generational differences, political differences, and regional differences as differences of *mentalità.*[10] When a woman from Calabria came to Women United, the caseworkers attributed her reluctance to leave her husband to her southern *mentalità.* When a young man spoke to me about the differences between his own relationship with his wife and that of his parents, he referred to generational differences in *mentalità.* And when a feminist lawyer spoke to me about particular judges who were unlikely to issue convictions in cases of domestic violence, she too spoke about *mentalità.* As used in Parma, the word *mentalità* encompassed more than just an outlook or frame of mind. Although it was often used to create boundaries of inclusion and exclusion, when my friends and colleagues spoke of *mentalità* they were referring not only to the ways in which individuals comprehend and interpret the world, but also to the decisions, actions, and utterances that flow from these interpretations.

In her work on the villagers of Los Olivos, Spain, Jane Collier (1997) provides a helpful example of how to study mentality as a device used in the construction of difference. In her study of the uses of tradition and modernity, Collier found that the younger generations differentiated themselves from their parents and grandparents by displaying a difference in "mentality" and through their determination to "think for themselves" rather than follow custom or the expectations of their elders. She also found that both proponents and critics of this "new" way of thinking "attributed the change in 'mentality' to a loosening of constraints on people's freedom to act as they wanted. Those who approved of the changes celebrated their liberation. . . . they painted a happy picture of progress from repression to freedom. Those who criticized the change complained of moral decline" (Collier 1997:5). Although Collier herself argues that people "always both think for themselves and let others think for them," the contrast she discovered between villagers who took stands on the two sides of the moral dilemma became a way to understand modern subjectivity, changes in family life, and the locally negotiated boundaries of tradition and modernity.

Among the people I worked with in Parma, as for most people, the divide between tradition and modernity was often framed in terms of the "old" versus the "new" way of doing things. People differentiated between doing things the old-fashioned way (*all'antica* or *nel vecchio stile*) and doing things in the style of today, and related these differences in style to differences in mentality. Like the villagers of Los Olivos, the people of Parma used mentality as a device to construct the dichotomy between tradition and modernity and place people on either side of the heuristic divide. As Kandiyoti explains in her work on the construction of tradition and modernity in Turkey, "the fact remains that attributions of 'tradition' and 'modernity' continue to be part of a political struggle over different visions of the 'good society'" (1997:129). In her extensive discussion of the *passeggiata* in a small central-Italian town, Giovanna Del Negro uses the promenade itself as a site for the negotiation of modernity and social change. For Del Negro, the *passeggiata* provides a key to understanding "how culture informs the ways in which modernity is manifested in a particular locale and the meanings that on-the-ground actors might give to that modernity" (2004:40).

In Parma, a distinction was often drawn between parents of the "old style" and parents "of today." An "old-fashioned" or "traditional" father was often described with the popular phrase *padre padrone*, which denotes a father who is authoritarian, controlling, and master (*padrone*) of the family. When the people I interviewed described this type of father, they spoke of a strict division of roles inside the home whereby the wife catered to every whim of her husband, from cooking and serving all his meals to drawing his bath and laying out his clothing and shoes in the morning. Men in this type of family were responsible for working outside the home; women often controlled nearly every aspect of household management. Many of the younger men I spoke with identified themselves as belonging to a new generation of fathers—fathers who helped out with household activities and took an interest in caring for their children. Those who favored the "old-fashioned" or "traditional" style of marriage and division of roles expressed concern about the blurring of gender categories and spoke about a rise in egocentrism and materialism, a decline in morality, and the emasculation of men. On the other hand, those who favored "new-style" marriages expressed a desire to change cultural assumptions about what it means to be mothers and fathers, and spoke about improved relations with children and increased freedom in daily life. Gender relations and what it meant to be a wife or husband, mother or father, woman or man were key sites for the negotiation of identity. Labels of tradition and modernity, old and new, were frequently invoked as a way for individuals to make sense of competing ideologies of gender.

Heather Paxson has found a similar process at work in her research on gender, reproduction, and motherhood in contemporary Athens.

She notes that "culturally distinctive negotiations of gender, family, nature, and citizenship" were "carried out in a self-conscious idiom contrasting past and present, 'traditional' and 'modern,' ways of thinking and doing" (Paxson 2004:6). Such negotiations of what it means to be "good at being a man or a woman" are part of what Paxson terms "gender proficiency" (12). It is through this process of negotiation that the Athenians Paxson worked with were able to "make sense of continuous, inconsistent cultural change" (8).

Gender is in fact one aspect of identity that is becoming increasingly linked with the process and project of modernity. As Dorothy Hodgson and contributors to her edited volume point out, "the assumptions, component processes, and consequences of Modernity are inherently gendered," and the "multivalent processes and projects of Modernity provide important sites for the negotiation and experience of gender relations" (Hodgson ed. 2001:8,9). Just as the processes themselves are gendered, local understandings of gender also "shape how Modernity/modernities are experienced, transformed and reproduced" (18). Indeed as Lisa Rofel points out, gender is "one of the central modalities through which modernity is imagined and desired" (1999:19). My work builds on the important work of Rofel and others who have brought gender to the forefront of modernity studies and demonstrated gender to be a key site for the expression of power and difference.[11]

Political and Economic Change

Of the many social and demographic changes that characterized life in Italy during the last two decades of the twentieth century, gender and family emerge as particularly salient. Ignited by the student protests of 1968, second-wave feminism in Italy took off during the early 1970s, when women marched in the streets to demand the right to divorce and the right to control their own reproductive decisions. Throughout the 1970s and 1980s numerous legal changes were sought and quite a few of them were achieved. By the 1990s, however, much of the activist fervor had died down. As the feminist movement changed direction in the 1980s there was a retreat from organized political activism. Then, in the early 1990s, people at many levels of society turned away from politics in general as they witnessed the fall of communism, corruption scandals, and the implosion of the Italian political system. By the end of the 1990s many of the earlier complaints against social inequalities had all but disappeared. The economy was strong, and "uncomfortable facts about structural inequality, both very old and very new, in the key areas of gender, class and race, were rarely the subject of public debate" (Ginsborg 2003:30). The political and social engagement of earlier decades had clearly declined. As Paul Ginsborg explains,

Two things were new about the 1980s and 1990s, both in Italy and Europe as a whole: the first was the profound uncertainty and division created by the rapid advance of information technology and the service economy. An already complex society seemed to be fracturing even further. The second was the contemporaneous weakening of institutions and ideologies which had previously formed identities and fostered social cohesion. Trade unions, mass parties, churches, all faced crises of cohesion and participation. Much more so than in the recent past, individuals were cast adrift in a world characterized by significant opportunities, but also by great risks. (2003:31)

It is within this larger climate of crisis and uncertainty that gender relations became particularly fraught. As Italians traversed a period of great economic and political change, there were significant adjustments at the level of everyday social relations. National feminist mobilization had subsided, but not without achieving real and identifiable change in Italian society. More women were educated, employed, and in positions of power than at any other time in Italy's history, and there were new laws designed to help women and families. Although there were many areas of continuing disparity, and Italy still ranked lower than many of its European counterparts with respect to women's employment statistics (Ginsborg 2003:35), there was nonetheless a perceptible change in the way in which women participated in the economic and political realms of Italian society. What is more difficult to measure are the lasting effects such changes had on everyday gender relations. "Women were moving *out*, making contact with a wider world," Ginsborg notes, "and few aspects of modernity were to produce so great a feeling of liberation as well as so much *angst*" (2003:35, original emphasis). Ginsborg goes on to cite the work of Italian scholars who discuss the paradoxes and ambiguities such changes brought to women's lives. The phenomenon of the "double shift" made famous in the United States through the writings of Arlie Hochschild (1989) and others was clearly present, albeit in a slightly different form, in the Italian context.

While Italian mothers worked to manage their numerous responsibilities inside and outside the home, fathers felt lost and a bit confused about where to devote their energy. As I will discuss at later points in this book, many men agreed in theory with ideals of parity, but when it came time to put these ideals into practice they experienced a difficult transition. Although "patriarchy had certainly lost some of its teeth," as Ginsborg notes, "a new model of paternity had great difficulty in emerging" (2003:77).

Many of these trends, particularly the "double shift" of working mothers and the discrepancy between ideology and action when it comes to gender identity, are hardly unique to Italy, but the combination seems particularly pronounced in the Italian context. Not only do women face the double shift of working outside and inside the home, but many also care for elderly parents, adult children, and even grandchildren on an everyday basis.[12] On top of it all is the emphasis placed on the need to *fare bella figura* by maintaining an impeccably clean house, cooking one and often two hot meals a day, and keeping the family dressed in style with clean, perfectly pressed clothing.[13] All of these factors, combined with ambiguous models for male participation in the *lavoro di cura*, or work of kinship and household, made daily life for Italian women particularly challenging.[14] It is within this climate of change that the categories of tradition and modernity became useful strategies for individuals struggling to make sense of what it meant to be a woman or a man in Italian society during the late 1990s.

Parma's Shrinking Birthrate

One of the major social changes that received front-page news coverage in Italy throughout my time in the field was the issue of population decline. Although a fertility transition is often subsumed under the category of "modernization" in Third World societies (see Fong 2004), a lower birthrate is not always interpreted as a sign of progress in First World societies. In fact, among many groups in Italy the low birthrate is seen as a sign of societal decay.

In December of 1999 the bishop of Parma issued holiday greetings to the residents of Parma and urged them to have more children. When asked by the local paper, "What issue is closest to your heart for the upcoming millennium," the bishop replied, "Children. Above all, Christmas is the holiday of a Child. . . . We live in a world where children are penalized. Parma has a birthrate that is less than the national average; in fact it is under one percent. We live in a situation of suicide. We are a people without trust in the future. The demographic decline also signifies a decline in religious faith and trust in life. The year 2000 could be the year for a new beginning" (*La Gazzetta di Parma*, Dec. 23, 1999:8).

Parma is clearly experiencing many of the demographic shifts that are affecting Italy as a whole. Throughout the 1990s, Italy had one of the lowest fertility rates in the world. According to statistics compiled by the Italian National Statistical Institute (ISTAT), Italy's fertility rate reached its lowest ever in 1995 with a rate of 1.9 (ISTAT 2005a:6). Statistics compiled by the World Resources Institute reveal that the total population of Italy is projected to decrease from 57,449,000 in 2002 to 52,364,000 in 2025 (World Resources Institute 2003). Such figures are slightly higher than what Italian demographers Antonio Golini, Antonio Mussino, and Miria Savioli predicted in their 2000 book titled *Il malessere demografico in Italia*. According to their figures, at current fertility rates Italy will have a population of 50,873,000 between 2020 and 2025 and drop to 38,245,000 by 2045–2050.

For the bishop of Parma, the shrinking birthrate signified a retreat from the Catholic Church and a decline in Christian values. For my friends and colleagues in Parma, there were a range of other factors to consider. Some attributed the decrease in the Italian birthrate to a rise in *egoismo* among young people. It is because of this selfishness, they argued, that young Italians place their own material pleasures ahead of their duties to family and society. Others found fault with the lack of state-sponsored programs to provide support and services for working families. Still others cited the legalization of divorce, increased educational and career opportunities for women, and the rising cost of living. Some reasoned that, in addition to the costs of raising a child, the need for two incomes in families and the trend of children living at home well into their thirties also factored into individual decisions to have fewer children. Such local explanations mesh with Elizabeth Krause's findings in her ethnographic work in the central-Italian city of Prato. She, too, noted "a great deal of fuss over the new Italian family," and devoted her project to examining "what happens when a whole society's patterns of making families changes dramatically" (2005:1,xiii).

The Italian demographer Antonio Golini attributes Italy's low fertility in part to the radical changes that were ushered in by the Italian feminist movement in the 1970s. He explains, "This revolution in the role of women has been so important and so rapid, but the problem is that it hasn't had a parallel reform in the social structure or the mentality of male behaviors which has basically remained the same. Women generally have only one child because the burden of raising the child still falls almost entirely on her shoulders despite all the changes in society" (Golini 1999).

Golini points out that even if the fertility rate were to rise in the near future, the population would continue to decrease for decades:" Italy is the first country in human history where the number of people over the age of 60 has surpassed the number of young people under the age of 20 years old" (Golini 1999). Marco Bottai, another Italian scholar, attributes the low birthrate to the "protracted and obsessive care" of Italian parents (Arkell 1994:14). The financial obligations of parenthood can be limitless, and with a job market especially difficult for young people, many Italian parents house, clothe, and feed their children throughout their twenties and sometimes into their thirties.[15]

Paul Ginsborg emphasizes the *"partial* emancipation" of women as one key to the puzzle of Italy's low fertility (2003:71, original emphasis). He reasons that even if many Italian women may have wanted to have more than one child, the realities of daily life made it impossible to do so. Not only were many women working outside the home, but they also had more household and kin work. Elderly parents living longer, adult children remaining at home for extended periods of time, and husbands who believed in parity but did little around the house may have convinced many women that having more than one child would be asking for trouble. Ginsborg adds that a rise in the average marriage age and a continuing preference, clearly strengthened by the influence of the Catholic Church, to have children within marital relationships may have also contributed to the decline in fertility (2003:71). In 1994 the average age for a first marriage was 29.3 for men and 26.5 for women, as compared to 1984, when the average age was 27.4 for men and 24.3 for women (Righi 1997:54–55).

As Ginsborg (2003) and Krause (2005) both point out, women are not the only ones who make reproductive decisions. A number of the young men I spoke with in Parma emphasized the importance of being *sistemati* (settled, or properly set up) before getting married and starting a family. For many this means waiting until after university (which can often take upwards of six years to complete) and after one has enough money to purchase a nice apartment and the furniture to match. Unlike in the United States, where young couples often rent apartments and make do with secondhand furniture in the early stages of marriage, in Italy it is very important to start off on the right foot with all the accoutrements of a "good life" already in place (see Counihan 2004 and Krause 2005).

Although some observers characterize the decisions of young people as selfish, Ginsborg warns that it would be a mistake to emphasize the *egoismo* of young men and women as a major reason for Italy's declining rates of fertility. On the contrary, Ginsborg claims that "a major contribution to fertility decline came not from a lack of responsibility, but an excess of it" (2003:72). In other words, young Italians realized the family responsibilities that awaited them as they transitioned into adulthood, and reasoned it was better to have only one child, if any. If Italians were *more* selfish, Ginsborg claims, they would not worry about caring for their elderly parents and supporting their children throughout their twenties and often into their thirties.

The region of Emilia-Romagna had one of the lowest fertility rates in Italy (and the world), with a rate of close to (or under) 1.0 for much of the 1990s (ISTAT 2005b:5). In the late 1990s the fertility rate began to rise, and in 2004 it reached its highest level in twenty-five years, with a rate of 1.32 (ISTAT 2005b:5). In the year 2000, Parma had 168,717 residents, of which 17,662, or 10.5 percent, were under the age of fifteen, and 37,395, or 22.2 percent, were over the age of sixty-four (Provincia di Parma 2001). According to Lamberto Soliani, a demographer I interviewed at the University of Parma, in order for Parma to have population equilibrium, every woman in Parma who was twenty-five years old in the year 2000 would have to have at least two children.

Soliani had an interesting explanation for why Italians are tending to marry late or not at all. Young women, more than young men, remain at the university and finish their degrees. Given the tendency in Italy for students to spend five to seven years completing a *laurea* (university degree roughly equivalent to a U.S. bachelor's and master's combined), many do not finish until their late twenties, and some continue studying into their thirties. These young women (and men) usually live in their natal homes, which not only extends the childhood period but also allows them to finish their studies and thus enter careers that require a high level of education. More young men than young women take manual-labor jobs (e.g., as mechanics or builders) right out of high school, and though they make good wages that are often equal to what an engineer might make, they end up less educated than their female counterparts. Soliani pointed out that it is difficult for a twenty-five-year-old woman to find a twenty-five-year-old man with the same level of *cultura* (education and sophistication), and estimated that 30 percent of women currently in their late twenties and early thirties will never marry. Although this demographer's explanation relies on certain assumptions about marital practices among young Italians, it is one potential answer to a question that has vexed historians, demographers, and anthropologists alike.

When I spoke with people in Parma about the low birthrate, their answers at times echoed the explanations of demographers, politicians, and representatives of the Catholic Church. Some told me it was a result of the selfish, materialistic desires of the new generations. Others told me it was due to the poor job market and the fact that young people live at home into their thirties and delay marriage until both partners have financially secure jobs. Still others spoke about the feminist movement and the many changes it brought to Italian society. While for some the low birthrate was a benign or positive consequence of social change, for others it represented a crisis for Italian society.

As Gail Kligman (1998) argues in her work on the politics of reproduction in Romania and the repressive pronatalist policies of the Ceauşescu regime, "reproduction serves as an ideal locus through which to illuminate the complexity of formal and informal relations between states and their citizens, or noncitizens, as the case may be" (1998:3). In Italy, the essentialist rhetoric employed by right-wing politicians—who are concerned about the future integrity of the Italian state, as a nation of Italians—combines with the rhetoric of the Catholic Church to create a discourse of population in peril. In Italy, as in many nation-states, the body, especially the female body, "is instrumentalized as a vehicle through which 'greater' goals than those of the individual are intended to be realized" (1998:7).

In her work on population politics in Italy, Krause (2001, 2005) notes that much of the discussion around Italy's demographic changes, especially among academics and the media, is conveyed through a discourse of crisis and warnings of impending doom. Krause finds that behind the public discourse of crisis there is a "quiet revolution" taking place among ordinary Italians. She suggests that "low fertility is the outcome of a deep, horizontal, quiet revolution that began nearly a century ago against the rigid pecking order of the patriarchal family" (2005:184). Although Krause argues that the demographic changes Italy experienced in the 1990s are "a consequence of society's embrace of an egalitarian model of the family, and of a generation's grappling with the implications for the cultural politics of gender in a context where the so-called culture of responsibility weighs most heavily on women" (184), she is careful to warn against the myth that "because Italian women have record-low fertility" they must therefore have "achieved record-high gender equality" (160). In fact, it is within this climate of low fertility that questions about gender proficiencies continue to be negotiated. As Krause aptly phrases the dilemma, "Low fertility is very much about struggles over male and female relations. It is about men figuring out how to be men beyond the rigid patriarchal family, and women puzzling over how to be women in this transforming gender regime that strives toward equality. Moreover, it is also very much about being Italian, being European, and being modern" (160).

The media, the Church, and politicians wonder what will become of Italy if women continue to have an average of only 1.2 children. Labels such as "irrationality," "selfishness," and "moral decline" are used by Catholics and conservatives as a way of speaking out against changes in family and gender roles. Just as some use the low birthrate to promote anxiety about the infiltration of Italy by immigrants,[16] others use it to sound an alarm about the blurring of gender roles. In this way, the low birthrate becomes a trope for talking about tradition and modernity and laying claim to an imagined past in which Italian women and men coexisted with separate and well-defined roles, produced children, and raised them to be morally upright citizens. For others, however, the low birthrate is a symbol of the difficult but necessary transition to new forms of gender relations.

New Forms of *Mamma*

Despite Italy's historically low birthrate, two derivatives of the word *mamma* have developed and gained attention in the popular press. There is the well-known term *mammone* (loosely translatable as "mama's boy"), which is used to describe the scores of Italian youths who are living with their parents throughout their twenties and often into their thirties; and there is the gender-bending term *mammo*, which is used to describe a man who participates in child-rearing duties once associated exclusively with women.[17] Just as there are varying reactions to Parma's low birthrate, so are there different understandings of the impact that changes in gender roles and household composition have had or will have on daily social life.

While in Parma, I noticed that fatherhood and the new role of *mammo* were getting considerable attention in local and national media. Articles devoted to family life in Italy not only documented changes in gender roles but poked fun at the "new" form of fatherhood by using the invented term *mammo*. In conversations about parenthood, many of my friends and colleagues in Parma explained that up until the preceding ten years or so, it had been rare to see a man pushing a baby carriage. Taking the children to school, going grocery shopping, changing diapers, and caring for children were not seen as "masculine" activities. During the 1990s, the pendulum shifted, and by the time I arrived to do my fieldwork in the late 1990s, a man pushing a stroller was a common sight on the streets of Parma.

In January of 2000 *L'Espresso*, a popular national weekly newsmagazine, published an article titled *"Mammo, hai fatto carriera"* (Simonetti 2000), a short but playful title that alludes on multiple levels to how gender roles are changing in Italy. In English, the title translates as "Mr. Mom, You've Gotten Yourself a Career." Use of the neologism *mammo* emphasizes how these men are placing the responsibility of fatherhood ahead of career ambitions. The phrase *fare carriera*—which is often used to distinguish between people who have pursued professional careers and those who work generally lower-paid jobs that require less education and training—offers a humorous poke at discussions that center on the new generation of women who have focused on building professional careers, sometimes at the expense of building a family.

In addition to providing short profiles of various men in Italy and abroad who have decided to take time off from their jobs to stay home with their children, the article raises fundamental questions about the way people think about gender and gender change. It sets up a division between the fathers of yesterday, "commanding, archaic, absent, demanding," and the fathers of today, "affectionate, playful," and speaks of daring men who "venture into spaces historically and culturally feminine" (Simonetti 2000:66,68). Although this popular-media article casts the changes in men's roles in a positive light and portrays men who put their children ahead of their careers as courageous and daring, other pieces in the media have questioned what these changes will mean for Italian society and for a generation of men who find themselves confused and in search of an identity.

According to an article that appeared in Parma's daily newspaper in November 1999, sociological studies conducted in the 1990s found men to be "insecure as husbands and as parents, scattered and bewildered at home and at work, victims of determined women who are in crisis themselves" (Luzi 1999). The article raised questions about the effect this insecurity could have on the next generation of children:

In reality, these men between thirty and forty years old have an alliance with their wives and search for an equilibrium between work and family that is often difficult to find. Are these new father and mother pairs a model for others to follow? Are they succeeding? If the maternal role remains the same and the paternal role changes to become increasingly less fatherly and increasingly that of a friend or older brother, isn't there a risk of neglecting particular aspects of child rearing? (Luzi 1999)

Though for some men and women the new visions of fatherhood provided freedom from the constraining gender norms of the past, for others the gender-bending ideology was deeply troublesome and a portent of danger for the country's newest generation of children.

Mammoni and Parental Dependence

The other popular derivative of mamma, the widely cited term *mammone*, has generated much discussion—both in Italy and abroad—about the new phenomenon of children remaining at home through their thirties. There was even a *60 Minutes* segment aired in the United States in 2001 that presented this new generation of mama's boys to an American audience.[18] In an article titled "Mama's Boy and Proud of It" that appeared in *L'Espresso* in 1999, a sidebar reads, "An army of thirty-year-olds who work half-heartedly, put off decisions, and live with their parents. . . . A generation that refuses to grow up? Maybe. But there are those who see the Italian model as an example . . . " (Arosio 1999:40). In a related article titled "Out of Necessity or out of Love?" Roberta Rizzo and Eugenia Romanelli interviewed thirteen Italians between the ages of twenty-eight and thirty-six who lived at home. For a thirty-two-year-old named Paolo with aspirations to become a university professor, living at home was a necessity while he awaited a grant to continue his research, but for a thirty-four-year-old named Marco, living at home was like living in a hotel and not having to pay the bill:

I have a medium/high salary, I dress elegantly, and I drive a company car, an Alfa Romeo 146. Economically I am well off and I could live on my own, probably in a nice apartment, but to tell you the truth I stay with my parents because it's comfortable. My house is like a hotel. I sleep, I wash, I have breakfast, and then I'm out the whole day working. In reality I spend more time in the office and in the car than with my folks. I have very stressful hours; I leave at 7:00 AM and come back at 11:00 PM. . . . Life is difficult and complicated: many of my peers are not able to start families because there are too many problems. (Rizzo and Romanelli 1999:43)

Although some media accounts, including the *60 Minutes* segment, portray a stereotype of *mammoni* as young men spoiled by traditional Italian mothers who wait on them hand and foot, in fact the phenomenon of *mammoni* is far more complex.[19] First, it's not just men who are living with their parents. Women are also choosing to stay in their natal homes through their thirties. Second, the practice is not necessarily interpreted by Italians as being "traditional." In fact, many posit links between the rising numbers of *mammoni* and the economic pressures of "modern" life.

Italy has one of the highest percentages of unmarried adults—men and women—who live at home with their parents (Arosio 1999:40). In 1995, 64.9 percent of men and 49.8 percent of women between the ages of eighteen and thirty-four lived at home (de Sandre 1997:68). According to data collected by ISTAT in 1998, 96.7 percent of children under the age of twenty-four lived with their parents, as did 43.8 percent of children twenty-five to thirty-four (ISTAT 2001:15). Although there are more young men than young women who remain at home through their thirties, the percentage of women living at home is increasing at a faster rate. From 1983 to 1995 there was a 23.3 percent increase in the number of women eighteen to thirty-four residing in their natal family homes, as compared to a 12.5 percent increase for men (de Sandre 1997:68). Through my research I found that many women live in the same circumstances as their male counterparts—with their mothers taking care of most household chores while they work long hours at demanding jobs or spend days and nights studying to pass university exams.

During my year in Parma I rarely met unmarried young adults in their twenties and thirties (from Parma) who were living on their own.[20] The few young adults I met who were from Parma and who had left their natal homes encountered a great deal of difficulty when they finally decided to move out. Their parents were hurt and could not understand why they would want to leave a warm family environment to live alone. Generally speaking, in Italy one leaves home for only two reasons: to study at a university in another city or to get married.[21] It can be a source of sadness but also embarrassment when a parent has an unmarried child leave the house only to move to the other side of the city. Many ask their children, "Was living here so bad?" and wonder what they did wrong.

Among the young people who do get married and move into their own home, both spouses usually work, and if there are children, the grandparents will often babysit on a daily basis. Some grandparents will take the children all day, every day, and many grandmothers will even do laundry and help with other household chores. With the lack of after-school programs and day care for older children, intergenerational help is increasingly critical for the current generation of parents. This intergenerational dependence is made easier by the tendency among Italians to live in close proximity to relatives (Cioni 1997).

For many Italians, the parent–child relationship remains extremely significant throughout the post-childhood period. According to data collected by ISTAT in 1998, 40.2 percent of Italians who do not live with their parents see their mother every day and 37.5 percent see their father every day. Close to 79 percent of Italians who do not live with their parents see their mother at least once a week, and 76 percent see their father at least once a week (ISTAT 2001). According to a study conducted in Emilia-Romagna that examined the residence patterns of women between the ages of twenty-five and fifty-five, "approximately half of their 'closest relatives' lived either in the same household or block of flats, while another 40 percent were found to be either in the same quarter or municipality" (Balbo et al. 1990:25,33, cited in Ginsborg 2003:75).

The proximity of relatives, whether within the same household or down the street, makes it easier for family members to depend on one another. Women are at the center of this kinship network. Married women often maintain ties with their husbands' relatives as well as their own; care for their own parents and their in-laws in times of sickness and frailty; and often provide day care for their grandchildren as well. With more and more women working full-time outside the home, the burden placed on middle-aged women has greatly increased. Children are living with their parents into their thirties, the elderly are living longer, young men and women are working longer hours, and it is often up to the mothers and grandmothers to fill in the gaps where the state-based welfare system leaves off and the family is expected to take over.

Multiple Modernities

Over the past decade, challenges to academic perceptions of modernity have come from many angles (Appadurai 1996; Bhabha 1994; Gewertz and Errington 1996; Rofel 1999; Hodgson 2001). Despite these (and other) attempts to sever the concept of modernity from a Western model of progress, Mary Steedly (2000) notes that many scholars still associate modernity with a singular break from the past. Although some of the most prominent social theorists of our time have recognized what Appadurai terms "the modern moment" to be "one of the most problematic legacies of grand Western social science" (1996:3,2), Steedly reminds us that "when modernity is taken to be an objectively given world-historical phase, the effect of some signal transformation, the desire to fix its moment (and, it should be added, its *place*) of rupture/origin seems almost inescapable" (2000:815).

Indeed, it is quite difficult for many scholars to separate their own Western understanding of modernity from modernity as a theoretical

concept. In a call similar to David Schneider's (1984) pathbreaking revision of kinship, Steedly suggests that our studies of modernity are
often clouded by our own folk models of what modernity is all about.
In Lisa Rofel's work on the politics of modernity in postsocialist China,
she takes scholars to task for equating modernity with "the invention of
humanism, the secularization of society, and the emergence of technical
reason" (1999:10). She argues against the assumption that modernity
entails a belief in the ideals of European Enlightenment and represents
a "noncontinuous break with what it constructs as the irrationalities of
tradition" (11).

In a similar vein, Dorothy Hodgson (2001) makes an important distinction between the Western project of "Modernity" based on a linear
idea of economic and social progress and the "modernities" that are
produced in local contexts. "Modernity," according to Hodgson, "has
multiple meanings and logics. It is always mediated by and through
local cultural forms and shaped by the actions and ideas of people op-
erating from different structural positions of power, knowledge, and
identity" (2001:7). Although Hodgson underscores the production of
modernities as a process shaped by local actors negotiating particular structural realities, she suggests that there are still some "common
characteristics" shared by the many forms of Modernity/modernities.
These characteristics include "a belief in ideologies of progress and im-
provement (although the meanings and objectives signified by these
terms may vary)" and the presence of modernity advocates who try to
convert others "through enticement, education, coercion, subversion,
or even force and violence" (8). Hodgson's distinction is a useful one in
that it allows for multiple understandings of modernity and multiple
definitions of what progress itself might entail. Although a notion of
"progress" is more likely shared by "modernity advocates" than by
modernity critics, the question Hodgson poses is certainly the right
one: "What do we in fact mean by 'modernity' given the coexistence of
multiple dominant modernities and the continuous production of new
forms of modernities?" (8).

The answer Steedly provides is both appropriate and useful. She suggests that by thinking of modernity as "a structure of feeling, a way of
thinking about time that is predicated on the idea of historical rupture
and steeped in the consequent inevitability of loss," our very definition of the term can be separated from a particular historical moment
and opened up to allow for the recognition of multiple modernities
that exist outside of "a grand European original" (Steedly 2000:815).

Although at first glance Steedly's argument seems most appropriate for recently emerged nation-states with a colonial past—indeed much of the anthropological discourse on "other modernities" seems directed at areas outside the West—Steedly's suggestion makes just as much sense for the West itself as it does for other areas. By thinking about modernity—and tradition—not only as structures of feeling or ways of thinking about time, but also as shifting categories of meaning, we can separate modernities from Modernity and draw connections with other processes of identity formation and difference.

Frederick Barth provides a classic theoretical approach for understanding how such processes of identity formation can take shape in local settings. In his groundbreaking essay on ethnic groups and processes of boundary maintenance, Barth issued a call for anthropologists to study the "ethnic *boundary* that defines the group, not the cultural stuff that it encloses" (1969:15, original emphasis). Although boundaries are certainly important, Daphne Berdahl (1999) alerts us to the idea that it may very well be the "cultural stuff" that can help us understand how such boundaries are produced and maintained. As Berdahl underscores in her ethnography of everyday life at the cultural and physical boundary between East and West Germany, "boundaries are constructed out of preexisting differences, which they, in their turn, act not only to reinforce but also to create; the sense of difference they mark is as important as the cultural forms and practices they enclose" (1999:5).

Building on Barth and Berdahl, we can apply a similar argument to symbolic constructions of tradition and modernity. Like any construction of difference, definitions of tradition and modernity are maintained by boundaries that vary through both space and time. The boundaries of tradition and modernity not only emerge out of difference, but also serve to reproduce such difference. The models, norms, ideals, beliefs, values, and ethics the boundaries enclose—that is, the "cultural stuff" they include—are continually in flux and, like categories of gender, are "at once empty and overflowing. . . . Empty because they have no ultimate, transcendent meaning. Overflowing because even when they appear to be fixed, they still contain within them alternative, denied, or suppressed definitions" (Scott 1988b:49). It is thus important to attend to the substance of tradition and modernity as well as to the processes of boundary maintenance.

David Sutton's analysis of the debate over the ritual throwing of dynamite bombs on the Greek island of Kalymnos provides an important example of how such boundaries are produced and maintained. Sutton suggests that dynamite represents "an idiom through which Kalym-nians can discuss and debate their own local identity, character, and tradition, and the island's relation to outside forces." Sutton points out that anthropologists can study "'tradition' and 'modernity' not as ana-lytical categories to be applied to different societies but as ethnographic objects—local categories with shifting meanings and contents for peo-ples trying to make sense of their place and their identities amid rapid change" (1996:66). Taking a similar approach, Vassos Argyrou (1996) demonstrates how, in the performance of the culturally central Greek Cypriot wedding ritual, labels of tradition and modernity not only are applied to differing tastes and practices in the ritual itself, but also are used to represent two sides of a class struggle between villagers and middle-class urban residents. Whereas villagers lay claim to "authen-tic" enactments of traditional practice, the urban middle class claims its own superiority through its connection to a reified notion of the "West" as symbolic of all things modern. Rather than predicate modernity on an understanding of progress, technology, or humanism, I suggest that we build on Steedly's rethinking of modernity as a "structure of feel-ing" and the continuing efforts of anthropologists such as Sutton and Argyrou who study tradition and modernity as shifting categories that are filled with meaning by local actors and used in strategic ways in both local and global contexts.

Resisting Reification

In the current period of feminist intellectual practice, there are many debates and unanswered questions about how to study gender, how to define the analytic category of "gender," and what feminist ethnography is all about (Visweswaran 1997). More than a decade after Judith Butler called upon feminists not only to address the invisibility of women in language and politics but to question "how the category of 'women,' the subject of feminism, is produced and restrained by the very structures of power through which emancipation is sought" (Butler 1990:2), feminist anthropologists still face an analytic dilemma: how to study and talk about "women" and "gender" without contributing to their reification.[22]

Paxson provides an intriguing answer in her formulation of an "eth-ics of gender" (2004:11). By examining gender as a "system of virtues" and questioning how people understand "what it takes to be good (at being) women or men," Paxson builds on a rich history of the perfor-mative (Herzfeld 1985; Butler 1990; Cowan 1990; Tsing 1993; Lancaster

1992), strategic (Ortner 1996), and narrative (Steedly 1993; Aretxaga 1997; Stewart 1996) approaches to the study of gender. If, in following Paxson, we turn our attention to the ongoing construction of "gender proficiency" in local and global contexts, perhaps we can indeed move beyond discussions of gender norms, gender identities, and gender models. Although such terms imply an understanding of gender as a symbolic category that takes shape in local contexts, they also ultimately reinscribe gender as a static collection of attributes.

In writing about my work in Parma I struggled with precisely this tension: how to talk about gender and gender change without reifying gender or the categories of "women" and "men." Similarly, I questioned how to talk about modernity without assuming a Western, teleological norm of progress. Ultimately, there is no perfect solution to such analytic binds, but as ethnographers we can endeavor to use local formulations and understandings as much as possible and allow our theoretical framework to grow out of the conceptualizations and logics of local actors. It is for this reason that I have chosen to contextualize within the wider theoretical context of modernity a project that was once primarily about intimate-partner violence. Because people in Parma did not talk about intimate-partner violence as a compartmentalized phenomenon to be analyzed apart from society itself, it did not make ethnographic sense to study intimate-partner violence as a discrete category of experience.

Such an approach may at first seem to distance my discussion from its initial focus on the intersection of gender and violence. In fact, my fieldwork did indeed move me away from a study of individual experience and toward a study of larger social processes. Some readers may question how this book can be an ethnography of intimate-partner violence and at the same time deal with topics as diverse and far-ranging as feminist activism, the micropolitics of organizations, the macropolitics of the state, kinship relations, and even law; to such queries I must respond that the very project of ethnography is to examine social life as it exists, in all its messy, overlapping, and inconsistent manifestations. I went to Parma determined to study community responses to intimate-partner violence, but ideas about gender, modernity, change, and tradition came up again and again in my conversations with friends and colleagues. Intimate-partner violence, it turned out, was one end of a hierarchy of subordination that women and men were continuing to sort out as they negotiated gender proficiency during a period of rapid socioeconomic and political change.

As Italian historian Paul Ginsborg states in the opening lines of his most recent account of Italian history, "Over the last twenty years Italy has witnessed a socioeconomic transformation as dramatic as that of the 'economic miracle' of the 50s and 60s, but strikingly different from it in both content and consequences" (2003:ix). Of all the changes Italy experienced during this time period, Ginsborg places particular emphasis on family and the *"connections* between individuals, families, society and the state" (xiii, original emphasis). It is within this climate of change, and within the realm of politics, feminism, family, and law, that I situate this ethnography of gender proficiency and everyday responses to intimate-partner violence.

Fieldwork Through Networks

When I went to Parma to conduct my year of fieldwork I was determined to capture the subtleties of local experience. But how to accomplish this in a city of 170,000 inhabitants? Though clearly too large to lend itself to the methodologies of a village study, Parma was also too small to enable me to focus primarily on a single neighborhood, as other urban ethnographers have done.[23] My challenge was to find a way to do a local study of a midsize city in a way that would allow me to utilize the insight that comes from the intimacy of the ethnographic project. By choosing three points of entry into the matrix of social life in Parma—Women United, Family Aid, and the Rocco di Marco neighborhood group—I was able to observe daily life in three very different settings. By shifting among these three locations on a weekly and often daily basis, I was able to become an active participant in three very different groups of people.[24] Through this methodology I defined the boundaries of my study in a way that did not conform to standard notions of "community" often defined by the lines that divide neighborhoods, towns, and ethnic or religious groups. My community was composed of three separate networks of people within the city of Parma, and each network included men and women of varying religious, political, class, and educational backgrounds.

After a few months of attending meetings and helping out with various activities, people became used to my frequent questions and constant note taking. I soon became one of the stalwarts of the three groups I participated in, and spent my days shuttling across town for meetings at Women United and Family Aid. I devoted evenings and weekends to attending meetings and activities with the Rocco di Marco neighborhood group, spending time with individual friends, and catching up on field notes. As the year went on, my daily calendar grew increasingly full. Working intensely with Women United, Family Aid, and the Rocco di Marco group enabled me to create lasting friendships with numerous individuals. My relationships with these individuals provided me with a social network that seemed to grow exponentially.

A phrase I heard many times during my fieldwork was *Parma è piccola, sai* (Parma is small, you know). When I bumped into friends and colleagues on the street or at the weekly market, they would often give me a big hello and say, *Parma è piccola, sai*. When a woman came to Women United as a client and turned out to be a local merchant with a very familiar face, my colleagues turned to me and said, *Parma è piccola, sai*. And when friends from one of my social networks met friends from another network and discovered they both knew the anthropologist from Boston, they told me the story and said, *Parma è piccola, sai*. Although a city of 170,000, Parma is still small enough that such coincidences happen from time to time. For an anthropologist, Parma's status as an urban field site that at times feels like a village presented methodological challenges as well as opportunities.[25]

Parma was large enough to enable me to cultivate friendships in a semi-anonymous fashion and keep my roles within my three fieldwork locations relatively discrete. All three locations were aware of my work in the other places, but there was rarely direct overlap. When there was overlap, it was often perceived as humorous. After I had been working with the Rocco di Marco neighborhood group for a few months, the members of the group held a meeting with a local social worker who was working to involve various neighborhoods in an after-school program for young teens. I heard later that at the end of the meeting, the group asked for a copy of the minutes so they could give them to *la ragazza* (the girl) who was working with them for her dissertation.[26] The social worker grinned and asked, "Could this be *la ragazza* from Boston?" When they said yes, she asked, "Could this be Sonja from Boston?" Everyone had a big laugh when they realized that Cinzia, the local social worker, was also a caseworker at Women United and knew me quite well. The more often these coincidences occurred, the more teasing I would get for being "famous" around town.[27]

The rewards of conducting fieldwork through three separate social and volunteer networks proved plentiful. By immersing myself in three social fields and tracing the many paths and interconnections that led from the physical field-site location, I was able to form a rich picture of the social, political, and economic dynamics of Parma. Remaining with only one of these sites would have given me a very narrow slice of the story. Although my research is necessarily partial, situated, and incomplete, the opportunity to move in and out of such diverse physical and social locations enabled me to gain a nuanced understanding of the city of Parma and the major issues and dilemmas in people's lives.

During my fieldwork, I learned something interesting about methodological choices. I had begun with a strong ethical determination not to interview the clients I met through my role as volunteer at Women United and Family Aid. Many friends and colleagues back home had advised against this approach, warning that I would be closing myself off from an important area of research. I gave careful thought to their concerns, but in the end I remained committed to my initial decision. Perhaps most important was my knowledge that the women were almost always facing tremendous stress and difficulty in their lives and were relying on the organizations for emotional and monetary support. As such, I was concerned the women might feel undue pressure to speak with me. In addition, I strongly suspected that the reason I was given such unlimited access to everyday life within the two organizations was because I repeatedly assured the caseworkers and volunteers that I was not interested in interviewing the women who came to the organizations for assistance. To stray from this commitment by requesting client interviews would have undermined my position as a reliable and trustworthy shelter worker and volunteer.

As it turned out, there was a different way for me to gain access to the stories of women who had lived with violence, and it emerged serendipitously through the fieldwork process. After I had established a reputation as a loyal member of both Women United and Family Aid, my colleagues began opening up to me, telling me bits and pieces about their lives. Roughly three months into my year of fieldwork, I began asking one or two of these women a week for a formal life-history interview. To my surprise, nearly everyone I asked was eager to sit down with me for a two- to four-hour chat.[28] They knew that my research was on intimate-partner violence, family, and gender, and they were happy to share their thoughts and experiences.

By the end of my year of fieldwork, I had conducted more than fifty interviews with women I met through my networks at Women United, Family Aid, and the Rocco di Marco neighborhood group. Without having planned to do so, I ended up interviewing five women who had experienced partner violence, some of whom had requested assistance from or actually worked for Women United and/or Family Aid. I met these women not as clients, but as colleagues and friends. Their stories came out over the normal course of the fieldwork process and were not obtained through violation of my commitment to Women United and Family Aid. In only two cases did I know about these women's experiences of violence prior to the interview. In every case I was both surprised and caught off guard by the desire of these women to tell me their stories when it would have been just as easy for them to gloss over certain aspects of their lives. For anthropologists, who are neither therapists nor counselors, there is a fine line between active listening and intrusion (George 1996). Whenever possible, I allowed the woman telling her story to guide both the conversation and the flow of her narrative. As I sat and listened to these very painful and poignant stories of betrayal, disillusion, shame, and silence, I questioned the limits of my role as an anthropologist within the intimate field sites produced by the very act of narration. Living-room couches, tables in coffee bars, and park benches were momentarily transformed into powerful sites of transmission and discovery.

For the women I worked with, the act of narration served as an opportunity to interpret their own experiences. For many, it was the first time they had retold their life story in such detail. The very act of narration—performed to an outsider—enabled them to attribute meaning to their stories of violence. They found themselves telling their stories to someone who would not disagree, would not offer advice, and would take no action following the narration. For many, it was the first time they were able to think of their own lives in ways that made sense to them. Their narratives reveal many forms of pain and suffering. I could have analyzed their experiences in medical and psychological terms, such as those discussed and challenged by Hacking (1996), Herman (1992), Young (1995), and others.[29] Instead, however, I have chosen to focus on what Geertz (1983) has called "experience-near" categories, by privileging the interpretations of the women who told me their life stories. As Arthur Kleinman suggests in his criticism of both the medicalization and anthropologization of experience, "What is lost in biomedical renditions—the complexity, uncertainty, and ordinariness of some man or woman's world of experience—is also missing when illness is reinterpreted as social role, social strategy, or social symbol . . . as anything but human experience" (Kleinman 1995:96).

It is the social intimacy of the ethnographic project that allows anthropologists to get beyond both the "cultural intimacy" (Herzfeld 1997) that prevents groups from revealing certain aspects of their cultural identity to outsiders, and the personal intimacy that prevents individuals from discussing particular details of their private lives. As a trusted outsider with an insider's view of daily social life, I was often privy to information that friends and colleagues would not normally discuss with casual acquaintances. The life stories I was able to record are thus more than mere catalogs of events or interpretations of reality; they reveal the relationships between individuals and their surroundings, and serve as a means of organizing experience: "personal stories are not merely a way of telling someone (or oneself) about one's life; they are the means by which identities may be fashioned" (Ochberg and Rosenwald 1992:1). I take a holistic approach to the analysis of these life stories and place them within the larger context of Parma's social, political, and ideological climate during the 1990s, what I've termed Italy's postfeminist period.

CHAPTER 2

Postfeminist Uncertainties

"FEMINISM WAS ITALY'S TRUE REVOLUTION. It changed everything. It changed the terms of production, reproduction, and language. It changed the identity of this country," said Giovanna, a former feminist activist living in Parma. But when I asked Giovanna how the feminist movement had changed everyday gender relations in Italy, she found the question difficult to answer. She sighed and told me,

I'm much less ideological than I used to be. It's not that I'm giving something up, it's just become the way life is. Every night I challenge my partner to take the wine out of the refrigerator and every night I'm the one to go get it. I remember one time there were three or four potatoes left in a pan and out of a disagreement over whose turn it was to clean up, a question of principle, we let the pot sit. The potatoes sprouted leaves, the leaves turned into flowers, and the flowers became new potatoes.

Such expressions of ambivalence were common among the former feminist activists I worked with. Many had fought throughout the 1970s to overturn a gender system in which women were subordinate to men in nearly all aspects of daily life. Thirty years later, at the end of the 1990s, they spoke proudly about the legal changes they had brought to Italian society, but were unsure what exactly had changed in their everyday lives, in their relationships with men, and in their experiences as wives, partners, and mothers.

Despite new laws and new ways of thinking about gender and women's lives, the legacy of the Italian women's movement of the 1970s and 1980s is still uncertain. A number of former activists spoke to me about their disappointment and disillusionment with the gains of the feminist period. As one former activist explained, "We left no path for the younger generations to follow."

Matthew Gutmann (1997b) suggests that successful ethnographies of gender "do not shy away from theorizing" but at the same time do not attempt to provide overarching theories of behavior. Instead, "by providing fine-grained documentation and analysis of particular historical contexts in lieu of sweeping generalizations, they highlight ambiguity as a central theme of the engendered aspects of men's and women's lives" (1997b:849) and propose new avenues and approaches for understanding the complexity of gender and gender relations.

In this chapter, I provide a short history of women's politics in Parma in order to suggest how ideas about women's subjectivity shifted throughout the feminist movement. Although Italian feminism has a rich history that extends back to the struggle for women's suffrage (achieved in 1945) and even earlier campaigns that emerged during the years of the *Risorgimento* (the nineteenth-century movement of Italian unification that culminated in 1870 with the capture of Rome), for the purposes of this book I will focus primarily on the feminism that developed in the latter half of the twentieth century.[1] The stories and memories of former leftist and Catholic activists who were part of this movement not only helped me understand the ideologies and divergences that gave rise to Parma's two main women's shelters, Women United and Family Aid, but also provided insight into the changes that sparked a period of gender ambivalence and uncertainty for many Italians.

The Postfeminist Period

Throughout this book I refer to the 1990s as Italy's postfeminist period, not because feminism as an ideology had disappeared but because feminism as a nationally organized political movement no longer existed. An overwhelming number of the women and men I spoke with in Parma referred to feminism as a movement that reached its prime in the 1970s, began to fade in the 1980s, and by the 1990s had become a part of history. Some celebrated the feminist period as a time of great spirit, camaraderie, and triumph; others scoffed at the extremism of the women who had taken to the streets to defy patriarchal norms. Regardless of the way in which feminism was discussed or valued, I noticed a widespread tendency to refer to it as something that happened in the past. It is for this reason that I define the 1990s as postfeminist and present the period as a time of negotiation and clarification.

It is important to note that my use of the label "postfeminist" is grounded in local cultural understandings of feminism as a movement and should not be interpreted to imply my own positioning in the debate over the use of "postfeminist" as a theoretical category.[2] As Shelley Budgeon points out in her discussion of the tension between second-wave feminism and postfeminist thinkers, some scholars interpret the term "postfeminist" as an antifeminist position and object that such language implies that the work of feminism is complete and that the goal of "equality has been achieved" (Budgeon 2001:13). In using the term "postfeminist" I do not in any way wish to imply that there is no further need for feminist politics in Italy, or elsewhere, but instead want to distinguish the ebb and flow of organized feminist politics and convey the dominant local understandings of feminism. I follow Budgeon in suggesting that "the prefix 'post' is used here not as a signifier of a complete break in previous social relations or as the overcoming of oppressive relations, but rather as implying a *process of ongoing transformation*" (2001:14, original emphasis).

Parity and Difference

Luisa Passerini (1996:145) notes that within Italy, as elsewhere, gender relations are enacted at a variety of different levels of society "and there may be contradictions between them at any given time." She calls attention to two levels that coexisted through much of Italy's feminist period:

The first is the level of laws, norms, and institutions. Here one discerns in the 1970s a distinct movement toward *parity* or formal equality between women and men. The second is the symbolic level, including politics, culture, and psychology. On this level in the 1970s there was a marked process of *differentiation* or pluralization in gender relations, toward a greater recognition of difference in the gender system and in sexual identities. (Passerini 1996:145, original emphasis)

As Passerini indicates, the 1970s stand out as a time of significant change in Italian society. There were momentous victories—and noteworthy battles—for the feminists who fought against decades of patriarchal norms and codified gender inequality. In 1970 divorce was legalized; in 1975 the set of laws governing marriage and family was significantly revised; in 1977 a law requiring equal pay in the workplace was approved; and in 1978 a law that gave women the right to choose to terminate their own pregnancies was passed (Birnbaum 1986:270–271).[3] At the same time, there was also a move within certain branches of leftist feminism toward the encouragement of relationships between and among women and the recognition of sexual difference.

In American feminist circles, the debate over equality versus difference has been highly contested and has created divisions within the American women's movement, but within Italy the debate took on a slightly different tone. Though there were certainly moments of tension, for the most part theories of difference prevailed, and there was far less angst and uncertainty about how to reconcile the importance of *parity* in the realm of institutions and *difference* in the realm of political and cultural practice. While the debate in America continued to swirl, Italian feminists decided fairly quickly that in order to accomplish their goal of recognizing a new female subject, the idea of being "equal" to men, in a cultural sense, had to be abandoned. Italian feminists seemed to anticipate the comments of Joan Scott, who suggests that rather than get bogged down in the quagmire of a binary opposition between equality and difference, we can "refuse to oppose equality to difference and insist continually on differences—differences as the condition of individual and collective identities, differences as the constant challenge to the fixing of those identities, history as the repeated illustration of the play of differences, differences as the very meaning of equality itself" (Scott 1988a:46). As Anna Paini puts it, "difference does not entail inequality" (1993:34), and although we may find it difficult to understand the meaning of "difference" outside of the hegemonic gender system within which many of us live, the recognition of sexual difference encompasses "a new project of practice that sees women as the negotiators: not an ungendered, neutral universe of equal women or women with a common destiny of oppression, but rather a new symbolic order built by women for (not 'on behalf of') women living in a real society made up by women and by men" (1993:34–35).

By the 1980s the recognition of sexual difference had become part of the mission of many Italian women's groups and organizations, but the nationally organized activism of previous years was beginning to disappear. As Bianca Beccalli explains, "Modern Italian feminism established itself in the early 1970s, expanding with remarkable strength and radicalism from its middle-class base to become a popular mobilization with an extensive network of activists throughout the organized labour movement. By the end of the decade, however, feminism was in decline; and the beginning of the 1980s saw it virtually disappear as a movement" (1994:86). Although feminism as an organized national movement had "lost its visibility in political struggles," Italian feminism moved into a different phase as women began to leave organized politics. Instead of working within mainstream politics, "they increasingly committed their energies to private projects and experiences, whether of an individual or communal nature" (Beccalli 1994:86) and focused their efforts on discussion groups and nonprofit service organizations. It is during this time that groups such as Women United and Family Aid grew into active organizations dedicated to sheltering women from their violent partners.

Parma's Women's Centers

Women United and Family Aid are private, nonprofit organizations that provide a range of essential services to women in need of counseling and shelter. Along with other service-providing organizations around town, Women United and Family Aid pick up the slack left by overburdened and underfunded government agencies that have neither the resources nor the experience to provide services for battered women and single women with children. Each organization has its own form of ideological discourse and practice as well as its own forms of control, all of which work to shape the subjectivity of women in distinct ways.[4] As in schools, hospitals, workshops, and barracks, the discipline at Women United and Family Aid is productive in that it creates particular forms of gender relations. At Women United the rules, regulations, and practices are intended to produce strong and independent *women*, whereas at Family Aid the rules, regulations, and practices are designed to fashion dedicated and capable *mothers*.

Women United is a volunteer association founded on the principle of providing help to women who are experiencing violence of any kind. It was created by a group of leftist women who were passionately involved with the feminist movement in Italy during the 1970s and closely connected to the Italian Communist Party (Partito Comunista Italiano; Pci) until the party's demise in the early 1990s. The help the association provides is based on an Italian feminist ideology that stresses the importance of recognizing the differences that exist between men and women in society and the need to build solidarity among women. What began in 1985 as a group that offered phone support and sponsored cultural events quickly grew into an organization that helped more than 150 women each year in the late 1990s, and offered legal and psychological support as well as a *casa rifugio* (shelter, or safe house) with accommodations for up to four women and eight children at any given time. During the time of my fieldwork, upon a woman's first arrival at Women United she was greeted by two caseworkers who listened to her story and worked with her to create a plan to achieve her personal goals. The organization was firm in its commitment to allow each woman to pursue her own path, even if that meant staying with a violent partner. This policy of respecting women's choices could not, for obvious reasons, apply fully to women requesting shelter. Such women had to commit to starting a new life, which included leaving their violent partners for good and maintaining the secrecy of the shelter's address. Without such a policy, the safety of the other women could be put in jeopardy.

Family Aid, on the other hand, is a national volunteer organization that was founded in 1975 (three years before the law approving abortion was passed) on the Catholic principle of helping women to "welcome life" by offering monetary and emotional support to pregnant women and women with small children. Although Family Aid had no formal connection with the now-defunct Christian Democratic Party (Democrazia Cristiana; Dc) or the Vatican, during the period of my fieldwork many local parishes helped raise money for the organization, and priests and nuns often served as spiritual advisors. A local chapter of Family Aid was founded in Parma in 1979, and at first it primarily provided assistance to young unmarried mothers or pregnant women, many of whom had run away or had been disowned by their parents.[5] Over the years, and especially during the mid-1990s, the demographics of the women seeking help began to change. By the end of the 1990s the organization was primarily helping older women, many of whom had violent and abusive partners. Although no one I spoke with at Family Aid was able to explain this shift, many speculated that it could be due to a change in social values regarding abortion and pregnancy out of wedlock. While Family Aid continued to uphold the welcoming of life as its guiding principle, the needs of the women seeking help had changed. The women were no longer pregnant teenagers in need of a surrogate family, but instead were adult women in their twenties, thirties, and even their forties who came from a diverse range of situations and experiences.

In addition to managing a food- and clothing-distribution center that helped more than 400 women in 1999/2000, Parma's Family Aid organization also owned several apartments that served as shelters for women and their children. The goal of the shelters was to help women become "good" and capable mothers. The shelter supervisors, or "educators," who worked in the shelters on a daily basis were responsible for ensuring that house rules were observed and that daily household tasks were completed. These supervisors were hired with the expectation that they would teach by example and serve as mother figures for the women living in the shelters.

After a few months of attending weekly meetings, observing daily interactions, and speaking with the women working at Women United and Family Aid, I could see that there was a clear correlation between the ideological and ethical systems of the two organizations and the models of gender, womanhood, and motherhood they invoked on an everyday basis. The organizations were founded on ideological models that were radically different and at the same time intimately related.

During my fieldwork in Parma, particularly during the time I spent with Women United and Family Aid, I often heard people emphasizing the political line between "us" and "them"—lines that invariably were used to divide communists (former Pci members) and Catholics (former Dc members). During the period of Italy's first republic—1948 to 1992—everything from trade unions to television stations to university departments was classified as either communist or Catholic.[6] Even supermarket chains allied themselves with particular sides of the political divide.[7] As David Kertzer demonstrated in his pioneering work about a neighborhood in Bologna during the 1970s, "*Il mondo cattolico e il mondo comunista*—the Catholic world and the Communist world—are among the most common terms of political discourse in Italy" (Kertzer 1980:2).[8] For nearly half a century, both the Communist Party and the Catholic Church (through the Christian Democratic Party, papal edicts, and the sermons of parish priests) called on individuals to think and behave in prescribed ways.[9]

Nearly thirty years after Kertzer's fieldwork—following the end of the Cold War and the widespread corruption scandals in Italy—both the Pci and the Dc were defunct, but the opposition between the two ideological systems remained strong in many aspects of Italian social life.[10] Although there was uncertainty in the minds of many Italians as to which party deserved their allegiance in the new political era (a flurry of new parties sprang up that claimed kinship with either the Pci or the Dc), there was still a clear distinction between the ideological principles of communists and Catholics, and the labels were still used to describe people as well as institutions.[11] Despite the new political landscape, the political opposition that had governed Italian social and political life for close to fifty years was clearly still prominent.

The women I worked with at Women United and Family Aid were

part of these two very different political and ideological trajectories in Italian society. Both Women United and Family Aid had been founded by women who were loyal to the Pci or the Dc, respectively, and to the corresponding women's organizations—Unione Donne Italiane (Udi) and Centro Italiano Femminile (Cif)—and the political distinctions were evident in many aspects of daily life within the two centers.

Leftist and Catholic Feminism

Although many who have written about Italian feminism do not refer to the women of the Centro Italiano Femminile as feminists, I have chosen to include the Catholic women's movement within the encompassing category of feminism. Rather than trying to decipher what should and should not qualify as feminism, I distinguish between leftist and Catholic feminists and let readers come to their own conclusions about whether the Catholic women's movement can indeed be called "feminist." The division of feminism into leftist and Catholic branches could be seen as an essentializing move in that it masks the many subgroups, subdivisions, and ideologies that are part of "feminism."[12] However, this very basic categorization is used simply as an organization tool and is not intended to blur the many different approaches to feminism that exist within these overarching categories.

The Unione Donne Italiane, commonly known as Udi, was founded shortly after the liberation of Rome in World War II (Birnbaum 1986:48). Originally intended to help recruit women to the newly organizing parties on the left side of the political spectrum (Kertzer 1982), at the very beginning of its political life Udi united women from the political and Catholic left in the fight against fascism. By the end of the war, however, cleavages had appeared in this union (Birnbaum 1986). Many Catholic women left Udi to join the Christian Democrats in the fight against communism, and they formed Cif, the Centro Italiano Femminile, as their own auxiliary women's organization. In 1948, the electoral victory of the Dc solidified the division between the political and Catholic left, and the Dc, "the anticommunist party of political Catholicism," went on to dominate Italian politics for nearly half a century (Birnbaum 1986:54).

Although both Udi and Cif were founded as auxiliary organizations to national political parties controlled almost exclusively by men (the Pci and Dc),[13] Udi and Cif organized and motivated thousands of women across Italy to fight for their ideals. Like almost every city throughout Italy, Parma had local offices for both organizations until Udi's national structure dissolved in 1982 and many local Udi offices were shut down. Parma continued to have an active Cif office throughout the 1990s, although many of its activities and services were transferred to Family Aid. In similar fashion, although there was no longer an Udi office when I arrived to do my fieldwork, many of the organization's principles, passions, and individuals were still alive and well in the form of Women United.

Throughout the post–World War II period, Udi and Cif were opposed to one another on many issues, particularly the questions of whether to legalize divorce and abortion (Birnbaum 1986). In many ways the fierce opposition between Udi and Cif mirrored the communist/Catholic divide that ordered much of daily social life in the second half of the twentieth century. Rather than a contrast between left and right or liberal and conservative, the opposition between Udi and Cif reflected a contrast between secular and Catholic approaches to strengthening women's position in society. Despite disagreement on many issues, Udi and Cif cooperated on several important initiatives, including woman suffrage in 1945 and new family legislation in 1975. In fact, toward the late 1970s Cif began voicing its support for many of the same issues that Udi women were advocating. Although the organization as a whole remained opposed to abortion, certain left-leaning Cif members even voiced their support for a woman's right to choose.

Lucia Birnbaum describes the 1978 regional Cif conference in Palermo as focusing on the theme of liberation, and points to the feminist undertones expressed by Maria Eletta Martini, a Dc politician who was vice president of the national house of deputies (1986:187). Birnbaum recounts that in her speech to the Cif audience, Martini "said she had been opposed to the recently passed abortion law because she was opposed to all violence, including violence to the unborn child, but stressed that responsible parenthood was an equal duty of women and men" (187). She voiced her agreement with Udi's assertion that "women should participate at all levels of social and political life." Birnbaum suggests that under the general theme of liberation, the women at the 1978 Cif conference were fighting for issues beyond just equality and were embracing the struggle for the recognition of gender difference. According to Birnbaum, the goal for the Cif women was "to recover genuine values founded on the conception of each human as unique, unrepeatable, with 'equality and difference'" (187).

As Birnbaum points out, "these statements by Catholic women were strikingly similar to the beliefs of women who called themselves feminists" (1986:188). Indeed, by the 1980s many Cif women were adopting themes from the leftist feminist movement. They spoke out against the traditional model of the Catholic family that held women to be subordinate to men, and actively worked to alleviate the double burden placed on working mothers, establishing day-care centers and working to pass new forms of family legislation. At the end of the 1990s, former members of both Udi and Cif spoke to me about the importance of recognizing gender difference, explained that the struggle for sameness between men and women was misguided, and expressed concern about whether and how the feminist movement had changed gender relations in Italian society. Although the most significant and radical transformations came from Italy's new-left feminists (women working outside the dominant political party system, as opposed to remaining within Udi and the Pci), the new understandings and approaches to gender reverberated far beyond women's collectives and research houses. Staunch supporters of both Udi and Cif were influenced by the ideas emanating from the new branches of the Italian feminist movement.

Feminist Transformations

The explosion of social activism in 1968 and the nationwide protests that began in universities, spread to factories, and in a short time permeated society generally (Ginsborg 1990:298) ushered in a new era for Italy's leftist women's movement. The 1968 student protests and occupations were fueled by poor conditions within Italian universities, but represented a wholesale rejection of hierarchy and authority. The protesters operated outside of any organized political party—in fact, according to Paul Ginsborg, "Some of the students' strongest disdain was reserved for the traditional forces of the left. The Communist Party was dismissed for the most part as an 'integrated opposition,' incapable of fighting the system" (1990:305). Although the new left criticized the hierarchical structure of the Pci and the exclusion of women and others with dissenting views, women were just as marginalized in the decision-making structure of the student movement as they had been in the traditional party system (Birnbaum 1986:80).

Italian feminism emerged from this period of widespread activism with new goals and strategies. Women's collectives began to form across the country. Built on the concept of consciousness raising (in Italy the practice was called *autocoscienza*, or self-consciousness), the collectives brought together small groups of women to talk about themselves, their personal experiences, and their identities as women (Milan Women's Bookstore Collective 1990). Sandra Kemp and Paola Bono note that this new form of Italian feminism "came at a moment when women were a lot less 'oppressed' in their daily and in their professional lives. At this point, the real discovery was that emancipation had not got rid of oppression—that it was part of it" (Kemp and Bono 1993:5).

A conflict soon emerged within Udi. There was a split between the younger women, who were forming collectives, and the more established Udi activists, who agreed with the criticism of the Pci but continued to support the mainstream political party system. The younger feminists, many of whom were part of the new left, emphasized the idea that "changing the culture and the political system must include changing yourself" and underscored the importance of being autonomous (Birnbaum 1986:106). They embraced the idea that having equality as a goal was neither helpful nor productive in solving women's problems. Of central importance was the idea that "women viewed the world differently than did men." These new-left feminists saw difference as an "existential fact that women have for millennia been excluded from history" (Birnbaum 1986:85). Rather than fight for equality within the very same structures that had oppressed women for centuries, these feminists sought to create political relationships among women. Difference was to be recognized and celebrated. As Carla Lonzi argued in her 1971 pamphlet titled *Sputiamo su Hegel* (Let's Spit on Hegel):

Equality is a juridical principle. . . . Difference is an existential principle which concerns the modes of being human, the peculiarity of one's own experiences, goals, possibilities, and one's sense of existence in a given situation and in the situation one wants to create for oneself. The difference between woman and man is the basic difference of humankind. . . . Woman's difference is her millennial absence from history. Let us profit from this difference. . . . Equality is what is offered as legal rights to colonized people. And what is imposed on them as culture. It is the principle through which those with hegemonic power continue to control those without. (Lonzi 1971, cited in Bono and Kemp 1991:41)

The link between Udi and the Pci was thus troubling for the new generation of Italian feminists. While some of the older Udi women remained with the Pci and focused on defeating the anti-divorce referendum of 1974, achieving new family-rights legislation, and improving social services, many of the younger feminists moved away from the party system and turned their attention to challenging the law against abortion (Birnbaum 1986:200). Others refused to work within any type of organized political structure and began establishing a new form of extraparliamentary feminist political action built on the recognition of sexual difference and the importance of relationships between and among women. De Lauretis explains that throughout the 1970s and "well into the '80s, Italian feminism was characterized by the widespread phenomenon of 'the double militancy,'" which involved two modes of feminist activism: working within party politics with a focus on equality and social reform and working outside organized structures of power with a focus on difference and personal experience (1990:6). As the latter mode gained popularity, ideals of *autonomia* (autonomy), *differenza* (difference), *autorevolezza*[14] (empowerment), and *relazioni fra donne* (relationships among women) became the touchstones of a new phase of feminist activism.

By the late 1970s, these new ideas had penetrated mainstream feminism. Udi became fully involved in the campaign for abortion rights and began actively challenging the men of the Pci who were intent on mollifying the Dc on the abortion issue. The Udi women who had at first been against the notion of working outside the system came to embrace the strategy of autonomy, and in 1982 Udi dissolved its national structure. The Pci subsidy that had supported Udi for decades was rejected, and power devolved from a vertical hierarchy of local, regional, and national chapters to a horizontal model in which each chapter was responsible for its own fate (Birnbaum 1986:201). At the same time, Cif began its own process of transformation by incorporating aspects of new-left feminism into their ideologies and approaches toward gender (204).

Following the legalization of abortion and the subsequent breakup of Udi, Italy's leftist feminists followed different paths. Some women abandoned feminist politics altogether, while others became involved with newly developed service-oriented activities such as women's shelters and health centers. Bianca Beccalli reasons that without a major national issue to address, "the feminists' autonomous activities lost the visibility they had achieved in the mid 1970s; moreover, the network of small collectives, which had formed the backbone of the movement, began to break down—most groups lost members or simply disappeared, and very few new ones emerged. As a political subject, Italian feminism altogether disappeared" (1994:100).

Despite the loss of an organized leftist feminist movement, the 1980s and 1990s in Italy saw the development of new applications for feminist ideals and values. Many women began incorporating the idea of sexual difference into their everyday lives and relationships. In her 2004 article that questions the meaning of contemporary feminism, Belinda

Giannessi suggests that there are three ways contemporary feminists can engage in the practice of feminism: "First, feminists could do feminism by organizing female energies (as in Women's Centres); second, feminists could do feminism in carrying out its work (that is, by adopting feminist principles as a personal way of living and doing feminism); third, feminists could write feminism" (2004:448). Notably absent from Giannessi's formulation is an activist agenda designed to achieve change on an institutional level. While many Italian women continued to work within political parties and within institutions throughout the 1990s on issues of *pari opportunità* (equal opportunity) and laws against sexual violence, such efforts were no longer part of a unified feminist movement. Feminist politics in Italy had shifted into a new era.

Contextualizing Italian Feminism ·

Although heavily influenced by British, American, and French feminism, Italy's feminists reshaped these schools of thought into their own theory and practice (Bono and Kemp 1991). It is impossible to speak of any of these feminisms in monolithic terms, for each has its own complex history with multiple and opposing branches, but it is nonetheless important to allude to some of the general characteristics that distinguish Italian feminism of the 1970s and 1980s from what was transpiring at that time in France, Britain, and the United States.[15]

Of central importance to Italy's new-left feminists (strongly influenced by French feminists such as Luce Irigaray) was their commitment to work outside of all organized institutional establishments. This meant working outside political parties, outside government agencies, outside universities, and outside any form of national women's movement. As Bono and Kemp point out, "Italian feminism helps bridge an uncomfortable inconsistency between feminism's theoretical refusal to countenance 'master narratives' and the political ascendancy of certain canonical texts in France, Britain and America" as well as the "gap between institutional, theoretical feminism and active/political feminism"(1991:3). Most of Italy's new-left feminists, including those involved with universities, refused to institutionalize their feminist activity and instead worked outside of any organized structure. This is an important distinction, as it reinforces the idea that women must enter into political relationships *with* women *as* women. Many of the central works that emerged in the 1970s were written collectively and attributed to groups of women rather than any particular individual.

Another feature of Italy's new-left feminism was the presence of numerous groups throughout Italy that were independently organized and funded. Throughout the 1970s and early 1980s these autonomous groups emerged in many Italian cities. The groups took shape in various forms—publishing houses, research centers, libraries, and bookstores— and often had very different agendas. Some of the most influential of these groups include Milan's Demau (a contraction of "Demystification of Patriarchal Authoritarianism"), Rome's Rivolta Femminile (Female Revolt), Milan's Libreria delle Donne (Women's Bookstore Collective), and Verona's Diotima, which identifies as a *comunità filosofica* (philosophical community). The groups were autonomous and distinct but united by their recognition of sexual difference, their commitment to work outside institutional structures, and their efforts to build political relationships between and among women. The goal was no longer "women's emancipation and equality, but the 'liberation' of women and the achievement of radical change through privileging the positive values embedded in women's difference" (Beccalli 1994:95).

With their focus on sexual difference, the new-left feminists in Italy diverged from many of their counterparts in Britain and the United States who were primarily focused on achieving equality and social change.[16] Even the work of radical feminists such as Shulamith Firestone (1970) and Kate Millett (1970), or of gynocentric feminists such as Nancy Chodorow (1978) and Carol Gilligan (1982), did not embrace "difference" in quite the same way as Italy's new-left feminists. Rather than constructing historical theories about why or how men and women are different, or examining how these differences take shape in daily social life,[17] the new Italian feminists accepted difference as a historical fact and used it as a basis for their own form of political action. For these feminists, difference did not refer to essential, biological differences between men and women. Nor did it refer to cultural differences in the construction of gender around the world. By difference, the new leftist feminists meant a symbolic difference embodied in the structures of Western society that account for only one subject, a subject that has always been male (Bono and Kemp 1991).

Teresa de Lauretis (1990) explains the project of sexual difference to an American audience. She draws from the work of the Italian feminist and philosopher Adriana Cavarero when she describes the project of sexual difference as the need to "rethink sexual difference within a dual conceptualization of being, 'an absolute dual' in which both being-woman and being-man would be primary, originary forms" (de Lauretis 1990:4).

Rethinking sexual difference requires rethinking the assumptions of Western philosophy that are based on a male/neuter subject. In arguing for difference, the feminists of the Milan Women's Bookstore Collective see the fight for equality as not only useless but wrong, as it "foreclose[s] the road to women's real liberation" (6). De Lauretis explains that although this insistence on the recognition of sexual difference may seem essentialist and reductionist, if viewed not as "the sexual difference that culture has constructed from 'biology' and imposed as gender, and that therefore could be righted, revisioned, or made good with the 'progress of mankind'" but instead as "a difference of symbolization, a different production of reference and meaning out of a particular embodied knowledge" (13), then perhaps it is easier to recognize this theory as a historically and culturally located project that allows women a way to affirm themselves "as subjects not altogether separate from male society, yet autonomous from male definition and dominance" (11).

For Italy's new-left feminists, the fight for equality was ill-advised because it only further established women's subordination to men. A quest for equality meant working within a system that was constructed to recognize a single (male) subject. As Bono and Kemp explain, "Becoming equal thus meant becoming like a man. But 'being-like' is never going to be as good as 'being'; and, on the other hand, being different is unacceptable if it means being inferior" (1991:15). Anna Paini clarifies that it is not equality per se that the new-left feminists opposed but "the notion of equality inscribed in the paradigms of Western thought and philosophy" (1997:129).

Whereas the early work of French feminists Luce Irigaray, Julia Kristeva, and Hélène Cixous has been criticized for its reliance on psychoanalytic theory and its distance from the "experience of ordinary women" (Moi 1987:4), the work of new-left feminists in Italy combined an attention to theory with a commitment to building political relationships between and among women. The growth of centers and groups around Italy enabled women to cultivate relationships with women from different cities, and the occupational heterogeneity of the women involved with these centers and groups ensured that the movement would remain connected to the everyday lives of women.

Although the new-left feminists were influenced by much of the feminist work going on in the United States, Britain, and France, the theories of Luce Irigaray played a particularly strong role in shaping the direction of Italian feminism. Like her predecessor Simone de Beauvoir, Irigaray was committed to the idea that within the structures of patriarchal

Western society there is one subject, and it is male (Schor 1994). A main point that differentiates Irigaray from Beauvoir is that "whereas for Beauvoir the goal is for women to share fully in the privileges of the transcendent subject, for Irigaray the goal is for women to achieve subjectivity without merging tracelessly into the putative indifference of the shifter" (Schor 1994:64). This is an important distinction and one that the new-left feminists in Italy incorporated into their own theorizing. Rather than fight to be included in a structure and language that are supposedly "universal" but in fact always masculine, Irigaray and the new Italian feminists sought to redefine difference and reappropriate what they referred to as "the feminine." As Schor explains, "Irigaray's wager is that difference can be reinvented, that the bogus difference of misogyny can be reclaimed to become a radical new difference that would present the first serious historical threat to the hegemony of the male sex" (1994:65).

Where the new-left feminists in Italy broke away from Irigaray was on the issue of feminist political practice. In contrast with Irigaray, who focused primarily on "sexual difference in the symbolic," the new-left feminists also embraced feminist political practice as a critical component of their work (de Lauretis 1990:16,17). A brief summary of the influential book *Non credere di avere dei diritti: La generazione della libertà femminile nell'idea e nelle vicende di un gruppo di donne* (Don't Think You Have Any Rights: The Engendering of Female Freedom in the Thought and Vicissitudes of a Women's Group), published in 1987 by the Milan Women's Bookstore Collective and translated in 1990 by Patricia Cicogna and Teresa de Lauretis as *Sexual Difference: A Theory of Social-Symbolic Practice*, will help clarify how the new-left feminists in Italy incorporated their theories of sexual difference into a form of feminist political practice.

The writers of the book begin with the statement, "This book is about the need to make sense of, exalt, and represent in words and images the relationship of one woman to another. If putting a political practice into words is the same thing as theorizing, then this is a book of theory, because the relations between women are the subject matter of our politics and of this book" (Milan Women's Bookstore Collective 1990:25). The book goes on to trace the history of a particular group of leftist feminists. The women who made up the Milan Women's Bookstore Collective write their own history and in the process say a great deal about the development of many of the critical theories and practices that came out of Italian feminism in the 1970s and 1980s.

Of crucial importance to the group's theory of political practice is

the relationship of *affidamento*, which Teresa de Lauretis has aptly translated as "entrustment." The word *affidamento* implies trust, security, and
even protection. For the women of the Bookstore Collective, the relationship of entrustment is one "in which one woman gives her trust
or entrusts herself symbolically to another woman, who thus becomes
her guide, mentor or point of reference—in short, the figure of symbolic mediation between her and the world" (de Lauretis 1990:8–9).
The women of the Bookstore Collective point to the biblical relationship between Naomi and Ruth as an example of such a relationship.
Other examples include the relationship between Virginia Woolf and
Vita Sackville-West, or between Jane Austen as a young writer and the
works of the great women writers she was reading at the time. A key
characteristic of such relationships, and one that distinguished the politics of Italy's new-left feminists from those of other feminists around the
world, is that they were not predicated on equality among women. The
very nature of entrustment assumes there will be a power differential,
there will be one woman who is the guide and mentor. As de Lauretis
explains, "Only a generalized social practice of entrustment through
disparity, the book implies, can change the affective contents, symbolic
meaning, and social value of women's relations to one another and to
themselves, and produce another structure of symbolic exchange and
other practices of signification" (1990:9).

Another important aspect of the feminist politics practiced by the
Milan Women's Bookstore Collective was the turn toward literature in
an effort to find "a female symbolic" or a way of expressing knowledge
in a "female gendered language" (Milan Women's Bookstore Collec-
tive 1990:108). The women of the Bookstore Collective began examin-
ing women's literary texts—novels, biographies, poems, and essays.
Among their favorite writers, later referred to as "mothers," were Jane
Austen, Emily Brontë, Charlotte Brontë, Elsa Morante, Gertrude Stein,
Sylvia Plath, Ingeborg Bachmann, Anna Kavan, Virginia Woolf, and Ivy
Compton-Burnett (109).

The reading and examining of texts gave rise to the Bookstore Collective's important identification of the inequalities that exist among
women. Much of the early American feminist theorizing on difference
initially ignored the differences that exist among women and "seemed
too often to involve homogeneous visions of womanhood" (Nicholson
1997:3); even the differences that were later recognized were primarily
differences of ethnicity, race, class, and sexuality. The difference recognized by Italian feminists focused on the basic inequalities that exist

among women. In a type of epiphany, the women of the Bookstore Collective who had gathered to discuss and debate literary works realized they were not all equal. The realization that some of them, "like their favorite writers, were seen as authoritarian 'mothers' prevaricating over the preferences and interpretations of the others, who thus felt cast in the role of daughters" (de Lauretis 1990:10) was a difficult one. As the women of the Bookstore Collective write, "When this simple truth was put into words that first time, the words had a horrible sound, in the literal sense of the term: sour, hard, stinging. But their meaning was crystal-clear. No one doubted they were true, and everyone understood that they had a close relation to our research" (Milan Women's Bookstore Collective 1990:110). The figure of the *madre simbolica* (symbolic mother) thus became a defining aspect of Italy's new-left feminism.

The symbolic mother enabled the cultivation of political relationships, not between equals but between some women who were seen as "mothers" and others who were seen as "daughters." In this way, knowledge was shared between women of different generations and backgrounds (de Lauretis 1990:11). As de Lauretis explains, these relationships enabled "a mutual valorization of the younger woman's desire for recognition and self-affirmation in the world, and the older woman's knowledge of female symbolic defeat in the social-symbolic world designed by men" (11). With this discovery, women were able to create a social contract (between women) that did not exist in the male structured society. Only when women paid the symbolic debt to the symbolic mother through relationships of entrustment with other women would women gain true freedom. For Italy's new-left feminists, this freedom was not found in the pursuit of equal rights under the law, but through relationships with other women and "a full, political and personal, accountability to women" (12). In other words, freedom was not found through equality but through agency and subjectivity as women. As Bono and Kemp explain,

The point is that the body itself needs to be signified and reconstructed, rather than negated. Women have to take upon themselves the task of signifying it, instead of negating its significance merely because, thus far, it has been interpreted to their disadvantage. That would be the risk of egalitarian positioning. Seeing men and women as equal in some abstract sense can easily result in identifying equality with sameness, where the model would be either the universal "male" or a "neutral" human being born of the combination of historically (male) created male and female characteristics. For Italian feminist theory, however, the subject would have to recognize itself in its partiality. Each subject would have to reconstitute him/herself, taking *him/herself* as a starting point. So far, this has been the case only for the male subject, who has negated women's subjectivity in the process. He has deprived her of a conceptual framework and of a language in which to give voice to, and therefore create, her own subject. (1991:16, original emphasis)

In Parma, the need to *partire da sé* (begin from oneself) was embraced by the new-left feminists who formed the collective Biblioteca delle Donne (Women's Library), a group with strong ties to the Milan Women's Bookstore Collective as well as other literary and philosophical collectives around Italy. Founded in 1979, Parma's Women's Library served as a meeting point for women interested in pursuing the politics of sexual difference. Although many of the Library's founders had previously been involved with organized political groups, in creating the collective they made a conscious choice to move outside the bureaucratic structures of society. Rather than provide any specific services to women, or actively lobby for or against legislation, the group focused primarily on discussing theoretical approaches to feminism and collecting important texts from the Italian and international women's movements. Their founding document was modeled on "the practice of doing" and involved recording the thoughts and opinions of all participants (Milan Women's Bookstore Collective 1990:95–96).

By adopting the principles of *autocoscienza*, Parma's Women's Library represented a counter-discourse and an alternative to the feminism promoted initially by Udi and Cif and later by Women United and Family Aid. By working completely outside of any type of institution, the group remained independent and devoted to the cultivation of political relationships among women. Although the group dissolved in 1997, its vast collection of books, magazines, and pamphlets was donated to a local library, and its members continued to meet with one another from time to time. In order to gain a more nuanced and local perspective of the history of Italian feminism, I now turn to the stories of Udi and Cif activists living and protesting in Parma during the 1960s and 1970s.

Udi Activists

Giovanna Riducci grew up in Parma. She joined the Italian Communist Party in 1972 and in 1973 she was asked by members of the party to take over the organization of the local Udi chapter. When I interviewed Giovanna about her experiences with the feminist movement, she explained that she began her experience with Udi in a "gender-neutral" way. She was charged with the bureaucratic task of reorganizing Udi following the organization's internal crisis of the early 1970s—one of many tasks handed out by local party leaders. Her approach was initially very practical and based on utilizing traditional party methods of organization, but as leftist Italian feminism began to change, so did Giovanna's approach to Udi.

In 1974, the already tense political atmosphere exploded with the referendum on divorce. According to Giovanna the referendum marked "a break with the past." It was not only a struggle for the right to divorce, but "a battle that put everything into play." For Giovanna and many other leftist feminists, the referendum opened a new chapter in the social life of women by creating new freedoms. Many women in Parma and the rest of Italy were directly involved in the political struggle over divorce, and their participation prompted critical reflection on the history of the Italian women's movement. The process of reflection created new tensions between men and women of the political left. Women began to realize the male power inherent in politics, and started to ponder the idea of political autonomy for women. The clash between Catholics and communists over the divorce referendum enabled many leftist women to discover the specificity and diversity of their own gender and profoundly changed the direction of Udi.

In my interview with Giovanna, she explained that in the mid-1970s the feminist question was no longer focused on why women were discriminated against at work and in other areas of society. Instead of speaking about parity, women started speaking and writing about difference. They realized that achieving parity was no longer enough because parity itself does not address the important issue of recognition. The feminists of this period began to speak out about the importance of being recognized as women and as political and social subjects.

As the women of Udi began to take a critical look at their own institutional structure and dependence on the Pci, women's collectives began to flourish. "Paradoxically," Giovanna explained, "the more a group was spontaneous, the more a group was disjointed, and the more a group lacked national organization and paid personnel, the more advanced and free the group was." There was no longer a need for a nationally organized group to unify the women's movement. The bureaucratic structure of Udi had been successful in galvanizing support to fight for and against national legislation, but the model had failed to achieve broader cultural change. Giovanna explained that the organization itself "was no longer useful." She asked, "What sense does it make to have ten thousand women as members of Udi if, when they get off the buses to go to protests and marches, they have a copy of *Grand Hotel* under their arm?"[18] For Giovanna, the fact that women were still following soap operas (in the form of comic books) meant that Udi had not been successful in its quest to change cultural models of gender.

According to Giovanna, it was very late in the game when Parma's feminists chose to embrace the notion of sexual difference. In Parma, members of Udi had continued to fight political battles and argue for parity between men and women. The law legalizing abortion provided Giovanna and the other Udi women in Parma with an important opportunity to change the modality of their activism. Giovanna was asked to administer the implementation of a new law that called for the establishment of *consultori* (advice/health centers) in the various *quartieri* (neighborhoods) of Parma. Women were involved in every phase, from planning to implementation, and they labored to ensure that sexual difference and the needs of women were recognized at every step. Birth control, abortion, pregnancy, birthing, motherhood, and sexual health were among the many issues addressed by the centers.

The women of Udi never reached the point of practicing "self-consciousness" like the new feminist collectives. Perhaps because of its organizational hierarchy, or perhaps because of its historical legacy, Udi was unable to transform itself from a national bureaucratic organization with offices and paid functionaries across Italy into a series of small-scale, independent women's groups. After the dissolution of Udi's national structure, local chapters continued for a few years, but eventually disappeared. In Parma, the women who had been involved with Udi splintered into various groups. Many women continued to be involved with the Pci, some ran for local office, others joined collectives, and still others left the women's movement altogether. Giovanna, along with a small group of women who were interested in women's health and legal rights, went on to found Women United.

When I asked Giovanna to define feminism, she told me, "Feminism was Italy's true revolution. It changed everything. It changed the terms of production, reproduction, and language. It changed the identity of this country." Giovanna defined the current women's movement as existing on three levels: the level of service-oriented associations such as Women United, the level of personal and collective reflection, and the level of women writers, journalists, and researchers who are committed to the recognition of sexual difference. When I pushed Giovanna to talk about how things had changed at the level of individual lives and individual relationships, she said she was no longer capable of saying what had changed. She explained that in recent years there had been a return to old ways of doing things. While there was more parity and more respect, and relationships between men and women had changed, still there was a return to old patterns, which made her think that "There is a big question that men have not been able to resolve." Giovanna agreed with those who described Italian men of the 1990s as weak and in crisis, but preferred to describe them as *sfigati*, unfortunates who had lost their place in society.[19]

Other women I spoke with who had been involved with Udi also expressed disillusionment with the current state of gender relations and cultural models of gender. Ilaria, one of Giovanna's friends and colleagues from Udi, pursued a slightly different path following the collapse of Udi. Rather than continue with politics, Ilaria concentrated on work and family life. She became a social worker for the local government, married, and had a child. Despite her departure from politics, she maintained her relationships with other Udi women, and together they transferred their skills as well as their goals to various locations within society: school, work, neighborhood committees, and so on. According to Ilaria, "Every place was an opportunity to construct a tiny piece of reality as we wanted it to be." The mistake, from Ilaria's perspective, was that she and many of her friends saw every aspect of their lives as a battleground. This was an error that weighed heavily on their personal lives and the lives of their families.

ILARIA: Autonomy was pursued even in the small things. For instance, I won't wash the plates if you don't wash them as well, I won't clean the floor if you won't wash the floor. At home the disagreements were over these things. The person you had next to you became the representative of everything that prevented you from feeling like an equal. . . . We forced the generation of our companions to change; with all the games and terrible fights many couples were destroyed.

SONJA: And why was this a mistake?

ILARIA: Because, I realized it afterwards and I think it was inevitable: there wasn't the possibility to look at oneself. We didn't look at the person next to us. We saw a symbol. Not that they [the men] were any better. On the contrary, they were firmly masculine . . . they expected what they had seen growing up, the traditional wife, welcoming and sweet. What they found was a ball breaker who fought about everything. This was not a great situation. We lacked the ability to talk to each other; the thing my generation absolutely did not know how to do was talk to one another.

SONJA: And did your husband change?

ILARIA: Yes, he changed, but I wouldn't want anyone to follow the same path. You can't spend thirty years of your life fighting a war that never ends. There was a time when I was determined to end it [the marriage], because I couldn't take it anymore. I found myself in the 1980s with a child and a tiring and frustrating job working with disadvantaged kids.

While Ilaria was struggling with her many pressures at work and at home, her husband was working in leftist politics and "pretending to be the good leftist father." From Ilaria's perspective, he didn't even know where to begin. He was busy helping the poor, the desperate, and the unemployed, and having a "ball-breaking wife" who wanted him to do things around the house was not part of the plan. He was an affectionate father, but his model of a wife and mother came from his memories of his own mother, who, according to Ilaria, was a *donna sottomessa* (submissive woman).

It was only in the few years prior to our interview, after nearly three decades of marriage, that Ilaria's relationship with her husband had started to improve. According to Ilaria it was because to a certain extent she accepted a subordinate role: "I accepted a more traditional female role, one of support and attention, limiting my own desires and needs in favor of his. To a certain extent I have followed this path. It was either leave the marriage ten years ago or else do this. Now I find we have an intense and reciprocal support, but it has been a long journey." Ilaria, like her friend Giovanna, fought for the rights of women throughout the 1970s only to admit thirty years later, with a disillusioned sigh, that she has been unable to incorporate the changes she sought for society into her own marital relationship. Only when she compromised on her goals and desires by assuming a more "traditional" role was she able to find harmony in her marriage.

Alessia was in her late forties when I met her, and had been a caseworker at Women United until she resigned in 1997. Along with a few other former workers and volunteers, Alessia went on to found a woman's cooperative in Parma that sponsors courses and social outings, houses women who are in economic difficulty, and works to help women suffering from depression and loneliness. When I went to speak with Alessia about the cooperative and learn about her experience with leftist feminism, she explained that the women's movement had failed to leave a legacy for the younger generations: "The women who fought in the sixties and seventies to change women's roles ended up following their own individual paths. I see aggression in the younger generations; they are confused. It gives me more security to see a man and a woman having defined roles than to see the confusion that exists today."

Alessia explained that many women in today's society have jobs, but very few hold positions of power. Women bring their "riches" to the workplace but are forced to change because the world of work is still masculine. The result is that there is "a return to traditional roles." According to Alessia, "women need to find a way to be in the family and also have a job." When Alessia and others from her cooperative visited local high schools to talk about gender and gender roles, they found that many young women envisioned their futures as consisting of motherhood and marriage. Careers were not part of the picture. Alessia had found a way to balance being a wife and mother with having a career. When I asked her if she considered herself to be a feminist she told me, "I was. The error that we made was to personally find our own paths, our own solutions to having a career and a family. We never found any general solutions, cultural solutions that could be used by later generations."

Emanuela, a member of Women United, spoke of similar frustrations. She came to Parma with her husband in 1967. She was nineteen and was quickly swept up in the passion and activism of the time. Like Giovanna, Emanuela told me that the fight for divorce and abortion radically changed the way women thought about themselves. She explained, "Women changed, their self-knowledge changed, they understood that they needed to pay attention to themselves and rely on themselves." Emanuela remembered her period of Udi activism very warmly. She went to evening meetings three times a week and participated in frequent demonstrations and protests. The women she met were inspired and driven to make changes in society that would create new freedoms and possibilities for Italian women. She met many women—local political visionaries like Giovanna as well as others—who remained colleagues and friends for years. From the way Emanuela talked about the years she was involved with Udi, it was clear that this had been a defining period in her life. The dedication and intensity of the women involved with securing a woman's right to abortion and divorce is unparalleled in the history of Italian feminist activism.

When I asked Emanuela to reflect on her experience with Udi and explain how relationships between men and women had changed since the 1960s, her response echoed the resignation of Giovanna, Ilaria, and Alessia. She told me,

Yes, relationships have changed, but they have gotten worse in the sense that men have not changed at all. They like their role the way it was. They're not able to understand the way women have changed. They don't understand what women want because they think women have always wanted the same thing. And they don't understand how they can change. I'm convinced of this.

Emanuela explained that she married her husband because, in the city where they grew up, he appeared to be "supportive of women's freedom and parity between men and women." At home, Emanuela discovered, "it was completely different, in the sense that he never washed the dishes or did other things around the house. Now he does more, but he still tries to get out of it." As is often the case, public support for gender equality does not always translate into gender equality within marriages and partnerships. Years after the dissolution of Udi, a friend of Emanuela's admitted to her that she had felt terrible going to Udi meetings because everyone was always talking about the importance of parity and rights. Meanwhile, she knew that in her own home her husband didn't lift a finger to help with household chores. Laughing as she recounted this story, Emanuela told me she had asked her friend, "Did you really think our husbands were any different?" With bursts of deep belly laughter, Emanuela told me her friend had "stayed quiet for twenty years because she was embarrassed she couldn't get her husband do to things around the house. She was convinced our husbands were better, that our husbands did housework!"

For many Udi women, the weekly meetings to discuss feminist principles and strategies for activism were liminal moments that gave them refuge from the pressures and demands of their everyday lives as wives and mothers. Although some had been able to incorporate feminist ideals into their daily lives, many were not able to significantly alter the gender dynamics of their own personal relationships. Unlike the woman who confessed her embarrassment years later, Emanuela and others did not see this disjuncture as a problem that barred them from continuing with their lives as activists. On the contrary, the disjuncture was accepted as part of the normal routine of being a wife, a mother, and a feminist, all at the same time.

David Kertzer discovered a similar integration of commitments in his interview with an Udi activist in the early 1970s. Before introducing in his article the narrative of Evelina Zaghi, one of Bologna's prominent local organizers, he explains that "Evelina's belief in the social, economic, and political liberation of women does not entail a personal rejection of all the traditional responsibilities of women" (1982:46). Evelina explained to Kertzer that she spent a great deal of time caring for her forty-two-year-old son, who lived at home, and her daughter, who was married with two children:

With my kids and everything, I don't have any spare time. I'm always busy. My son comes home every day to have lunch, so I have to be here to prepare it for him. Then, when I get a little time, I have to go to my daughter's, because she has two children and a job, so I have to take care of things. (Kertzer 1982:59–60)

More than twenty years later, Emanuela's story was similar to Evelina's, except that Emanuela recognized the contradiction and expressed optimism about the new generations. She told me that young men were doing more work around the home and spending more time with their children: "It used to be embarrassing for a man to be seen pushing a baby carriage; now men take them out, all happy to be with their children." Despite the confusion and ambivalence she saw in contemporary understandings of gender, Emanuela explained that women in their twenties and thirties are more confident and focused on their careers than the women of her own generation. According to Emanuela, they are not politically involved, and enjoy the fruits of the feminist project without stopping to think why and how these gains were achieved.

The passion and activism of Udi was unique to a particular generation of leftist women across Italy who were united by their dedication to fighting for women's rights. Although the collapse of Udi in 1982 marked the end of a nationally organized leftist women's movement, the values and ideals lived on, albeit in a different form, in the numerous service-oriented associations and cooperatives run by women, organizations such as Women United.

Two Generations of Cif in Parma

Gina Bianco was thirty years old at the time of our interview, and was on the board of directors for the Parma chapter of Cif. I met with Gina one sunny afternoon. We had arranged to meet at a park in one of Parma's residential neighborhoods, just outside the city walls. Gina arrived a bit late and out of breath. She explained that there had been an emergency at work and she had not yet had time to pick up her baby daughter from her mother-in-law's. As we walked the few blocks to her mother-in-law's apartment she explained that her mother and her mother-in-law alternated taking care of her daughter, which avoided hurting anyone's feelings. Gina and her husband lived just a few blocks away from both sets of parents, so the childcare system they had worked out was very convenient for everyone involved.

When we arrived at Gina's mother-in-law's apartment complex, Gina buzzed up and her mother-in-law brought the baby down in a stroller.

We chatted for a few minutes, and then Gina and I went off on our own for a walk around the neighborhood. As we walked, Gina pushed the stroller and I carried my tape recorder. Gina explained that Cif was founded both to advance the rights of women and to reflect on the relationship between men and women in society. The mission was, and still is today, "to support the participation of women in all aspects of society." According to Gina, Cif sponsored the very first courses on political education for women, organized the first courses on sexual education, and instituted the first social services intended to help families. In Parma, Cif ran *consultori*, summer camps for children, and day-care centers. Although during the 1990s the services Cif offered were greatly reduced, they still administered two day-care centers and one summer camp.

Gina pointed out that whereas the early phases of leftist feminism focused on the fight for equality, "today there is more of a focus on the valorization of difference. We don't want to be the same as men; there are differences and we want the differences to be recognized and to be valued." When I asked Gina to describe the differences between Udi and Cif, she said the difference really lay at an ideological level:

Today Udi no longer exists. The principal battle was over abortion. It was a cultural difference. The Catholic culture was absolutely against it and the leftist culture saw abortion as a great freedom for women, the ability to control their own bodies. Today it is really an aspect of history. Today it is an opposition that no longer exists. The great risk for feminism of today, as pointed out by an important feminist scholar, is that we are not able to transmit anything. . . . If you ask young girls today when women gained the right to vote they'll say we've had it forever.

Although both Cif and former Udi members have mutual respect for each other's work, there is still some reticence and resistance to collaboration. Although Gina herself did not feel any opposition to former Udi members, she confessed that she had not found it easy to collaborate with Women United.

Gina herself identified with the center-left of Italian politics and found no contradiction in identifying herself as both feminist and Catholic:

In my opinion there is no opposition between being Catholic and being feminist. On the contrary, the first person to liberate women was Jesus Christ. I think that the Catholic message is to help people to be as free as possible and to be as free as possible yourself. The relationship between men and women is central. In my opinion, each of us is called to give the maximum we can give, and if we're caught in the bind of a particular role we won't be able to give the maximum. I find that the reason I'm feminist is because I'm a believer.[20] . . . In my opinion, all Catholics should be feminists because feminism is the pursuit of rights.

In her own household, Gina divided all the household duties equally with her husband, but since they both worked outside the home they decided to dedicate part of their income to hiring a person to help with the cleaning. When I asked Gina whether they had discussed the division of duties before getting married, Gina explained that before getting married her husband had been enthusiastic about the idea of dividing all of the household labor. He had gone with her to conferences and meetings to discuss relations between men and women, and they shared the same opinions on how to construct a relationship and a household. "But," Gina explained, "Thinking and agreeing is one thing, doing is another." After they married, Gina realized that her husband was not one to spontaneously do things around the house. Whereas for Gina it was normal to come home and immediately start getting dinner ready, her husband needed to be told, "Turn on the oven and start cooking." Whereas Gina came from a family where both her parents worked and divided nearly all of the household duties, her husband came from a family where the father "came home and asked what's for dinner," and the mother did everything.

I found this disjuncture between theory and practice to be common among the men and women I spoke with in Parma. Just like the Udi activists who went to meetings to talk about equal rights and equal duties but went home to serve their husbands and clean the house, Gina and other women her age struggled with men who agreed in principle with an equal division of household duties but did not translate this theoretical stance into everyday action.

Gina, however, was a rarity among her peers. She was one of a small group of young women who were active participants in Cif. When she went to national meetings (she was also a national representative), she was often the youngest person there. Gina identified the lack of young people as one of Cif's central problems. Out of the 150 women associated with Cif in Parma, about 15 were of a younger generation (in their twenties and thirties). Most of the Cif women were the ones who had been with the organization since the 1960s and 1970s.

Carmela Vitali was one of these women. She was seventy-seven when I met her, and had been involved with Cif for more than thirty years. Although no longer on the governing council, Carmela continued to be actively involved with the organization. One morning I sat with Carmela at her dining-room table and heard about her many years of experience with Cif and women's politics. When I asked Carmela to tell me about the goals and objectives of Cif, she quickly set the organization's principles and values in opposition to those of Udi. She explained,

The objective of Cif has always been to help women gain awareness. At first the goal was to increase women's participation on a civic and political level, in local government, in organizations, in women's health centers, but always from a Catholic point of view. Now everything has changed. They [referring to Udi] have also changed; they now understand that you have to maintain certain fundamental values. They've seen how the number of births has decreased, how many babies died because of their campaign for abortion. They too have become frightened. And now things have changed. When I say them, I'm referring to the women of Udi and the women who used to be involved with Pci politics, women we worked together with on many issues, women we met with, discussed with, women for whom I have the utmost respect. They worked tirelessly, but from a different set of objectives and principles.

Although the women of Udi and Cif had great respect for one another, they also disagreed vehemently on a number of issues. Just as the Pci and Dc were intimately tied through their opposition to one another, so were Udi and Cif. Carmela explained that members of Udi and Cif would often attend the same meetings. Called in for consultations by local and regional government, both Udi and Cif would voice their points of view at these sessions. Laughing, Carmela remembered many late-evening meetings when the Udi members would stall until midnight, when the Cif members could no longer stay awake. Then, once Carmela and the other Cif representatives had gone home, all the important decisions would be made. During the 1970s and 1980s, the left was in power in Parma and Bologna. Government agencies were therefore almost always allied with the Udi point of view. Nevertheless, Cif members continued to attend meetings and continued to argue for their position on various issues.

When I asked Carmela if she and the other Cif members called themselves feminists, she laughed softly and said,

Ah, that's a good question. You could say feminists, but not in an extreme way like other feminists, especially the feminists of my time, the 1970s. We are for equal opportunity between men and women, but not for equality itself. We've seen that equality isn't enough, we want equality in all fields but we want women to be recognized for what they bring to society. In this sense we are a bit feminist. We realize that women can do certain things, maybe more than men. But in my time there were women who threw out their bras to prove they were equal to men. That was absurd.

Like the Udi activists I spoke with, Carmela underscored her conviction that women can do anything and everything men can do, but that women are different from men. She agreed with the theory of gender difference and said, "We are not for fixed roles . . . we can't say that a woman must stay at home, but she must have the possibility of staying home if that is what she chooses." Carmela pointed out that despite efforts to secure a salary for housewives (including a legislative proposal by the Dc in 1979), there was still no adequate support from the state for women who stay home to raise their children.

Carmela was several decades older than Gina and had been an active Cif member during the most turbulent period of the women's movement. Unlike Gina, Carmela frequently mentioned her Udi counterparts. She reminisced about the great divide between the two organizations but expressed deep respect for the hard work and perseverance of Udi women. For Carmela, Udi women were

incredibly strong, the organization was able to train very good people. They were able to pay their leaders whereas we were all volunteers. They went on to become very important women, they became representatives in local and regional government, they became the heads of organizations, and they became top managers. . . . I always admired them for their dedication to Udi.

Although Carmela identified with the center-left of Italian politics, she no longer had any type of party allegiance. With the fall of the Pci and the Dc, many people found themselves confused by the plethora of new parties. Former Dc members were especially confused, as the Dc had been essentially a centrist party that united Catholics from both the left and the right. Carmela did not support the major rightist parties such as Forza Italia (Go Italy), Alleanza Nazionale (National Alliance), and the Lega Nord (Northern League), but she also could not ally herself with the major leftist parties such as Democratici di Sinistra (Democrats of the Left) and Partito della Rifondazione Comunista (Refoundation Communist Party). When I asked Carmela about politics, she explained,

Today it is very difficult. I still haven't figured out whom I can trust. Everything is a big mixture and people's positions are not clear. They say that a new center will be born, but I'm not so sure. I think it will just continue like this, with a left that moves closer and closer to the center and a right that claims to be the new Dc. Catholics are divided. I feel bad for young people who don't know how to orient themselves. It is very difficult to find young people who are involved with politics.

In fact, many people I spoke with, especially leftist former Dc members, expressed confusion about the current political situation. The end of the Cold War, the dissolution of the Catholic/communist opposition, and the proliferation of new political parties had made the negotiation of political identity a difficult process. When I asked Gina if there was a particular party for Catholic leftists, she said, "I couldn't say, I have trouble understanding. It changes every day."

When I spoke with former Udi and Pci members, they expressed similar confusion and frustration with the ambiguous political climate. They also showed frustration with the male-dominated political arena. According to Manuela Amoretti, a former functionary of the leftist party Ds who held a seat on the regional government of Emilia-Romagna but lost her reelection bid in 2000, the political situation is not good for Italian women: "Even in the Emilia-Romagna region, where almost all women work and many women have important positions, the world of politics remains male." Indeed, instead of steadily increasing, as was the case in many other European nations, the percentage of women in representative government in Italy decreased in the 1990s. Following the elections of 2001, women made up only 9.2 percent of the Italian parliament (Tonelli 2001).

When I asked Amoretti to list the most important issues facing women at the beginning of the twenty-first century, she cited the importance of opportunities for work, the importance of having more flexible schedules in order to balance the needs of work with the needs of the family, and the need for a more equitable distribution of *lavoro di cura* (caretaking work) between men and women. Despite legislation in Italy that encourages equal opportunity for men and women and allows men as well as women to take leave from work to care for children, Amoretti pointed out that unless legislation is accompanied by cultural initiatives, nothing will ever change. Amoretti's views are echoed by scholars such as Luisa Passerini, who notes, "Some of the laws passed in the 1970s were little used in practice (the legislation allowing fathers leave of absence to care for children is a case in point) and this reluctance shows how slow the pace of change has been in some areas" (1996:156).

When I asked Amoretti whether she thought it would be useful to have an organization like Udi to help coordinate these initiatives, she explained that it would be very difficult to have a national women's movement in today's political and cultural climate. She pointed out that in recent years there has been a retreat from collective experiences, and that a national movement of women in Italy, on the scale of Udi, has not existed for a very long time. There is general apathy on the part of many Italians, especially among young people, and in large part it is due to an alienating and confusing political atmosphere.

In the early 1990s, the collapse of the political dualism that had governed Italian political life for nearly fifty years created a climate of instability in society as well as in politics. Continual government crises (between 1992 and 2002 Italy had eight different governments),[21] the exposure of far-reaching corruption in the 1990s,[22] and the proliferation of political parties[23] all contributed to apathy on the part of many Italian voters.

Confusion about political orientation, combined with ambivalence about the state of gender relations, led many women to stay out of politics altogether and devote their time to service-oriented organizations with clearly delineated principles and goals. During the 1990s there was no longer a national organization for leftist women. Many of Parma's former Udi members directed their activism to Women United and other such institutions. On the Catholic side, Family Aid continued to expand, with new office space, additional shelters, and volunteers of all ages, but Cif struggled to attract youthful participation and stay relevant in the confusing political and social environment.

In 1996, writing in English but addressing herself to an Italian audience, Luisa Passerini noted that "in the confusion and disillusionment of the 1990s, we do well to remind ourselves of the irreverent energies which broke through twenty years ago. That remembered passion can encourage us to take stock of our own times, and to press once more for a recognition both of equality and of difference, between the sexes and between individuals" (1996:157). In these closing lines of her review of gender relations in Italy, Passerini conveys the mood among many former activists I spoke with at the end of the 1990s, who were proud of the changes that had been achieved, aware of the enduring aspects of a patriarchal society, and unsure what the future might hold.

CHAPTER 3

Politics of Gender and Shelter

THE DIFFERENCES BETWEEN the ideological visions of Women United and Family Aid illustrate two points on the continuum of gender proficiency (what it means to be a good man or a good woman) in Parma in the late 1990s.[1] Whereas the women involved with Women United interpreted "modern" forms of gender relations as a positive step toward increased freedom and autonomy for women, many of the women involved with Family Aid feared the impact that such new forms of gender relations would have on the institutions of family and motherhood. These contrasting visions of gender not only shaped everyday interactions within the shelters—and produced very different experiences for the women receiving help and assistance—but also mirrored the range of ideas about gender proficiency I was reading about in local publications and hearing about in casual conversations with friends and colleagues.

Monica

When I first met Monica in September of 1999 she was living with her two children in an apartment known as a *casa rifugio*, or safe house, administered by Women United. While living in the safe house, Monica was encouraged to learn how to manage money and was given a weekly stipend to use for groceries and personal items. Childcare was not provided, and she was responsible for adjusting her work schedule to take care of her children. Although caseworkers would stop by each day, and there were rules of the house, most of the time Monica and the three other women living in the apartment were on their own to manage their time and their lives.

At the point when I met her, Monica had been living in Women United's safe house for more than a year. She had developed close bonds with the caseworkers and volunteers, and they were proud of the way she had taken control of her life. Monica would greet the caseworkers with big hugs, which they would reciprocate. Monica's name continually came up in discussions as an example of a woman who was a pleasure to work with—easy to talk to and get to know.

A few weeks after meeting Monica, I found out that she was scheduled to move to an apartment administered by Family Aid. Although she was no longer in danger, and therefore no longer in need of a shelter with a secret address, she did not have enough money to rent her own apartment. As a single mother and a legal resident of Parma, Monica was eligible to sign up for one of the subsidized apartments rented out by the city government, but there was more than a year's wait. As an interim solution, her social worker made arrangements for her to move to one of Family Aid's apartments. Although the women at Family Aid had agreed to provide shelter, each week Monica seemed to hear a different story regarding her future living arrangements. First she was told she would be getting an apartment to herself. Then she was told she would be sharing the apartment with another woman. Finally, on the day she moved in, Monica found out that she would indeed be sharing the apartment with another woman, who had two children of her own, and she would also be sharing the space with three rotating shelter workers who were responsible for supervising the apartment twenty-four hours a day.

The first few months were extremely difficult. Monica became depressed and frustrated, often calling upon the women of Women United for support and advice. From the perspective of Women United, it seemed as if Monica had gone from an atmosphere based on trust back to an atmosphere of control, supervision, and hierarchy. When I asked the women at Family Aid about Monica, I was told that initially she was placed in the supervised apartment purely for security reasons (to make sure her ex-husband would not come after her). After a few weeks, however, the supervisors reported that she had no control over her children, was manipulative, and continually broke the rules of the house. It was then decided that Monica would need to learn how to be a "good" and "responsible" mother before she could be allowed to move to an unsupervised apartment.

The supervisors who lived in the house with Monica were theoretically there to make things easier—they helped with childcare, did the food shopping, and at times prepared dinner—but Monica did not welcome their assistance. After eight frustrating months for both Monica and the shelter supervisors, the board of directors at Family Aid agreed to move her into an unsupervised apartment.

Intrigued by the discrepancy in the ways Monica was perceived by the two organizations, I asked one of the caseworkers at Women United whether they had ever had any problems with Monica while she was living in the safe house. The caseworker explained that Monica would occasionally exaggerate or evade the truth, but she never caused any problems. The caseworker laughed and told me that although Monica was known to tell a white lie every so often, they were always easily recognizable and just part of her outgoing, robust personality. Seeing Monica in two very different shelter environments, and hearing the very different reactions of the shelter workers, provided me with a clear example of the political and ideological differences between Women United and Family Aid and, by extension, between the leftist and Catholic women's movements in Parma.

Women United

As byproducts of the communist/Catholic political dichotomy, Women United and Family Aid were founded on very different understandings of what it means to be a woman in Italian society. Although the Pci itself did not actively work toward change in gender relations,[2] many women who were part of the Pci became very involved with the leftist feminist movement of the 1970s and campaigned for the rights to divorce and abortion, and for new roles for women in society. The women of Women United spoke and wrote about the need for continued change in Italian society—more support for working mothers, more equitable division of tasks within the family, more opportunity for women to occupy positions of power in business and politics, identities for women outside the roles of wife and mother, and greater acknowledgment of gender difference. They saw themselves as promoters of a "modern" cause, and differentiated themselves from the Catholic women of Family Aid, whom they labeled "traditionalists" with very different definitions of womanhood. The women of Family Aid defined themselves as supporters of the sanctity of life, and underscored the importance of teaching women how to become "good" mothers. They saw the women of Women United largely as the "feminists" and "abortionists" of the 1970s who did not recognize the importance of the unborn life and the word of God. Family Aid did work to help unmarried or divorced mothers become economically self-sufficient, but for them ultimate success lay in finding a good man (in order to marry and procreate). The ideological differences between Family Aid and Women United were reproduced in their methodologies for helping women. By examining these methodologies we can form a picture of how proponents of "new" and "old-fashioned" visions of gender, motherhood, and marriage responded to issues such as partner violence, abortion, single motherhood, and self-sufficiency in Parma in the late 1990s.

Women United was founded in the early 1980s when a group of women who were collecting signatures to demonstrate support for the law against sexual violence asked themselves how they could create a place where women could discuss and question the problem of violence. As explained in the organization's 1991 brochure:

Seven years ago there were women on the street encouraging people to sign a petition in favor of the law against sexual violence. I found a leaflet that said, "Come and study this problem with us." I went to the meeting and discovered that there were many of us who wanted to create a new solidarity among women. I discovered that there were many of us—from different social, cultural, and professional positions—who wanted to rewrite aspects of the social rules. We wanted to create "a place" in which to work out life paths, in which to reinforce the potential of every woman, a place in which there would be no room for violence: this place became Women United.

In its 1998 brochure, the organization defined itself in similar terms:

Women United is a place where women can address the problem of violence, outside of a context of culpability. Any woman who has experienced or is experiencing violence in any form—psychological, physical, or sexual—is welcome to visit.

We are volunteers and workers, united by the common goal of producing freedom and autonomy for women. Our political stance emphasizes the importance of building relationships among women, the need to overcome a neutral or male point of view of the world, and the promotion of gender difference and the feminine gender in all its variety and richness.

The organization's political stance was based on leftist Italian feminist ideology rooted in the fight for the recognition of gender difference. Instead of arguing for "sameness" between men and women—which many women I spoke with said is an impossible goal—the women of Women United followed the lead of other leftist feminists who were arguing for a "symbolic revolution" whereby women would become "the subject, rather than the object, of the 'woman question'" (de Lauretis 1990:5). The women of Women United placed great importance on working for wider societal recognition of *la differenza di genere* (gender difference). They described the project of gender difference not as the need for women to engage in political relationships with other women but as the need to recognize that women and men have different qualities and traits, all of which should be equally valued and appreciated.

When I met Isabella she was thirty years old and one of three caseworkers at Women United. Isabella was unusual among the young women I met during my year in Parma. Nearly all the other women in their late twenties and early thirties were unmarried and working or studying while living with their parents, but Isabella was separated from her husband and raising their five-year-old daughter.

One afternoon during an interview in Isabella's living room, I asked whether she thought the women working and volunteering at Women United were feminists. Isabella took a moment to think, and then explained:

> It depends what you mean by feminist. Feminist in the sense of a party, or how feminism was initially interpreted? That women are the same as men and everything is the same therefore we dress like men? No. With respect to equal rights and duties, yes. But it is important that I am a woman, I want to be different from a man, I want to maintain my femininity because it is part of me. It's not true that in order to do a man's job I need to dress like a man, speak like a man, or give up having children. . . . We are different, and the differences between man and woman need to be *valorizzate* (recognized and valued).

Ghita, one of the youngest volunteers at Women United, who midway through my year in Parma was hired as a caseworker, responded in a very similar way to my question. She too said that it depended on the definition of feminism, and explained that it would be impossible for her to identify as a feminist because she was just a baby when all the historic feminist battles were taking place. Ghita said she believed in parity between men and women, but did not agree that men and women are the same.

The organization's older volunteers and caseworkers, primarily women in their fifties, more readily identified as feminists. Emanuela, the same activist I talked about in the previous chapter, had moved to Parma in 1968, just as the student movement was gaining momentum, and became actively involved with the various waves of feminist activism. According to Emanuela, the word "feminist" had become a stereotype, but in her opinion being feminist meant "thinking that women have rights to citizenship exactly the same as those afforded to men, and therefore have the right to do the same jobs as men, have the right to speak, and have the right to equal opportunity." When I asked Emanuela whether women my age (I was twenty-seven at the time) could be classified as feminists, she explained: "Women your age, for the most part, reject the word. I have a daughter who is about your age, and the women of this age don't want to fight in the feminist sense, but they are absolutely feminists, in the sense that they claim equal rights for themselves."

The women of Women United—both the younger and older generations[3]—incorporated the ideals of equal rights, gender difference, and gender solidarity into their everyday interactions with each other and the women they sought to help. During meetings, caseworkers and volunteers continually reinforced the idea that they were there to help, not as social workers or professionals but as women extending a helping hand to other women. There were lawyers and psychologists who volunteered at Women United, but meetings with professionals always came as a second step.[4] The initial point of contact and point of reference was always a caseworker or volunteer, whose most important qualification was her identity as a woman.

The primary goal of Women United was to help women build the confidence and self-sufficiency they needed in order to leave abusive partners, become financially independent, and rebuild their lives. The organization aimed to give women the tools they were denied by the rest of society—a safe place, a sense of self, a sense of autonomy, an appreciation of the female gender, and a sense of the strong bonds that can be created among women. Cinzia, another young caseworker, described the organization as a place of *solidarietà femminile* (female solidarity). According to Cinzia, female solidarity meant that as a woman she could better understand other women, she could listen to a woman's story and think "maybe I've gone through a similar experience in the past or maybe I will go through a similar experience in the future."

In my conversations with the women of Women United, they had difficulty defining what it meant to be feminist in the late 1990s, but were resolute about the importance of promoting female solidarity and the recognition of gender difference.[5] When I asked about the origin of the "difference" between men and women, they cited culture as the primary culprit. They explained that the differences between men and women stem from centuries of patriarchy and the almost universal subordination of women. Although the women of Women United recognized differences among women, especially the cultural differences associated with class, regional identity, and ethnicity, they embraced a larger commonality that transcended such differences. This commonality was the worldview born of generations of subordination and restriction to the duties associated with raising children and maintaining a household.

Structure and Organization of Women United

Women United was founded through perseverance by a small group of women dedicated to challenging violence against women. After applying to the regional government numerous times for funding, in the mid-1980s the group succeeded in securing its first grant of £150 million (US$75,000). At this point, the group wrote its bylaws and formed an association. The purpose outlined in the founding charter was "to activate the fight against every form of violence against women" and to develop "tools and structures that promote solidarity among women who experience violence." The organization was classified as a voluntary association, which meant that although it was allowed to have a minimal number of paid employees, it was not allowed to profit from its endeavors and had to be governed by a board made up entirely of volunteers.

Women United was the second organization of its kind in the region of Emilia-Romagna, and one of the first in all of Italy. In its early years, the headquarters were very small and poorly located—in a distant residential zone and right above a municipal office, which made it difficult for women concerned about privacy to come in for meetings. During this period the organization focused on providing a telephone support line and promoting cultural events to increase public awareness. Over the years, Women United increased its funding and expanded its services, and in 1991 Parma's city government gave the organization a lease for its current location. The new, larger offices enabled Women United to begin having face-to-face meetings with women. The hours of operation were expanded, and the association decided to start hiring paid caseworkers, as the organization was no longer able to function with only volunteer labor.

As an active volunteer from 1999 to 2000, I observed the caseworkers attending to the business of the organization—writing letters and working on funding proposals, organizing conferences, scheduling appointments, and managing Women United's many community awareness projects. Office hours were Monday through Friday from 9:00 to 1:00, and on Tuesdays and Thursdays the office reopened in the afternoon from 3:00 to 6:00. Each day there was usually at least one scheduled appointment with a woman, and often there were walk-in consultations as well. The phone rang frequently throughout the day, and the caseworkers fielded calls from women calling to check in or schedule an appointment. Many initial conversations with women seeking help took place over the phone, but the caseworkers always encouraged women to schedule face-to-face meetings. Caseworkers recorded only a first name and encouraged women to use a pseudonym if it would make them feel more comfortable.

From 1991 to 2000, more than 1,400 women visited Women United. By 1996, the organization had gained enough community recognition and funding to open a *casa rifugio* (safe house) in another area of the city, and began offering shelter to women in need of protection from violent spouses and partners. The safe house was an apartment with a secret address that could house up to four women with their children. It enabled women to leave their violent partners and create new lives for themselves and their children.

The caseworkers I met—Maura, Cinzia, Ghita, and Isabella—were paid to work for the organization, but they were very committed to the cause and often worked many more hours than their contracts stipulated. Only one of the caseworkers had a salary and a contract that entitled her to vacation days. The others were paid on an hourly basis and were not entitled to any benefits.

All administrative business was taken care of at the main office, which was also the place where caseworkers, lawyers, and psychologists met with women. The safe house, on the other hand, was a home for women escaping violent partners and husbands, and was run as a separate entity. The caseworkers helped the women living in the safe house find jobs and get their children into day care. The caseworkers also provided ongoing emotional support and were on call to help with any emergencies. When the safe house was full, the caseworkers would spend many hours each day making sure everything in the house ran smoothly. Even though the house was *autogestita*, or self-run, which meant that the women purchased groceries on their own and shared cooking and cleaning duties, there were still many things for the caseworkers to manage. When the women got into arguments with one another, the children were sick, or the women had problems at work, the caseworkers were always called in to iron out the difficulties.

Each week, the women living in the safe house were given an allowance to pay for all food and personal items. The caseworkers saw this as a way of helping the women gain experience in saving and managing money. For many of the women, managing money was a new skill that required practice. Prior to entering the safe house, many had lived with husbands who prohibited them from having anything to do with household finances.

Due to a decrease in funding available from local and regional governments, in the late 1990s economic concerns became increasingly worrisome for the organization. Women United began charging a high daily rate for women and children living in the safe house. In order for a woman to enter the safe house, the social services of the town in which she was a resident had to agree to pay a daily fee for her room and board. On occasion Women United would waive this requirement if the woman had no place of residence or was in extreme danger. With a paucity of outside funding, the organization was forced to rely increasingly on the safe house to generate enough money to support the organization.

Women Helping Women

The style in which potential clients were received was another indication of the ideology of the organization. When a woman came to Women United for an appointment or an unscheduled drop-in meeting, the first thing a caseworker would do was greet her at the door and invite her to have a seat in one of the four large, comfortable armchairs that were arranged in a circle in one corner of the room. Once she was seated in a chair, two caseworkers or a caseworker and a volunteer would sit down with the woman and provide prompts for the woman to tell her own story. During an initial meeting, the caseworker would usually just listen, interrupting only occasionally to ask for clarification or more detail about a particular point. The caseworkers would not take notes during the meeting, as they preferred to maintain a more intimate atmosphere. Only after the meeting would the caseworkers begin writing up notes on a woman's story. Women come to Women United for many different reasons (sexual harassment, rape, incest, depression, etc.), but according to archived records, in any given year roughly 60 percent came because they were living with violent husbands or partners.

In an interview with Maura, I asked what she tried to do during a meeting with a woman. She explained: "I try to pull out of the woman whatever strengths she has left, and I try to work with these. They all have strengths, it might take two hours, or even three, four, or five, but they come out, and they come out strong." Cinzia, another caseworker, explained that she did everything possible to make sure the woman felt comfortable. Then she tried to understand what was making her suffer, and worked on whatever that was. The help could be very concrete, such as how to look for a job, or how to obtain a legal separation, or it could come in the form of moral support, when just talking about a particular situation could be helpful. For Ghita, another caseworker, a meeting could be deemed successful when a woman left feeling lighter, as if a load had been lifted from her shoulders.

The emphasis Women United placed on female solidarity was exemplified by the way Isabella, another caseworker, discussed women who had the opportunity to leave their violent partners but ended up staying with them. Although caseworkers often privately expressed frustration with women who chose to stay with violent partners, in discussions about the organization's ideology the caseworkers always emphasized the importance of providing women with the opportunity to make their own choices. Only when women sought shelter in the safe house were they required (according to the rules of Women United) to leave their partners. In an interview, Isabella explained the importance of this methodology:

They may say they want to leave but there is something that for them is stronger than the desire to leave, and it makes them stay. . . . In many situations it is important for a woman to have someone who believes her; even today in rape trials a woman will be asked, but how were you dressed? Why were you out at that hour of the night? Knowing that there is an association of women who understand you and won't ask you these absurd questions helps a lot. . . . Often just coming to Women United is a step forward for a woman.

Isabella went on to explain the importance of understanding a woman's request:

If a woman comes in and says she is experiencing violence you might just assume she wants to separate, but maybe the woman isn't asking how do I separate, maybe she is asking how can I get my husband back, or how can I get along with my husband. . . . I am convinced that if during a meeting a woman is coming to ask what she can do to live in a peaceful way with her husband and I say to her, Signora, you need to separate, then we're talking about two different things. Again the woman goes to someone who doesn't listen to her. . . . If I don't listen to what the woman is telling me then it is always that the woman doesn't understand anything, she always has to take advice from someone else, her husband who tells her how to dress, what kind of makeup to wear, what to make for dinner, if she can go out, if she can't go out, and the caseworker from Women United who tells her Signora, you need to go here, you need to do this . . . you can't do that. I don't want to put myself in that position because in my opinion it's a form of violence I'm committing against this woman. It's like saying, you'll never make it, you'll never be able to do it, you haven't understood a thing. Instead you have to help her see her own value, help her see things from a different perspective.

After a meeting with a woman, the caseworkers would usually sit down and write up their notes about the meeting. In addition to recording short narratives, the caseworkers answered a battery of questions pertaining to the type of help the woman requested, the type of violence she experienced, biographical information about the woman and her partner, and other places where the woman had sought help. Each woman was assigned a client number, and every time she returned in the course of the calendar year, additional information was added to her file.

As a volunteer caseworker at Women United, I was able to obtain data for the years 1991–94, 1996, 1998, and 1999. I found that the number of women coming to Women United had increased from approximately 100 per year in the early 1990s to 180 in 1999. The percentage of married women remained between 43 and 48 percent, and roughly 60 percent of clients indicated that they had physically violent partners. The majority of women seeking help at Women United were between eighteen and thirty-nine years of age, and in any given year, between 11 and 20 percent of the women were older than fifty. Close to 80 percent of those with violent partners characterized the violence they experienced as "repetitive," which for some meant a few times a month, and for others meant every day.

Classification has long been a focus of anthropological inquiry. From the historic debate between Alfred L. Kroeber and W. H. R. Rivers over classificatory systems and the derivation of kinship nomenclature, to more recent discussions of race and ethnicity, why and how people classify has been a topic of interest to anthropologists.[6] Mary Douglas (1966) emphasized the importance of classification when she posited a link between the anomalous and the profane. Thirty years later, Michael Kearney traced the development and use of the term "peasant" and reminded us that "labels—constructed identities— are important because of their constituting power" (1996:171). What emerges from Kearney's argument is that the act of classification—the construction of categories—has political and social implications for both the classifiers and the classified.

Women United engaged in its own form of classification. Along with other similar organizations in the region of Emilia-Romagna, Women United divided violence into four categories: physical, economic, sexual, and psychological. These categories are important in that they determine the way violence is conceptualized. When the caseworkers filled out the forms that went into a file for each woman, they marked off on a sheet the type or types of violence a woman indicated that she had experienced. Under each form of violence there were also subcategories, of which one or all could be checked off. Under physical violence there were the subcategories "with visible signs; without visible signs; with physical damage; with the use of objects and/or weapons; attempted murder; locked in or out of the house." Under economic violence there were the subcategories "control of all household money; control of woman's salary; impedes woman's ability to look for or maintain a job; refusal to allow woman to assume economic or legal responsibilities." Under sexual violence there were subcategories for "sexual molestation; forced sexual relations; sexual aggression without rape; rape; forced prostitution." And finally, under psychological violence were the subcategories "betrayal; lies and deceit; refusal to communicate; refusal to take part in domestic work or raising of children; humiliation and denigration; harassment; voluntary damage to objects and/or pets belonging to the woman; stalking; limitation of woman's freedom of movement; refusal to allow woman to leave the marital household; violent threats against relatives or children; threat of violence or murder." This list illustrates the range of actions Women United (and other leftist women's organizations in the region of Emilia-Romagna) defined as "violence against women," but it also illustrates the range of situations the organization has seen in the past and expects to see in the future.[7]

By categorizing violence—and distinguishing violence from non-violence—the organizations engaged in a knowledge production that is at odds with the discourse of local and state norms for gender relations. Embracing a Foucaultian approach to classification, we can see that just as "madness and non-madness, reason and non-reason are inextricably involved," so are violence and non-violence bound to one another and definable by the very "exchange which separates them" (Foucault 1965:x). By classifying violence and labeling the various acts that can be recorded and defined as violence, Women United and other women's centers placed violence itself along a continuum of gendered hierarchy and subordination.

Caseworkers

In the spring of 2000, after seven months of volunteering at Women United, and after having conducted interviews with all the caseworkers and selected members of the board, I conducted case-specific interviews with Maura and Cinzia. These interviews focused on the caseworkers' experiences with selected women who had come to Women United between 1999 and 2000. I chose a total of fifteen to eighteen cases of women who had come to Women United because of partner or spousal abuse. I specifically chose women who did not live in the safe house, and who spanned a range of ages, classes, and professions. I did not include immigrant women in my sample, and I did not include women coming to the center for other forms of violence—stranger rape, sexual harassment, incest, or child abuse.

For each caseworker I chose six to eight cases with which they had been directly involved, and as we went through each case I encouraged them to tell me everything they remembered, from the woman's story to the atmosphere during the meetings to their own emotions regarding the case. Before discussing a case, the caseworker would take a few minutes to read through the file and re-familiarize herself with the woman and the story. We would then begin our recorded discussion.

Maura's Clients   When Bianca came to Women United in the spring of 2000, Maura recognized her immediately. Although she had never met with her personally, she remembered having seen her in the office a year or two earlier. According to Maura, Bianca was "absolutely determined to separate" from her abusive husband, who continually hit her. Bianca came to Women United with her young son and a car packed with suitcases. When she sat down and started speaking to Maura and the other caseworker, she explained that the night before, her husband had threatened her repeatedly with a knife saying he would kill her.

Within a few minutes of beginning to talk about Bianca, Maura made a point of telling me that had she been alone in the office when Bianca stopped by, she would have taken her directly to the safe house. Instead, because of a rule requiring that any new entry to the safe house be discussed and approved by the board member responsible for overseeing the house, Maura and the other caseworkers ended the meeting encouraging Bianca to go to her father's house for the evening, and to call in the following day. As Bianca was leaving, she said to the caseworkers: "Once again you are sending me back home."

Maura explained that this meeting with Bianca continues to torment her. The fact that they never heard back from Bianca makes Maura think of all the possible places she might be—with her father, back with her husband, or perhaps even dead. Maura felt that, in an emergency, caseworkers must be allowed to assume the responsibility of deciding whether or not to offer a woman shelter. At the moment when Bianca had been ready to leave her husband and start a new life, Women United had not been able to welcome her. Maura noted the failure of the organization as a whole when she summed up the meeting:

Out of fear of going over a board member's head, because we have to go through a series of procedures, we were forced to say things we didn't want to say. I believe I had the capacity to decide that this was a woman who wouldn't have told anyone where the safe house is, who would have maintained our secret address, who with our help would have looked for a job, and who perhaps would have begun to live a better life.

When Maura spoke about the women who came to Women United, she divided them into two groups: women who were determined to work toward starting a new life and women who came to vent their emotions but always found another excuse to stay with a violent partner. Maura pointed out that from her conversation with Bianca, she could tell she was "a smart girl who knows how to speak, who knows how to interact with others, but stopped relating to people out of fear." Maura described Viola, a young woman who came to Women United in 1999, in completely different terms:

She is a spoiled child, a child who hasn't grown up despite the pain she has suffered, despite understanding that if she doesn't change her situation social services could take away her child. She is controlled by her dream of this man who buys her expensive clothes and takes her to the most expensive hotels in the world. She always ends up going back to him. She is one of the people I call a "repeater," she goes from one violent situation to another. I often ask myself why these women, who have lived through terrible violence, instead of freeing themselves end up falling back into situations of violence.

According to Maura, in addition to talking about all the wonderful places this man took her, Viola also discussed the fact that he hit her and treated her poorly, and that they lived in a crumbling house in a town outside Parma. Every so often her partner would go out of his mind. He would hit her, yell at her, and leave the house, only to return some time later. Maura explained that Viola was in a very complicated situation and was very confused. In violation of the policy that called for caseworkers to provide the space for women to make their own decisions, Maura encouraged Viola to go back to work in order to "rediscover the satisfaction it seems she once had while working with her mother's business." She told her that "she needs to walk on her own two legs" and that it was very important she look out for her children's well-being. Only by working and supporting herself could she ensure that her children would not be taken away. Maura expressed her frustration with Viola throughout our discussion: "She is an ambiguous person who says, yes, yes, yes, and then does what she wants. It is right for her to do what she wants, but then it's hard to understand what the role of Women United should be."

When I asked Maura how she distinguished between women who were determined to work with the caseworkers to create a plan for leaving a violent partner and those whom she termed "repeaters," she explained that she could tell after two or three meetings:

As long as a woman continues to say he hit me, he said X to me, he did Y to me, and tells a series of things about her partner without realizing why these things happen, there is almost always a return to violence. If, instead, a woman has in some way faced her pain, not that the other women don't feel pain, but those who are able to leave violent partners and husbands have examined themselves and their situations. Accompanied by us they take a huge and difficult step toward leaving a violent partner. They are the women who used to hope their husbands would change and now know they never will.

Cinzia's Clients   In my interviews with Cinzia, she explained that many women who stay with violent partners have "an umbilical cord with these men who mistreat them." Sandra, a woman in her fifties, came to Women United "after many episodes of violence, including a time when her husband slammed her against a wall, causing her to break her collarbone." Cinzia learned through her meeting with Sandra that she had a daughter in her thirties and another daughter who had died at an early age. Sandra's husband had always been violent, but after the death of their daughter he became even more violent. He had a pension that he spent almost entirely on alcohol and gambling, and Sandra managed to pay all of the household bills out of her pension and the sewing and embroidery work she did out of her home. While meeting with Sandra, Cinzia tried to help her see her own strengths and realize she could make it on her own. Sandra's biggest preoccupation was whether she would be able to support herself economically if she left her husband. Cinzia explained,

I didn't want to tell her a fairy tale, but I tried to show her that despite all the violence she had experienced, she still had many sources of strength, in the sense that even though her husband practically kept her sequestered in the house, she was still able to continue earning money through odd jobs from neighbors and acquantainces. I tried to show her that without her husband she would be able to expand her list of clients because she wouldn't have to worry about inviting people into her home not knowing when her husband might start yelling and throwing things.

At the time of our interview it had been two months since Cinzia had met with Sandra, and there had been no word from her. Cinzia explained that although Sandra would be eligible to receive free legal representation from the government, without children to support she would have little chance of winning any type of alimony were she to separate: "It may seem like a paradox, but usually women who have grown children, who sacrificed their own lives for their children and finally say, now that my children are out of the house, enough is enough, now I will separate, encounter the most economic difficulty. These women find themselves at age sixty with no job, no income, and often these women don't separate out of economic necessity."

Cinzia went on to explain, however, that in addition to being a question of money, it was also a question of habit. After forty years of violence one gets used to it. Cinzia remarked that she herself fell into the trap of saying "these women are unable to separate because of economic problems."

Sandra doesn't have any reason to stay with this man. One can say I don't want to separate from my husband because of my children, one can say I don't want to leave this town because of my children, but Sandra's children are grown and her daughter lives in a different town. There's the economic factor, but in my opinion it's not the real reason.

When I asked Cinzia how many of the women she worked with eventually decided to separate from their husbands and start new lives, she explained that it would be difficult to determine because many women would come for one meeting and never be heard from again. It would be easier, she said, to tell me about the women who had lived in the safe house, because they usually stayed in touch with each other and the caseworkers. Of the eleven women who stayed in the safe house in 1999, two returned to their husbands. According to Cinzia, the ones who returned to their husbands were the ones who, after staying in the safe house, moved to a Catholic shelter run by nuns: "Many of the women who go to Santa Lucia end up going back to their husbands. It's not because we [Women United] are better than them [Santa Lucia], it's because of the Catholic conception of the family union. They start saying to the women, 'you know, life will be difficult without a husband.'" Cinzia explained that when two of the women living in the safe house went to see a former housemate who had moved to Santa Lucia, they came back and told the caseworkers about a conversation they had had with one of the nuns. The nun, who according to Cinzia was "very nice" but ended up doing irreparable harm, told the women: "Think hard before you leave your husbands because at the age of thirty-five it's not easy to find another man. I know—not out of personal experience—that once you have sex it is difficult not to have it again and it can drive you crazy."

Cinzia explained that these types of comments and warnings can be very persuasive for women who are insecure about the choices they have made. As a caseworker, Cinzia had seen many women make the difficult decision to leave their husbands and partners only to return home a few months later. It made her angry to see a woman like Maria-bella—who made many sacrifices to separate from her husband and worked many long hours as a cleaning woman to pay for the separation—return to her husband:

With these women, honestly, it is difficult for me. On the one hand I understand, but on the other I don't. I understand that those who return to their husband or choose a new partner who is a carbon copy of their ex are women who experienced violence or witnessed violence as children, and that it is a cycle of violence that continues. . . . I have seen that women who return to violence, and continue to submit to violence, do so because they have a history of violence.

Just as Maura divided women into repeaters and non-repeaters, during my discussions with Cinzia she also divided the women she worked with into two categories. While discussing Sandra's story, Cinzia made it clear that she did not hold out much hope that Sandra would eventually separate from her husband of forty years. On the other hand, with a thirty-five-year-old woman named Luciana, Cinzia remained optimistic.

Cinzia described Luciana as being "very Catholic," a label Cinzia used to convey a picture of a woman who would be hard-pressed to consider divorce and was likely to believe in the value of self-sacrifice for her husband and children. Luciana met her husband during a Catholic youth-group outing, and after a brief period of dating they were married. When Luciana came to Women United she had been married for three years and had a baby girl.

According to Cinzia, Luciana's problems began the minute she married her husband and went to live with him and his family. Cinzia explained that Luciana's living arrangement was the classic farmer household in the style of the "old patriarchal family," where the entire family—brothers, their wives, and their children—lives together in the same house. Prior to marrying her husband, Luciana had a job with the local town government, and though she reduced her hours to part-time, she did not leave the job completely despite the requests of her husband and in-laws. According to Cinzia, Luciana found herself fighting against not only her husband, but his entire family. She was shut off from the rest of the world and lived in an environment where her father-in-law was the head of the family and made the decisions for everyone in the household. Luciana had never had the courage to tell her elderly parents that her husband was violent toward her. When she would say that there were problems and tell them about her general unhappiness, they would tell her, "have patience, he's your husband, you have to forgive him." Although Luciana repeatedly told Cinzia that she saw separation as her only option, Cinzia noticed inconsistencies in Luciana's remarks, and explained that she was a woman trapped by both her religious beliefs and her reluctance to cause her elderly parents any emotional pain.

Cinzia explained that in addition to being violent and aggressive, Luciana's husband "behaved in a very denigrating way toward her" and any time she tried to tell him something he would knock his knuckles against her skull "to remind her of her inferior position." According to Cinzia, knocking on a person's head was "an ugly gesture" that in the past a man might have done to a child or the village idiot. For Cinzia, this gesture was worse than a punch or a slap because it was "as if you want to enter the head of another person because you're convinced he or she doesn't understand a thing." Known as a *marucco*, the gesture was once widely used in the province of Parma.

When I asked a friend from Parma what she knew about this gesture, she said she had never heard of it. Intrigued, she decided to do a bit of research. A few weeks later I received an e-mail message with the information she had collected from three friends who lived in a small town outside Parma. According to them, a *marucco* could be a gesture either of affection or of punishment, and to receive one "brought an electric sensation." They explained that the gesture underscored the hierarchical relationship between an adult and a child or between the *padrone* (boss) of an agricultural business and his workers. The gesture was a way of "lowering you" and "putting you in your place." By using this gesture, Luciana's husband emphasized her subordinate role in their relationship. As a gesture that, depending on the context, can bring either pleasure or pain, the *marucco* symbolizes both the comforts and humiliations of hierarchy and domination.

For Luciana, it was humiliating to be treated this way by her husband. Cinzia described Luciana as being out of her element in her in-laws' farming household. When Luciana married she left her "normal" life in a large town to live with her husband and her husband's family in an isolated mountain village, far from her family, friends, and community. Despite Luciana's lucidity, Cinzia found countercurrents in her story. Throughout the meeting Luciana repeated phrases such as, "In reality my husband's not a bad person." According to Cinzia this meant she either was still in love with her husband or was fearful of being alone. Nonetheless, Cinzia told me she was convinced Luciana was a woman who had the capacity to leave. She was a woman who could eventually find a way to leave her violent home life "because she is young, because she has only lived with her husband for three years, because she has many resources, because she is independent and has a job, and because she understands herself."

After her first meeting with the caseworkers at Women United, Luciana made another appointment, but then called to cancel saying she was not feeling well. At the time of my interview with Cinzia, a few months had passed without word from Luciana. Despite this, Cinzia assured me, "This woman will return. I am sure she will return, maybe not for a while, but I am positive she will return. Maybe she won't yet be separated, but at least she will have told her parents the truth. She will return, and if for some reason she doesn't, then she will do it on her own."

Explaining Violence

Women United was committed to helping women regardless of whether they chose to stay with or leave a violent partner, but caseworkers often expressed frustration with women who defended their husbands or continually came up with reasons not to seek a separation. The younger and more highly educated the woman, the more hopeful the caseworkers were that she would decide to leave a violent partner.

During one of my interviews with Cinzia, I asked what she thought might be the reason for spousal violence. She hesitated and then explained that for her it was cultural, there is a culture that holds that women are the weaker sex and a man "needs to prove, above all to himself, that he has the louder voice." Cinzia went on to explain that men are exasperated with women and find themselves unable to deal with the social, political, and legal advances women have made.

Men are realizing that women can do everything without men; by now with artificial insemination they can even have children on their own. Men don't feel so great about this. Men need women, but I see that women in their fifties who become widows rarely remarry. They take their trips, they do tons of things they never did when they were married. Men who become widowers, even if they were completely in love with their wives, two or three years later always have a new companion. In my opinion this happens because a man finds himself lost without a woman. . . . In my opinion men feel psychologically violated by women because men now realize that women can graduate from college, have careers, and maybe the only thing men still have is their ability to hit.

Maura used similar terms in her explanation for spousal and partner violence. She attributed much of it to a lack of dialogue between couples and within families. In addition, Maura explained, "Violence has always existed—because of a power that is decisively male. The family was always thought of as having a father who worked, a father who brought home the money, and a father who could decide everything. This imprinting has remained with men, that men are worth more."

Emanuela spoke of similar problems between men and women. She explained that the biggest changes for women in Italy came with the laws of the 1970s allowing abortion and divorce. With divorce, women started realizing that they no longer had to rely on their husbands for financial support, and with abortion, women started realizing that they had a choice whether or not to have children. Instead of relying on their husbands or their families, women began understanding the need to take care of themselves. According to Emanuela, these changes to a woman's sense of self caused rifts between spouses and partners. While women were going through great changes, men stayed the same: "Men haven't changed at all, and they have difficulty understanding the changes that have occurred because they like the role they used to have. They don't understand what women want and they don't understand how they themselves can change."

Women United offered women a feminist ideology that called for the valorization of womanhood and a sense of self as an alternative to the Catholic and societal values that call for the preservation of a family unit and the importance of sacrifice, duty, and forgiveness. In my interviews and conversations with caseworkers, they recounted numerous stories of women who were told by their priests, "have patience and forgive"; or by local policemen, "you don't file charges against your own husband"; or by their mothers, "you're a woman, you need to make sacrifices to hold the family together." Though public awareness is growing and Women United has established good relationships with the various groups that make up Parma's police force,[8] in the towns and villages outside the city it is still difficult for a woman to report the violence of her own husband, and there are still many police officers and doctors who continue to ignore intimate-partner violence.

In addition to encouraging the city of Parma to pay more attention to the needs of women experiencing violence in their lives, Women United sought to create a safe and supportive environment for women to come forward and share their experiences with other women. Although the caseworkers I worked with often had personal feelings of frustration with women who refused to leave violent partners, they were resolute about the importance of providing women with the space to make their own decisions about their lives. At Women United, women were encouraged to find their own interior strength and power. A few blocks away, at Family Aid, the goals and methodologies were quite different.

Family Aid

The first branch of Family Aid was founded in Florence in 1975, on the Catholic principle of helping women to "welcome life" by offering monetary and emotional support to pregnant women and women with small children. By 1999 there were more than 220 Family Aid organizations located throughout the country. Parma's Family Aid was founded in 1979, one year after abortion became legal in Italy. Planning and organizing for the Parma branch began in 1976, when abortion was still illegal but the "cultural movement" in favor of abortion rights was gaining power and influence. A group of upper-middle-class women who were members of the Catholic Centro Italiano Femminile (Cif) began meeting to "reflect on their commitment to the unborn life and their conviction that life must always be welcomed and promoted" (internal 1989–1999 Family Aid document). Two years later they decided to open up an office to provide ongoing support for pregnant women and women with small children.

The main office for Family Aid was located in the heart of Parma's historic center. Like Women United, Family Aid is a nonprofit, volunteer association. The organization's bylaws declare the association to consist of "volunteers united by their conviction of the humanity of every fetus and the value of every life." The primary goal was to welcome every life, provide women with the freedom not to abort, and promote the value of life beginning with conception. Family Aid sought to help various categories of women—Italian, foreign, married, single, younger, older—face their problems and build independent lives.

For Elisabetta Mancini, the president of Parma's Family Aid organization during the period of my fieldwork, the primary objective of the association was "undoubtedly to support difficult motherhoods and privilege the emerging life." At a ceremony to celebrate the beginning of the fiscal year, Elisabetta reminded the gathered crowd of volunteers of the importance of saying "yes" to every emerging life, and of ensuring that there are no single mothers forced to abort simply because they are alone or without money. In addition to providing economic and psychological assistance to pregnant women, a corollary goal of Family Aid was to help mothers achieve personal, parental, and economic autonomy.

In one of Family Aid's internal documents, the women defined their ideology in opposition to that of other women's groups that were prevalent in the 1970s. They wrote that Family Aid was founded as a response to a "cultural movement that saw maternity as a negative event" and an "obstacle to achieving full emancipation for women." The founders wanted to provide an alternative to the prevailing feminist ideology and offer support to pregnant girls and young mothers with small children. Although Family Aid was officially a lay organization and open to people of any religious affiliation, the organization was still Christian in character and was based on a fundamentally Catholic value system. Meetings I attended often began with prayers led by the association's spiritual advisor, and there were ongoing collaborative relationships with the local diocese, parishes, and convents. The organization itself did not actively try to change the legality of abortion, but it had close ties with other organizations that did engage in political advocacy.

Just as the founders of Women United were actively involved with the Italian Communist Party (Pci) and its associated women's organization, Unione Donne Italiane (Udi), the founders of Family Aid were actively involved with Italy's Christian Democratic Party (DC) and the associated women's organization, Centro Italiano Femminile (Cif).[9] Although Catholic and leftist women worked together to obtain, in 1945, a woman's right to vote, relations grew increasingly strained after 1949, when the Pope excommunicated Catholics who supported the Pci or Psi (Birnbaum 1986:269) and Cif became engaged in the battle against communism. The two groups of women worked together again in 1975 when they fought for family-rights legislation, but faced a great divide in the 1970s on questions of abortion, contraception, and divorce.

During the late 1990s, Women United and Family Aid had cordial relations with one another despite being quite vocal about the differences in their ideologies and approaches to helping women. The women of Women United categorized the women of Family Aid as Catholics who reinforced "old-fashioned" ideas about gender, preached ideals of self-sacrifice in order to save a marriage or prevent abortion, and would stop at nothing to keep a family intact. On the other hand, the women of Family Aid viewed the women of Women United as feminists who ignored the sanctity of life and the importance of motherhood. However, these differences did not prevent the two groups from collaborating with one another to help individual women and increase public awareness of the resources that exist for the women of Parma, even if the collaboration was at times difficult.

Structure and Organization of Family Aid

During the period of my fieldwork, Family Aid was engaged in a number of different programs and projects to help pregnant women and mothers with young children. These projects included food and clothing distribution, skills-based training, financial support for pregnant women, and the administration of a number of shelters. Although the organization provided some sort of assistance to more than 400 women a year through its various programs, the shelter program was by far the one that required the greatest amount of resources, and was the one I chose to focus on for my research.[10]

In the late 1970s, when the organization was founded in Parma, there was only one shelter in operation. In 1999, when I became a volunteer, there were several first- and second-stage shelters. First-stage shelters were characterized by the twenty-four-hour presence of a supervisor who purchased food, organized a chore chart, helped with childcare, and attended to many other household duties. Second-stage shelters were apartments that housed one or two mothers who were economically self-sufficient and deemed responsible enough to care for their own children and run a household without the constant presence of a supervisor. In 1999, a total of eighteen mothers and twenty-four children were housed in Family Aid's first-stage shelters, and thirteen mothers and seventeen children in their second-stage shelters.

As an official volunteer association, Family Aid was able to hire a limited number of employees, but all members of the board of directors as well as people in elected positions (president, vice president, treasurer) had to be volunteers. First-stage shelters had paid supervisors who rotated shifts. The number of supervisors varied during my year of fieldwork, but at any given time there were at least five salaried supervisors, along with four to six substitutes who were paid hourly and worked primarily nights and weekends. The women who coordinated the volunteers, organized food and clothing distribution, and managed the adoption program were all volunteers. Even the president of the organization, who seemed to work all day, every day, was also a volunteer. When I commented to another volunteer, who spent at least three mornings a week working at the organization, that I was amazed the president worked such long hours, she told me, "She does it as a sacrifice to God. Just like all the other volunteers. I'm a grandmother, I have many things to do at home, but I come here because of God. Praying is important but it's not enough. You also have to give to others." Many of the women I spoke with emphasized that their dedication to volunteerism stemmed from their personal connection to God and their conviction that only through faith, good deeds, and sacrifice can one achieve salvation.[11]

Family Aid's administrative office was a small apartment in the center of town. The space was cramped, with just three small rooms that functioned simultaneously as the offices of two paid social workers, the administrative and bookkeeping office for the association, and the storage and distribution center for used clothing and food items. The office was overflowing with files and donations, and there was always a buzz of activity. The entrance to the social workers' office was often a revolving door of volunteers, employees, and women seeking help. The social workers' first meeting with each woman seeking help was aimed at determining her needs. The social workers then created individual "plans" to help each woman reach self-sufficiency. The women who were offered a room in one of the first- or second-stage shelters were added to the list of cases to be closely monitored.

As at Women United, the posters and decorations at Family Aid revealed much about the ideology of the organization. Whereas in Women United's offices the walls were adorned with posters proclaiming the unity of women, the walls of the Family Aid offices were decorated with crosses, portraits of the Virgin Mary, and posters proclaiming the sanctity of life. One poster had a picture of a fetus seven or eight months old still in the womb, with the words: "Look at me! You love me, you respect me. Why . . . because you see me? But I was also to be loved and respected when I was inside my mommy and you couldn't see me!"

Women Helping Women

Until the mid-1990s, Family Aid provided shelter and assistance primarily to young women who had become pregnant out of wedlock and were abandoned by their partners, their families, or both. The original shelter is still widely known—by taxi drivers and others throughout town—as a home for *ragazze madri*. The goal was to provide a place for young women who might otherwise look to abortion as the only solution to their predicament. In creating a home for these women, strict rules were established and round-the-clock supervisors were hired to help train them to become "good" mothers and household managers. These supervisors were encouraged to assume the role of surrogate mothers for the women, and to teach through example.

When Tiziana, one of the supervisors in a first-stage shelter, was hired in 1994, almost all of the women living in the shelter were teenagers. The first thing Tiziana was told in her interview was that the shelter was run like a home. When Tiziana started at Family Aid, she had already worked for twenty-eight years as an office worker, was married, and had raised two children. When she heard that her job would be to treat the shelter as if it were her own home, she thought to herself, "For better or for worse I've been able to run my own household for many years. If this job entails running a household, I'll give it a try." When Tiziana arrived for her first day of work there was no one to welcome her, or explain her role, so she just introduced herself to the women and began working as she would in her own house. Reflecting on her position within the shelter, she explained, "I don't know if this is a handicap or something positive, but I see that acting as a mother here means that I behave in the exact same way as I do in my own home. I don't distinguish between the two places. I say the same things to the girls here—whether they are fifteen or thirty—as I say to my own children. I don't know to what extent this is the right thing to do."

The connections Tiziana drew between her own family and household and her position as a shelter supervisor were connections encouraged by the ideology and methodology of Family Aid. In daily conversations as well as official documents, the women receiving help were always referred to as *mamme* (moms) and never as "women." Even though a good number of the women, especially the teenagers, who came to Family Aid were in the early stages of pregnancy and had no other children, they were still called *mamme*. In addition to emphasizing that the women they helped were mothers, the women of Family Aid also actively promoted the cultivation of a mother/daughter relationship between shelter workers and the women coming in for help. By using the informal pronoun "tu" instead of the customary formal "lei" with women they did not already know, the women of Family Aid underscored a mother/daughter or giver/recipient relationship with women requesting assistance.[12] Despite the fact that the moms they admitted in the 1990s were quite a bit older, this aspect of their methodology did not change. During the time of my fieldwork, I rarely saw pregnant teens in the first-stage shelters, whereas women in their twenties and thirties were quite common.[13] When I asked volunteers and supervisors why there had been such a noticeable shift in the demographics of women seeking help, many pointed to a change in societal values, which made pregnancy out of wedlock less of a stigma. They also pointed to an increase in the number of women having abortions. Statistically, however, there are fewer abortions performed in Italy now than ten years ago.[14] Although societal values regarding pregnancy changed throughout the history of Family Aid and single motherhood became more acceptable, the language and methodology of the organization remained largely the same. During the period of my fieldwork, the women who received shelter and assistance were always referred to as *mamme*, regardless of their age or life experience.

When I arrived at Family Aid, Elisabetta had already been president of the Parma branch for five years. When she began her tenure, one of her primary goals was to increase the activities sponsored by the organization and the number of mothers helped each year. In an interview, she told me she had inherited an organization that was practically in "a state of abandonment," with only one first-stage shelter and one second-stage shelter, which were barely half-full at any given time. Elisabetta explained that the rules of acceptance were quite stringent, and one of the first things she did as president was to relax the standards of acceptance and "open the doors of the shelter a bit wider" to help the many mothers who were in need. As the admission criteria were relaxed, more and more mothers with older children began coming to the shelter. Before long, the organization had enough applications to warrant the opening of another first-stage shelter and numerous second-stage shelters.

According to Elisabetta, the characteristics of the average woman coming to Family Aid had changed significantly: "In the early years there were girls who were either frivolous or lacking in culture who found themselves pregnant and were sent away from their families. . . . Now we don't have young girls but women in their thirties and forties with troubled histories. Many have experienced physical or psychological violence from aggressive partners or husbands." When I asked Elisabetta why there has been such a radical shift, she explained that life has changed and probably the parents of her generation are to blame. During the postwar economic boom, parents began giving their children everything they asked for. Parents who had been children during World War II did not want their children to feel any of the deprivation they had experienced. According to Elisabetta, and many other people I spoke with in Parma, this created a generation of people who are irresponsible and want everything at their fingertips without having to work for it. They feel entitled to many things but have little sense of duty. Elisabetta explained that nowadays, couples get tired of each other, or angry at each other, and instead of working to save the relationship they just split up, causing great trouble for the woman who is left alone with the children.

For Elisabetta, one of Family Aid's great success stories is the story of a young mom who was brought to the organization by the police. She had left her violent partner many times before, but had always returned to him. This time the man was put in jail and the young mom, who had a baby daughter, came to live in a first-stage shelter. Elisabetta told me,

There was a long period in which she continually went to see him in jail and even brought her daughter. We found her a job and she responded very well to our help. She demonstrated that she was a great worker and as time went on she decided to stop seeing this man. She found a different man, she married him, and they are doing very well together.

Elisabetta explained that when the young mom started dating this new man, "He came to the office to introduce himself and we acted as if we were the parents. We asked him his intentions, and even though she didn't want to tell him about her past we felt very strongly that he should know everything." As she told this story of success, Elisabetta spoke as a proud parent who had re-educated her daughter and married her off to a good man. The organization took on the role of family by proxy for Elisabetta and many other young women.

During my time at Family Aid, the women who came to live in the first-stage shelters were almost always sent by social services. More often than not they were women who had lost custody of their children. Family Aid was a last resort for these women and a chance for them to prove their ability to care for their own children in a supervised environment. For each woman who moved into a first- or second-stage shelter, a plan was created to help put her on the path to economic, personal, and parental autonomy. Violence and abuse experienced by women prior to their arrival at Family Aid was rarely discussed. Of primary importance was helping these women create new lives for themselves as good and responsible mothers. By providing shelter, food, and childcare for the women living in first-stage shelters, the supervisors at Family Aid hoped to give the women more time to concentrate on gaining new skills, finding a job, and/or separating from an abusive or negligent partner. In meetings and casual conversations, the volunteers and supervisors often questioned how these women—who had everything provided for them and still were unable to hold down a job or control their children—would ever be able to run a household on their own.

As one of the substitute supervisors, I spent a number of evenings and weekends working at the first-stage shelters. My responsibilities included overseeing meal preparation and ensuring that chores were completed in accordance with the weekly list created by the supervisors. The women were required to observe curfews and were instructed to sign out whenever they left the shelter. If they wanted to travel outside Parma they needed the approval of the president of the association. In practical terms much of my time was spent breaking up fights among the children and mothers, and watching out for the safety of the smaller children. I was also the bearer of the keys, and as such was continually asked by the mothers to open locked doors (play room, laundry room, storage closets) and bring up food items from the pantry.

The moms were not allowed to have access to the food-storage area, and the subject of waste was a common topic of conversation among shelter supervisors. I was told repeatedly that the moms wasted food and were not allowed to have more food items in the kitchen than what they needed for a particular day's meals. All food items and supplies were kept in locked pantries, and as the shelter was continually running out of supplies I spent large percentages of my shifts running up and down the stairs with food and cleaning items. I was also told that the laundry room was to remain locked and could only be opened for the person whose turn it was to do laundry. The laundry detergent was kept in a nearby storage room and was to be doled out by the supervisor in order to prevent any waste.

By creating a very controlled environment much like a disciplinary institution (Foucault 1979), Family Aid aimed to give women the time and energy they needed to move toward personal, parental, and economic autonomy. Some women utilized the benefits the shelter provided and stayed focused on their goal of saving enough money to eventually move out on their own; others rejected the controlling atmosphere, as well as the help the supervisors tried to provide. Many came to Family Aid as a last resort and did not share the goals of the "plans" that were tailored for them. Although some women moved smoothly through the system—from first-stage shelters to second-stage shelters and thence to subsidized apartments owned by the city government—others ended up leaving Family Aid to move in with family members or return to abusive or negligent partners.

In the case of Ottavia, she came to live in the Family Aid shelter as the last step before her son was taken away. Her husband was suspected of abusing their child and was scheduled to go on trial for the abuse of children he had had with previous partners. By coming to the shelter, Ottavia was able to continue living with her son. Family Aid's primary goal was to separate Ottavia from her partner. After a few months of trying to distract Ottavia with courses and other activities, the staff realized that as long as she lived in the same city as her partner, they would never separate. Many supervision meetings were spent devising new strategies for separating the couple, but Ottavia continued to proclaim her partner's innocence and refused to stop seeing him.

Carolina, on the other hand, left an abusive husband and came to Family Aid of her own accord, with a desire to become self-sufficient and care for her children. Family Aid had two goals for Carolina: to gain job readiness skills and to learn how to be a better mother to her four children (three of whom lived in the shelter). Although Carolina successfully completed a sewing and tailoring class, when I left Parma the supervisors were still not satisfied by her ability to rear her own children and were worried that she might decide to return to her ex-partner. They often debated whether to let her take out-of-town trips by herself, and occasionally sent along chaperones to make sure she did not visit her ex-partner.

Although Family Aid helped many women who had experienced physical, emotional, and sexual violence, their principal mission remained to welcome every unborn life and mold capable, responsible, and autonomous mothers. Family Aid's vision of womanhood was synonymous with motherhood, and very much in line with the teachings of the Catholic Church. Ideals of sacrifice for God and for family were underscored in many aspects of daily life. Although single motherhood was accepted, it was viewed as far from ideal. In fact, the president on occasion encouraged women to return to their husbands when in her opinion they were "good" men. The women of Family Aid felt it was very important for children to have a male influence in their lives. As such, *obiettori* (conscientious objectors to the army) who signed up for a year of civil service work were routinely hired to provide a male presence within the shelters. In addition to helping with odd jobs, the young men routinely drove the children to and from day care and played with them after school. For one of the social workers, not having a father was the equivalent of missing a limb: "In my opinion a child needs a father, do you see how they attach themselves to the *obiettori*?" The most important goal, however, was for the mothers to create serene, caring environments for their children. When African or Chinese mothers sent their children back to their native countries to live with relatives, or when the courts ordered that children be taken away from their mothers and placed in foster care, the women of Family Aid felt they had failed in their mission to promote and facilitate motherhood.

On March 25, 1999, the holiday of the Annunciation, Family Aid celebrated its twentieth anniversary. Volunteers, board members, and employees gathered to "follow the example of the Virgin Mary" and renew their faith in God and their responsibility to defend life—both born and unborn. The women of Family Aid had also gathered to celebrate twenty years of an association that is "a living testimony of a fatherhood and motherhood, not to biological children, but to mothers who are alone and in difficulty . . . it is a fatherhood and motherhood that knows how to start from the beginning when the path becomes difficult, and renew faith and hope for many women" (remarks recorded from the anniversary celebration).

Although the "typology of the moms living in the shelters has changed," the celebration underscored a belief that the primary goals of the association remained the same: Family Aid was founded as an alternative to an ideology that portrays motherhood as an obstacle to a woman's full self-realization, and to offer women an ideology rooted in Catholicism that calls for the valorization of the unborn life and the importance of motherhood.

Even though the women of Family Aid and Women United often defined themselves in fierce opposition to one another, there were many spaces of overlap between the two organizations. As a volunteer for both groups, I could see that the two organizations worked with similar groups of women, many of whom had experienced violence at the hands of husbands and partners. I could also see that both provided support and counseling to help women lead healthy and productive lives. Finally, although they had starkly different ideas about what it should mean to be a woman in Italian society, I could see that both were engaged in a process of negotiating state, Catholic, local, and feminist discourses about gender and gender proficiency.

CHAPTER 4

Two Sides of Shame

WHEN I FIRST MET LUISA, she was fifty-seven years old and trying to get over the breakup of her second long-term relationship. Talkative and feisty, Luisa frequently voiced her opinion to the other women at Women United whenever she disagreed with the way something was being handled. When I arrived at Luisa's apartment for our scheduled interview, she brought me into her living room, where we both sat down on the couch. I placed the tape recorder between us and we began by talking about her work with Women United. I was surprised when Luisa explained that she decided to begin volunteering because she herself had experienced a physically and psychologically violent marriage. I certainly had not expected to hear Luisa, an outgoing woman who often voiced her opinion, tell me that she had received her first punch from her husband when they were still boyfriend and girlfriend. She explained, "I took it badly, but I accepted it and I excused him because I thought I had provoked it. And this is the mistake. He gave me a punch that sent my head spinning for a week. I went home but I pretended nothing had happened. I was embarrassed about what others would say."

At first I thought I had misunderstood the sequence of events and asked Luisa, "And this was how many years after you were married?" She quickly corrected me and said, "No, no, it was before we were married. This is why it's absurd. When you see a woman who endures violence and ask why . . . well, I endured it as well, I also tried. You aren't able to accept it right away, you think there is no way this can be happening to me. You say this is impossible. You say wait a minute, maybe I said a word too much, maybe if I had done X or hadn't done Y, if, if, if."

Pia, a volunteer for Family Aid, conveyed a similar story of violence when we sat down to record her life history, and I was just as surprised by her story as I was by Luisa's. Although Luisa and Pia volunteered at organizations with very different ideologies and methodologies for helping women, both told me similar stories about the everyday violence they had experienced. The oppositions I had been hearing about through my daily work at Women United and Family Aid began to blur as I listened to their very articulate and poignant narratives of violence and shame.

In this chapter I present the life histories of Pia and Luisa—along with the stories of other women—in order to illustrate the continuum of gender proficiency in Parma and the difficulty that women from various ideological perspectives faced in resisting particular aspects of their marriages and partnerships. I suggest that the *vergogna*, or shame, that some women experience is shaped by the intersection of feminist understandings of gender and local, state, and Catholic norms of family and household.[1]

Violence and *Vergogna*

Luisa began volunteering at Women United because she wanted to share her experience as a *donna maltrattata* (mistreated woman) and as a woman who realized she no longer wanted to be part of "a tradition that says even if your husband hits you, a man can do that." She stayed with her husband for four years before deciding to request a separation. Despite the fact that both her parents and her in-laws called her husband a "bum," recognized that he would leave the house without warning and stay out all night or even for days at time, and repeatedly said that he did not deserve her, when Luisa finally gathered enough courage to ask for a separation, all of a sudden she became the one to blame. As Luisa explained, "You're good because you endure, because you put up with it. But then when this girl who is so good says, 'enough,' then he becomes the victim and you become the one who ruined the family." Up until the moment Luisa decided to leave her husband, she remained "good" in the eyes of her relatives. She was fulfilling her role as a married woman, sacrificing her own happiness for the greater good of maintaining her marriage and preserving the reputations of both families.

As Luisa's marriage was ending, she met another man, Davide, and fell in love. Shortly after Luisa's husband moved out of the apartment, Davide moved in. He stayed for twenty-six years. Davide asked Luisa to marry him many times, but Luisa always said that one marriage was enough for a lifetime. In the early years they were very happy together, but by the time I met Luisa the relationship was ending. At Luisa's request, Davide moved out and leased his own apartment. They continued to see each other, but according to Luisa it was more out of loneliness and habit than anything else. During my first interview with Luisa she said very little about Davide other than that they had been together for a long time. Throughout my year of fieldwork I learned very little about the nature of their relationship or why Luisa had decided to end it. It was not until the very end of my stay that she began telling me more about Davide and why she could no longer continue with the relationship.

"The relationship was stifling me, suffocating me," Luisa explained, "I just couldn't take it anymore." Davide refused to participate in any of the household tasks. All the cleaning, washing and ironing of clothes, food shopping, and food preparation were Luisa's responsibility.[2] Both Davide and Luisa worked outside the home; Davide was a professor and Luisa had a part-time job at the local hospital. Whenever they went on vacation they had to go where Davide wanted to go. According to Luisa, "He always had to command, had to be the one in charge. I served him for twenty-six years until I finally said no more."

Luisa identified herself as part of a generation of women that struggles to reconcile the gains of the feminist movement with the advice passed down from mother to daughter to "endure because he's your husband." Her life story calls attention to the ambivalence many women feel toward their own sense of self and their experiences as women and as wives. When Luisa refused to marry Davide she was asserting her desire to maintain a certain degree of independence and freedom. Although she accepted a subordinate and subservient role for close to thirty years, she had remained unmarried and lived in an apartment she owned, so that when she decided she had had enough, all it took to end the relationship was to ask Davide to move out. Luisa disagreed with the ideology that calls for women to serve their husbands and be responsible for all the household duties, and yet she occupied this type of role throughout much of her adult life.

Luisa had a close friend with many similar life experiences who helped clarify this incongruence between ideology and action. Together, Luisa and her friend Allegra helped me understand the layers of shame that women with violent partners often experience. Close friends from girlhood, both women married young only to find themselves in relationships underscored by routine violence. Although Luisa and Allegra did not learn of the other's experience until many years after they had left their violent partners, the similarities in their stories are striking. By speaking with Luisa and Allegra, I learned that the *vergogna* I had heard about throughout my time in Parma could not be translated as merely feelings of guilt, embarrassment, or disgrace. Instead, both women spoke of *vergogna* as a multilayered emotion shaped by the achievements of the feminist movement and the enduring vestiges of a masculinist and Catholic legal and moral code.[3]

Glossing Shame

In anthropological discussions, particularly of southern Europe, any mention of the word "shame" inevitably raises questions about its alleged counterpart, "honor," and the now thoroughly challenged honor/shame dyad. According to the honor and shame model developed by Peristiany (1966) and Pitt-Rivers (1966), and later reformulated and criticized by Herzfeld (1980), Wikan (1984), Brandes (1987), Delaney (1987), Gilmore (1987), and others, shame was one pole of a moral system that divided society into those with honor and those without. Although the notion of "honor" (glossed as male by many of the honor/shame theorists) was rarely discussed without its partner, "shame," the value of honor was usually placed on a higher pedestal in analyses of how a specifically "Mediterranean" code of morality could help explain everyday social interactions among people living in southern Europe and the Middle East. During my fieldwork experience, not only did the idea of shame go far beyond notions of modesty or sexual restraint, the daily discourse of shame rarely included any reference to *onore*, or honor. In fact, as Unni Wikan (1984:636) has suggested, it was shame, rather than honor, that was the "predominant concern" for the people I worked with. Men and women frequently used the word *vergogna* to describe or explain everything from a conversational gaffe to spousal rape, and it repeatedly came up in discussions of the largely hidden phenomenon of intimate-partner violence.

Although a superficial translation of *vergogna* might lead us back to the old dichotomy of honor and shame, a more nuanced analysis will demonstrate *vergogna* to be a multivalent symbol women employed to make sense of their complex reactions to intimate-partner violence.

By focusing on the construction of shame, and the ideological puzzles women negotiated in their daily lives, we can understand women's experiences as indicative of larger tensions playing out in Italian society in the decades following the social movements of the 1960s and 1970s. On the one hand, Italian feminist activism achieved great legal and social changes for women, including the rights to reproductive freedoms, marital freedoms, and enhanced career opportunities. On the other hand, many aspects of the Italian legal system and daily family and social life continued to privilege the rights of men. In my interviews with women who had lived with violent partners, I learned that the shame they experienced was shaped by two distinct emotions: the embarrassment that comes from submitting to mistreatment in a time and place where women are expected to stand up for themselves and the fear that comes from wondering whether the violence they experienced could be retribution for their failure to adequately—and simultaneously—perform the roles of wife, mother, and lover. The *vergogna* they experienced thus took shape through the intersection of locally formed categories of modern and traditional gender proficiencies.

Silence Between Friends

Luisa and Allegra came of age at the height of the Italian feminist movement, but both had mothers who stayed at home and fathers who worked and expected to be served by their wives. Luisa did not introduce me to Allegra until the very end of my year of fieldwork.

Luisa surprised me the first time I went over to her house by telling me the story of her marriage. She surprised me a second time when she told me she had arranged an interview with a friend of hers who had also left a violent husband. Luisa entrusted me with her own story when we were just casual acquaintances, but it was not until we had spent many hours together talking and taking walks together that she entrusted me with the story of one of her closest friends.

Luisa arranged a lunch date at her home so that the three of us could chat and Allegra and I could get to know one another. After lunch, Luisa went into the kitchen to do the dishes and Allegra and I sat down on the couch—the very same couch where Luisa had told me her own story ten months earlier—to begin the interview.

Allegra described her relationship with her parents as "formal." When she became an adolescent her father became very possessive and controlling. Allegra explained that it was the 1970s and she wanted to wear miniskirts and go out with friends, but faced opposition from her father: "My father was very possessive of me. He had to be the man of the house. My mother had to be at his service, the children had to be at his service."

Allegra explained that her mother and father had married young and were very much in love: "I always saw them as young and in love, but I would say that my parents' marriage lasted because my mother *subiva*[4] (endured), because my mother put up with my father's possessiveness, his nervous attacks. . . . She served him in everything. She had to prepare breakfast in a certain way, lunch in a certain way. She served him at the table, prepared his clothes in the morning, cleaned his shoes, she did everything."

Luisa, listening from the kitchen, interrupted, "But this was normal, this wasn't an exception. It was what women had to do." I asked Luisa whether her mother did these things for her father and Luisa said, "Yes, my mother also did these things but so did we, at the beginning we did these things for our husbands. We're of an intermediary generation."

Allegra agreed and added, "Until we were fifteen we grew up with a mentality of the early 1900s because that's how our parents grew up and that's how our parents' parents grew up. The only difference was that you no longer used the formal 'voi' when addressing your parents."

Like Luisa, Allegra served her husband in the same way she had seen her mother serve her father. Pregnant at age seventeen, Allegra left home to marry her boyfriend. She explained:

He was a person who spoke a lot. He won me over with his words and all the attention he paid me. . . . I found a person who covered me with attention and words. Then, once we were married, he revealed himself to be an entirely different person, immature, infantile. . . . My husband was a baby even though at the time he was twenty-eight years old. He was a child because he had never been responsible for anything. He began working for the first time when we married. He was accustomed to getting whatever he wanted.

After describing her husband's character and why she was initially so attracted to him, Allegra moved on to describe their life as a married couple:

The violence started right away. I was seven months pregnant the first time it happened. And it was for such a little thing. My friend had come to visit me on Christmas day, and since I had the brain of an eighteen-year-old I was late coming home and wasn't ready on time for Christmas lunch with his parents and his brother. That was the first time he hit me. I stayed quiet. I pretended nothing had happened and told no one. And this was my first big mistake, because from then on he felt free to react in this way. Either I gave in to him or he was violent. It continued like this until the moment I said, enough. I reported him to the police, I left our house, and I was free.

In telling her story, Allegra compressed ten years of a violent marriage into just a few sentences. Throughout those years Allegra did not tell a single person what she was experiencing at home. The biggest fights with her husband were at meal times. Allegra did not know the first thing about cooking when she first got married. As she put it, her husband was "a perfect cook, or almost perfect," and he constantly criticized her cooking. For Allegra, cooking turned into a nightmare. She was constantly worried about whether her husband would erupt in anger if something was not prepared properly. Despite the fact that Allegra and Luisa, two close friends, were going through very similar experiences as young wives, neither knew about the other's true daily existence until well after both women had separated from their husbands.

When Luisa finished the dishes, she came into the living room and we talked about why she and Allegra never told each other what they were going through until many years after the fact. Allegra explained that the reason she never went to the hospital or told anyone about her experience was because of the *vergogna* (shame or embarrassment) she felt. For her, the shame came from

having to admit to others that I had made a mistake, for others to see I had made a lifelong mistake, married the wrong man, to admit publicly that I made such a big mistake. I think this is why I never said anything to my parents. Because my parents, I mean my mother, told me not to marry him, she told me he wasn't right. To return home two months after the wedding to say he hit me would have been to admit I had been wrong. I was proud, too proud to admit that I had made such a big mistake. And it was the same with other people. You didn't speak of these things, you endured and that was it. If you were to say your husband hit you, it was seen almost as if you must have done something wrong, something to provoke it.

The shame Allegra described to me had two facets: the shame of admitting that she had chosen the wrong mate and the shame that if her husband hit her it must have been because she deserved it. These layers of shame can trap women and keep them from seeking help. One layer stems from the gains of the feminist movement and the conviction that it is wrong for a husband to hit his wife. The other derives from the perpetuation of a moral and legal code that allowed men to hit their wives when they fell out of line. The embarrassment of the first combines with the self-doubt of the second to create a complex shame that is unbearable to many women. Rather than face the shame head-on, many women decide to continue enduring in silence.

After ten years of violence, Allegra broke her silence when she decided to file a police report against her husband. The decision to file the report came after a particularly violent period. Whenever Allegra tried to bring up the subject of a separation, her husband reacted with violence. In addition to being afraid of her husband's reaction, Allegra also had misgivings about reporting her husband to the police. Even after she went to the police station and filed a report with the help of her older brother, Allegra still had thoughts about retracting the report: "It was a very difficult thing to do because it was like putting on display in the central square everything that happened in my home, intimate things about my family life. And I constantly had anxiety about reporting my children's father to the police."

Allegra explained that she found the courage to file the police report and leave her husband only after her mother-in-law had passed away. She felt very close to her in-laws. They were also the only ones who knew the truth about her marriage. They knew that Allegra's husband had been having an affair since the day he married her and they knew that he was prone to episodes of violence. When Allegra finally decided to leave her husband, her in-laws blamed her for the end of the marriage despite what they knew about the relationship. Such a thing had never happened in their family—it was a black mark, and they blamed Allegra just as Luisa's in-laws had blamed her.

Not only did Allegra fear the reactions of her family and in-laws and worry that exposing the violence she experienced might bring shame to her entire family, she also feared the reactions of friends and colleagues who might wonder how an educated woman could endure a violent husband for so long. This second side of shame, shaped by the gains of the feminist movement, raises the question of whether feminist politics may, in some cases, inadvertently collude with masculinist legal and moral codes to prevent women from confiding in family and friends. For women involved as activists and volunteers, this layer of shame can be particularly difficult to overcome.

Enduring Violence

Pia is a woman who has ambivalent feelings about her husband but continues to invest time and energy in the relationship. I met Pia when I started volunteering at Family Aid. During my first few weeks at Family

Aid, I spent many hours in the central office, just watching the flow of activity and helping out with whatever people needed help with. Often this had me sitting in the main conference/work room at the long table where all the other volunteers worked. As the women sorted clothing and food donations and organized supplies, I typed letters, collated papers, entered information into the computer, and helped with other administrative tasks. I often chatted with Pia—who stopped by the office from time to time—and the other volunteers.

When I asked Pia if I could interview her for my project, she immediately agreed and we made plans to meet one morning for a coffee. After we had ordered our coffees and settled down at a table in the back of a local coffee bar, I explained that the interview was more of a life history than a series of structured questions, and suggested that she begin by describing her experiences as a child. Pia didn't skip a beat. She jumped in right away by telling me all about what it was like to grow up in Parma. She began walking me through various phases of her life and didn't stop talking until we had finished an entire cassette. Pia's narrative followed a very linear path. It began with the mistakes she made when she was young and ended with an emotional crisis and the various steps she had taken to put her life back together.

Pia was born in the early 1940s to very young parents. Although she had not been unhappy as a child, reflecting back on her childhood she realized that her parents had not provided the type of structure and guidance she needed. Despite the fact that they had lived in the apartment below her for entire adult life, Pia did not feel very close to either of her parents.

Pia married her husband when she was seventeen. Looking back, she realized that her life had followed a familiar pattern: "I followed the same path as my mother, despite all the criticism I voiced about the way she lived her life." For Pia, following the same path as her mother meant marrying young, becoming a mother very early, halting her education, and never finding a career. Pia had her first child when she was eighteen. At the time, her husband's income was more than enough to support the family, and since her parents-in-law worked and her own mother was not interested in helping with childcare, Pia chose to stay home and "be a mom." Once her daughter started to get older and have her own activities, Pia began feeling lonely and depressed. She faced a difficult decision. She was reluctant to go to work and leave her child at home, but on the other hand she needed to think of her own well-being. She then had a "great idea." She explained in an ironic tone, "Instead of trying to emancipate myself by finding a job, I decided to try to have another child." Despite her husband's protests, Pia decided to get pregnant again, and at the age of thirty she had her second daughter. At about the same time, her husband was getting over a health problem that had plagued him for ten years. He had an operation, and according to Pia, "It was like he had been reborn." It was at this point that the problems with him began.

"I found myself with two children, one older, one very young, and a husband who had another woman. I was without work and I had no idea what to do," Pia explained. She tried looking for a job but had no experience and found that employers were looking for younger people. The problems with her husband got worse, and Pia began staying in the house and closing herself off even more. As Pia sank deeper into depression, her husband found himself gaining responsibility at work. He was promoted to a new position that required him to take frequent business trips. Pia also knew he was spending a lot of time with one of his female colleagues.

Pia never told anyone other than her priest about her marital problems. She explained that the problems began when her husband had an emotionally intimate extramarital affair: "At this point, I was very scared. The other time my husband had had an affair it was really only about sex, but this time I realized it was something more. . . . At this point I said, oh my God, now what will I do. And that's when I went into a serious crisis."

Pia began closing herself off even more from her husband and the other people in her life. She remarked, "I have patience. I don't know if it is a virtue or a flaw, but I have a lot of patience." After a few years, Pia saw signs of her husband coming back. They started talking and going out together, but also began to have economic problems. His salary was no longer enough to support Pia and two growing children.

Pia began thinking seriously about her life, questioning her options and rethinking many of her previous decisions. Her husband was still emotionally and sexually involved with his colleague at work. Pia began to feel confused and trapped. She lacked the strength to tell her husband to leave and feared a separation would create further economic problems for her family. She felt guilty because she had never gotten a job and was not sure what she wanted. Part of her hoped her husband would leave and part of her hoped he would stay. It was at this low point in her life that Pia met Father Morava.

Pia was introduced to Father Morava by an acquaintance. At the time, Pia felt the need to confess a sin she had committed several years earlier and asked friends and neighbors for recommendations. Until our interview, the only people who knew about her marital problems and the sin she had committed were Father Morava and her husband. With tears in her eyes, Pia told me that soon after the birth of her second child she had had an abortion. Already worried about her family's economic problems, Pia had feared that having another child would cause her husband to leave her for someone else. At the time, she put the abortion out of her mind and refused to deal with all the emotions surrounding her decision. But when her marital problems began reoccurring, all of her emotions resurfaced. Pia initially went to Father Morava in an attempt to grapple with her guilt about having had an abortion, but she ended up talking to him at length about other issues in her life. She returned every three weeks to talk about her problems at home, her depression, and her confusion. In the end, as Pia explained, Father Morava helped her more as a psychologist than as a priest.

As part of their religious and community duties, many priests devote time to listening to the narratives of their parishioners. This listening takes place both inside and outside the confessional. During the course of my research, I observed that in some ways, the position of the anthropologist mirrors this long tradition of sacred listening. Like priests, anthropologists are often removed from everyday social relations within a community, and like priests, they are often seen as sources of both confidence and suspicion.[5] Although some of the people I worked with in Parma dismissed priests as being out of touch with current social life and as being protectors of traditional gender norms that subjugate women, others explained the important role priests can play as counselors, mentors, and listeners.[6]

I was struck to hear Pia tell me that prior to our interview the only person who had heard her life story in such detail was Father Morava. In this respect, the priest/parishioner encounter often exists outside of normal space and time, producing an effect similar to the liminality of ethnographic intimacy. In our interview, Pia spoke a great deal about Father Morava. She connected her newfound confidence and control over her life to their regular meetings. Even her newfound dedication to volunteer work was a result of meeting Father Morava. When Pia decided to start looking for a place to spend her free time and a way to give something positive to others, Father Morava sent her to a nearby nunnery. The nuns, in turn, sent her to Family Aid, where she ended up becoming a dedicated volunteer. The irony of the situation was not lost on Pia. She pointed out with a smile that she, of all people, ended up as a volunteer at a place whose primary purpose was to discourage the practice of abortion. As Pia began volunteering and trying to make sense of her life, things at home were getting worse. Pia's husband started having trouble at work and became increasingly angry at home. According to Pia, her husband was not well. He had completely lost his equilibrium. Pia saw that her husband was suffering and that this suffering was coming out against her. She explained, "Sometimes he became very mean—very, very mean. I was once again patient. I told myself I should send him out of the house, but I didn't want to create problems. . . . I tried to at least save the children's tranquility and serenity. It was a very ugly period."

Pia ended her life story by telling me that her volunteer work had helped her enormously. It enabled her to find new ways to relate to other people as well as a new sense of spontaneity within herself. Despite her husband's attempts to prevent her from going to her volunteer shifts, she never gave in and always found a way to go. In recent months, she told me, her relationship with her husband had reached an "unspoken compromise" of how to live together. She was happy to tell me they had even gone out together a few times as a couple. In addition to helping her look at her life in a new way, her meetings with Father Morava encouraged her to read the Bible and think more about religion. Although she still found it difficult to believe that everything she did, "the good and the bad," was part of God's plan, she said she believed in the existence of a superior entity.

Throughout Pia's narrative, there were certain aspects of her life that she alluded to but did not directly discuss. One was the violence she experienced at home. It was clear to me that when she told me her husband was sometimes "mean" and "unstable," she was alluding to either physical or psychological violence. Without being intrusive, I wanted to understand how she dealt physically and emotionally with these experiences. When I asked if her husband became violent in particular situations, Pia told me, "No, he is not a violent person. Absolutely not. On the contrary, he is a person who is very affectionate. He became violent because he had a lot of anger that he didn't know what to do with. He had problems at work, problems with his other woman, and he became violent. But I was always patient." I asked if she ever called anyone for help and Pia said she always took care of things on her own. When I asked if she ever went to the hospital, she explained:

No, no, he's not a violent person, he's not a bad person. Maybe that's the reason why I was able to put up with the violence. I understood it was his suffering that made him this way. He just ended up exploding. . . . I dealt with my suffering by closing myself off, he dealt with his by exploding. But he's not that type of person; on the contrary, he is full of affection.

Pia defended her husband's actions in the same way as many of the clients I had met at Women United. By defending her husband, she was able to defend herself and the decisions she had made. As Allegra pointed out in her discussion, women who are living with partner violence often feel embarassed to admit they were willing to put up with violence and ashamed that they may have somehow provoked the violence. By continually referring to her husband's good qualities, and attributing his violence to problems beyond his control, Pia was able to displace these two sides of shame and continue with her daily life.

Near the end of my interview with Pia, she showed me two necklaces. One was a pendant of the Virgin Mary and Baby Jesus, given to her by Father Morava, and the other was a cross, given to her by her husband. Pia told me that the cross had been torn off her neck many times during fights with her husband and that she had had it fixed every time. During the last fight they had, three months before our interview, he had tried two times to tear it off her neck but it never broke. From then on, Pia told me, their relationship began to improve.

Luisa, Allegra, and Pia are women on different sides of Italy's communist/Catholic divide, yet all three faced similar pressures in their daily lives—the pressure to perform their roles as "traditional" women dedicated to their husbands and families, and as "modern" women capable of making independent decisions about their lives and their physical and emotional well-being. This multilayered experience of gender proficiency may have been most pronounced in situations of violence, but it was also quite evident in the daily negotiation of household labor. I learned from many of the women I met through the Rocco di Marco neighborhood group that women from diverse political, religious, educational, and generational backgrounds faced similar dilemmas when it came to negotiating gender proficiency in their relationships with husbands and partners.

The Nightmare of the Laundry

One afternoon, following a leisurely lunch with Franca and Annalisa, two women in their mid- to late fifties, Franca brought up *l'incubo del bucato*, or the nightmare of the laundry. It was not the first time I had heard this expression. Nor was it the first time I had heard women complain about the piles of clothes they had at home waiting to be washed and ironed. Franca explained that as she got older she enjoyed cleaning and other household tasks less and less. Smiling, she told us that in addition to being behind with the ironing, she was upset that the other day her husband had "humiliated" her when he took out a rag and cleaned the windows himself. Annalisa nodded knowingly. She confessed that sometimes she and her daughters would hide the clothes that needed to be ironed so that her mother, who came to clean the house every day, would not see how far behind she was. For Annalisa, hiding her unfinished household work was a way for her to appear the perfect homemaker and *fare bella figura* in front of her mother.

The conflict women face between their responsibilities as workers outside the home and the high standards of housekeeping with which they were raised is common in many cities across Italy. In her work on food and gender in Florence, Carole Counihan relates the experiences of Cinzia, a woman who works full time and "feels her mother's disapproval" when she gets behind with housework and leaves beds unmade and laundry unironed (1988:58–59). According to Counihan, throughout the 1980s many Florentine women were "struggling to manage the claims of family and the need and desire to work for wages" (2004:80). Counihan suggests that the women she worked with were concerned about their ability to perform their domestic duties, regardless of whether they worked outside the home. As one of her informants, a "career woman" named Marianna, confessed, "I have learned to make many things since I married Renzo—but, of course, I didn't know how to make anything. However, I live always with the fear that it won't come out right. Will it be ruined? But look what I've made. Will it be good?" (83).

The tensions women experience when they work outside and inside the home clearly resonate in a variety of cultural contexts, but the situation may be especially difficult in a place like Italy, where the cultural standards of order and precision are particularly high when it comes to household tasks. I think of myself as a fairly neat and orderly person, but I too felt the burden of making sure my apartment was impeccably clean before inviting Italian friends to come visit. Counihan (2004) recounts numerous stories that demonstrate the exacting standards of household order that her Florentine informants faced on a daily basis. As one of Counihan's informants, Caterina, explained,

Look, when I do the cleaning, I do it right. Rest assured that if I clean the bathroom, I clean it so that there is not even one hair on the floor. But then maybe five minutes later Sandro arrives, and bam, he goes into the bathroom and leaves the whole sink dirty. All he did was wash his hands. Madonna, that makes me angry! So then I say, "How is it possible? I washed the bathroom yesterday evening. We're only the two of us and we're hardly ever at home and yet the bathroom is already dirty. What will people think?" . . . Oh he's not one of those men who come and check on you and say, "Oh, Caterina, the bed needs to be made." If the bed isn't made when he comes home, he doesn't say a thing. It bothers me more than him, because for God's sake, if people come over and the bed isn't made, it looks bad. . . . So I do the work; I make the bed. I don't want to appear disorderly. . . . Our friends are young people like us, but it still bothers me if the house is a mess. Why? Maybe because I've been conditioned. Furthermore, don't think that our friends will say, "But look at these two, they still haven't made the bed at nine in the evening." No, they say, "Look at her. She is a real slob. She left the bed unmade." That is how it is. Rest assured that if people come over to the house, it's not the man who sees the bed unmade. The woman sees it—for example, my mother, or Sandro's mother. . . . They don't say anything to him. They say it to me. I'm the one who looks bad. (2004:164–165)

Some of the younger women I interviewed would have welcomed a more equal distribution of household tasks, but other women I spoke with expressed discomfort with the idea of men performing certain household duties. Cooking was the exception. Although meal preparation was generally done by women, men also cooked occasionally. I attended a handful of dinners for which the husband had prepared the *pastasciutta* (pasta with sauce) or sliced the prosciutto in preparation for company.[7] Ironing, however, was a household duty that fell squarely on the shoulders of nearly every woman in Parma, married or single. It was seen as part of women's work and was very rarely done by men. There were certain tasks—such as cleaning, washing clothes, and ironing—that were naturalized by many as feminine activities. A number of the women I spoke with, particularly women in their forties and fifties, told me it would be shameful to see their husbands doing tasks such as dusting or ironing. Counihan reports similar views among her informants in Florence:

Florentine men and women concurred that housework was not men's work. As forty-five-year-old Rinaldo said, "For me to sweep or mop the floor, I just can't see it. It's stronger than me (*è più forte di me*). Sure, at home with just the family, I could sweep if I really had to, but I just couldn't mop the floor. I wouldn't be able to do it—not physically—but I don't know; it would really bother me. I just don't have the inclination to do it (*non me la sento proprio*). I don't know— doing the laundry—come on, it is not men's work. Traditionally it is just not men's work. Maybe in the United States the men iron, but for me to iron, Sergia would have to be sick—no, not even then would I iron. I would send my clothes out." (2004:91)

In Italy, the process of washing clothes and linens is both time- and labor-intensive. Although washing machines are common, dryers are scarce, both because of the energy they consume and their reputation for being hard on clothing and linens. Many families that could easily afford the cost of a dryer have no interest in purchasing one. Once the clothes and linens come out of the washing machine, they must therefore be hung out to dry. For those fortunate enough to have terraces or backyards, the clothes are hung on lines with clothespins. For those without outdoor space, the clothes are hung on folding metal drying racks that can be set up inside. The next step is ironing. In addition to shirts, blouses, pants, and dresses, the pile of items to be ironed includes sheets, bath towels, tablecloths, napkins, dishtowels, socks, and often even underwear.

In Parma, as in the rest of Italy, it is the women who are primarily responsible for cleaning and ironing clothes as well as for the rest of the *lavoro di cura*, which involves caring for children, caring for the elderly, looking after the house, and managing the household.[8] Many women attend to these responsibilities in addition to working full- or part-time jobs. Rossella Palomba (1997) analyzed the results of data collected by the Italian statistical agency, ISTAT, and charted the hours women and men devoted to the following: activities for the family, housework, work outside the home, personal needs, and free time. According to Palomba's analysis, marriage marks a change in the daily routine for both men and women, but it is the women who experience a radical and fundamental shift in priorities. Palomba found that married women without children spent more than 2.5 hours more per day on housework than their unmarried counterparts (4 hours and 36 minutes as compared to 1 hour and 54 minutes), whereas married men actually experienced a slight decrease (36 minutes as compared to 42 minutes). Palomba suggests that men "pass from the care of the mother to that of the wife," and although a man's free time diminished a bit with marriage, the structure of his day remained more or less the same (Palomba 1997:165–166). With the birth of children, the amount of time women devote to domestic work again increases. Men, on the other hand, devote more time to work outside the home in an effort to earn more money. It is no surprise that women, more than men, experience difficulty balancing time spent with children with time for themselves and household chores. When men do devote time to domestic activities, the work tends to center on the purchasing and preparation of food, small repairs, and gardening, while the making of beds, cleaning, and the washing and ironing of clothes almost always remain the wife's responsibility. According to a study conducted by the universities of Modena and Reggio Emilia, women who work outside the home dedicate an average of thirty-five hours per week to household duties, whereas men on average dedicate only eight (*La Gazzetta di Parma*, Dec. 16, 1999:1).

The burden of the "second shift" (Hochschild 1989) is intensified in Italy because the activities involved with *lavoro di cura* are generally more laborious than domestic activities in the United States. As Counihan (1988) argues, working women in Florence are "caught in a bind." The women Counihan interviewed wanted to work at full-time jobs outside the home, but at the same time felt "incomplete and incompetent" if they were not also "perfect housewives." In Italy, it is nearly impossible to excel both inside and outside the home because of the great amount of time and labor that goes into *lavoro di cura*. In addition to the importance of ironing, among many families it is still common practice to have two multicourse hot meals each day; shop daily for fresh fruits, vegetables, and meats in small, family-owned stores in town; and keep bedrooms, living rooms, and kitchens impeccably clean and orderly. Although many people I spoke with placed an aesthetic and health-related value on home-cooked meals and immaculate living spaces, the desire to *fare bella figura* in front of neighbors, friends, and relatives is also a strong motivating factor.

During the 1980s and 1990s, shopping in large supermarkets and preparing meals with packaged ingredients became more widespread as women worked increasingly long hours outside the home, and the business climate shifted to resemble more of a U.S.-style workday with only an hour off for lunch. Counihan (1988) suggests that Florentine women gain power and influence through the control of food, and that the contemporary shift toward commercially prepackaged, ready-made meals moves food out of the domain of women. As a result, food becomes less important in the shaping of female identity, and "foods increasingly represent not the values of home, family, and women, but the values of consumerism" (Counihan 1988:58). Dishwashers and washing machines, now common in many homes, have also changed the nature of women's household responsibilities. Despite such timesaving tools and products, women still shoulder a great burden when it comes to the work of family, household, and kinship.[9]

Counihan (2004) recognizes the power that many of her Florentine informants exerted through their control of the household realm, but she also underscores the stark difference in economic power that caused many women to become trapped in unhappy marriages. Regardless of whether women controlled household finances or not, when the source of monetary support came from a husband's paycheck, women had little recourse other than to stay put and endure for the sake of financial security. As one of her informants explained,

There are many reasons why a husband and wife stay together in spite of not getting along. Sometimes there are reasons of economic interest. My God, if a woman is independent and can survive by herself as well as she can with her husband, well then at a certain point she can say, "I'm self-sufficient and I'm washing my hands of this, and that's that." But if the woman is economically dependent on her husband, how can she make it without him? So then she bows her head and stays there. (2004:110).

Italy's social welfare system relies in great part on the family network—the idea that in times of difficulty it is the family that one looks to first for support. Throughout Italian history, family solidarity has been seen as the solution for the societal dilemma of how to care for those who cannot care for themselves. Facilities for the elderly are few and far between because it was always assumed that most people would care for their own aging parents. The same is true for other types of social services. Although medical care is available to everyone through a public healthcare system, other services such as day care and public housing are difficult to find and often have very long waiting lists. In the 1970s, the institution of basic social services for children, the elderly, and the disabled was controversial and viewed with apprehension. There was a persistent fear that such services could undermine family solidarity (Barbagli and Saraceno 1997:24). Despite the implementation of basic social services, the widespread lack of day-care and elder-care facilities, combined with the desire among many families to care for relatives in the home, has created a generation of overburdened Italian women.[10] It is the current generation of grandmothers, many of whom spent thirty years or more working inside and outside the home, who must care for their elderly parents and in-laws, as well as their grandchildren and unmarried children still living at home. When a relative falls ill and needs constant attention, it is the women who spend day and night in the hospital or bedroom, rotating shifts with other female relatives. When children who work full-time jobs decide to have children of their own, it is the grandmothers who become full-time babysitters.

Liliana is an energetic woman who is always smiling and on the go. She is in her mid-fifties and works full time for a local bank. Liliana gets up at 5:00 AM and works a 7:00 to 2:00 shift, Monday through Saturday.

In addition to her full-time job, she picks up her two grandchildren from day care at least three afternoons per week and cares for them until her daughter and daughter-in-law return from work. Liliana does all the shopping, cooking, cleaning, washing, and ironing for herself and her husband. Somehow, she also manages to squeeze in daily visits to her elderly mother. Liliana gave up on her husband helping out many years ago, and now just accepts the fact that he goes to work every day and comes home to read, relax, and enjoy his free time.

It is common knowledge that in many Western societies, as women enter the labor force, their partners and husbands "in the aggregate do not increase the amount of child care and housework they do" (Di Leonardo 1984:193). Although this trend may be changing within certain segments of Western societies, in Parma the situation I observed for working women with families closely mirrored the "double day" written about by American feminist scholars in the 1980s (Di Leonardo 1984; Hochschild 1989). In her work on Italian immigrants in the United States, Micaela Di Leonardo found that the women she worked with participated in three forms of labor: "work in the market . . . , work in the household, and the work of kinship" (1984:194). The work of kinship, as Di Leonardo defines it, consists of a range of diverse activities, all of which enable the creation and maintenance of ties between households. Although the women I worked with did not compartmentalize their labor in this way, they did perform work in each of the areas Di Leonardo mentions. Nearly all my women friends and colleagues worked or had worked in the labor market, were responsible for most household and child-rearing duties, and performed the work of kinship by organizing holiday gatherings, visiting or phoning relatives, attending to elderly parents, and babysitting grandchildren. Single women are far from exempt from the work of kinship, and in fact often fill in for married sisters. Flavia, a friend who is divorced and without children of her own, routinely helped out in the bakery owned by her sister and brother-in-law, and babysat for her young nephews. Angelina, another friend, took turns with her sisters in caring for her invalid father during his many years of illness, and sacrificed a full-time job to devote more time to her kinship obligations.

As two-income families become increasingly the norm in Parma and other cities across Italy, the domestic arena is becoming uncertain for both women and men.[11] Work outside the home has become both a financial and intellectual necessity for many women, but kin relations (maintained primarily by women) are still at the center of the social welfare system. Household duties and expectations have changed only marginally over the past fifty years, and yet young people are living with their parents until well into their thirties, and middle-aged parents, especially mothers, are continuing to care for their adult children and elderly parents as they begin to become elderly themselves.[12] As people marry later and live longer, the demands on women have intensified.[13]

The women and men I spoke with in Parma expressed ambivalence about gender and marital relations. Young women told me that men their age were confused about what they wanted in a woman. Middle-aged men told me that they were a generation in crisis. And middle-aged women told me that they were both disillusioned by the theoretical gains of the feminist movement and confused about what to expect from their husbands.

On Saturdays It's Sandwiches for Dinner

Franca and Paolo live in the Rocco di Marco *quartiere* (neighborhood) of Parma. They are in their late fifties and have lived in the neighborhood for close to twenty-five years. I first met Franca at meetings of the Rocco di Marco neighborhood group. After a few casual conversations, she invited me over for lunch, where I met her husband Paolo. As the months went on I returned for other lunches and dinners with Franca and Paolo, and met their two children: thirty-three-year-old Luca and twenty-eight-year-old Regina.

When I met Franca and Paolo they were retired. Franca had worked as an elementary school teacher and retired at a young age to spend more time with their two children. Paolo had worked in the office of a local food-exporting business until his late fifties, when he too decided to retire. They lived on the third floor of a modern condominium building in a two-bedroom apartment with one bathroom, a kitchen, a living/dining room, and a terrace. Franca and Paolo were both very involved with parish and neighborhood activities. Franca participated in the Rocco di Marco neighborhood group and Paolo was a volunteer with *Avanti*, a parish group made up almost entirely of men who administer the parish bar and activity room and organize various social outings for members of the parish. As a couple, Franca and Paolo attended mass every Sunday morning, usually the 11:00 service, and frequented the couples' group led by don Bernardo, the parish priest, that met one Sunday evening per month. Every summer they would go away together for two weeks, often to the mountains, and spend their days swimming and walking. Occasionally they would go away with other couples, but usually their first priority was to vacation with their children and grandchildren.

Their son Luca and his wife, Carla, decided to get married when they were in their mid-twenties. Despite warnings from family and friends, they decided to go through with it while Carla was still at university and before they had been able to save any money. Luca had not gone to university and was already working, but his entry-level salary was barely enough to support one person, let alone two. Their first home was a tiny, dark apartment above a café in an old, decrepit building in the center of Parma. The bathroom was on the floor above their apartment, and Carla often joked that when she went to the bathroom in the middle of the night, she never knew whom she might meet on the way upstairs. Franca told me she was appalled when she first saw the apartment, but after a few weeks was amazed to see how homey Luca and Carla were able to make the place and how happy they were just to be living together.

Shortly before Carla's graduation, she and Luca once again shocked their friends and family by announcing that they were expecting a baby. Carla graduated, had the baby, and began working part-time. The three soon moved to a larger apartment in a *quartiere* outside the city center. By the time I met them in the fall of 1999, Carla and Luca had had a second child, and Carla was hoping to find a full-time position as a translator. When I returned to Parma for a follow-up visit in May of 2001, Carla had found full-time work, but as an office assistant. Although it was not her ideal position, the new job was a big help financially. When Carla started working full-time, Franca also gained a new job, as the afternoon babysitter for her two grandchildren.

One day during my follow-up visit, Franca invited me over for lunch. It was a nice day, so I decided to borrow a friend's bicycle to get from the center of Parma to their condominium complex. When I arrived outside the building, Luca and Carla were just getting out of their car. It was a bit after 1 PM, and they had come directly from work (although the lunch break had shortened in recent years, nearly all organizations and businesses in Parma still closed for at least a two-hour *pausa*, or break, in the middle of the day). We rode up together on the elevator and caught up on one another's lives.

When Franca opened the door she was wearing her cooking apron. She greeted us and said the pasta would be ready in just a few minutes. The table was set just as I remembered. There was a white tablecloth,

cloth napkins, and a plate and bowl at every setting. On the table there were two bottles of water, one sparkling and one still, a bottle of orange soda, a bottle of sparkling white wine, and five or six hunks of bread placed directly on the tablecloth. The time and care put into meal preparation on an everyday basis becomes even greater when other people are invited over. Depending on the situation, and whether the guests are family members, friends, colleagues, or even strangers, there can be both a desire to provide for others as well as a desire to *fare bella figura* and demonstrate one's ability to present a good meal.[14]

We sat down at the table and Franca brought out a large pot full of *tortelli d'erbetta*, a first course typical of Parma and often served on special occasions, especially when there are out-of-town guests. *Tortelli d'erbetta* are thin, tender, square envelopes of pasta filled with a delicate combination of spinach and ricotta and parmigiano-reggiano cheeses, and served with an abundance of melted butter and grated cheese. After we finished our generous servings of *tortelli*, Franca brought out the second course, *prosciutto e melone*, also typical of Parma's local cuisine.

As we ate our prosciutto and cantaloupe, we chatted about the United States, presidents Clinton and George W. Bush, and Italian politics. Everyone at the table was disappointed by the recent victory of Berlusconi (the media tycoon and founder of the Forza Italia party), and concerned about what it would mean for the country's future. Although practicing Catholics and former Christian Democrats, both Franca and Paolo had joined the center-left following the disintegration of the centrist Christian Democrat party. We continued to talk through to the final course of fruit and gelato—until eventually Luca and Carla had to return to work.

After we said our goodbyes, Paolo went out to the terrace to read, and Franca and I sat down at the table to continue chatting. As we talked about the neighborhood group, the parish, her daughter who lived and studied in Rome, and other things going on in Franca's life, I gained more insight into her daily routine. Every afternoon Franca picked up her two grandchildren from preschool and took them back to their house, where she gave them a snack and watched them until her daughter-in-law, Carla, got home from work. Franca usually gave Carla a hand with the housework by preparing something for dinner, doing the ironing, or making the beds. In her own house, Franca did the cleaning, the laundry, and the food shopping, and made lunch and dinner every day for herself and Paolo. When I asked what she prepared for lunch and dinner she explained that she always served a *primo* and *secondo* (first and second course) because Paolo liked having them, even if the first course was just soup or something light. Every so often they would go out to dinner with friends, but she explained that usually they preferred to just stay at home.

Ever since Franca could remember, Paolo and his friends from childhood spent Saturday afternoons and evenings together. The men would usually go on a hike, or a drive, or out to dinner, and Franca was happy to stay home and have some time alone to relax or do housework. When I asked what she prepared for dinner when Paolo was away, she smiled and exclaimed, "Sandwiches and tea." Saturday nights were a break from the normal routine.

Franca helped her daughter-in-law with childcare just as Franca's mother-in-law had done when Franca had small children and was working as a teacher. When Franca talked about watching her grandchildren and helping out with Carla's household chores, she never complained and always referred to it as helping her daughter-in-law, not her son. Franca told me that when she first started going over to their house she was careful not to step on Carla's toes and always asked before doing things to help.

Like so many other women I spoke with, Franca pointed out that despite the many changes for women that had occurred over the preceding twenty years, the brunt of the household and childcare responsibility still fell on the woman. She told me that although roles were changing, and should be changing, it was also important not to feminize men in the process. Whereas Franca's father did nothing to help her mother and would sit at the table barking orders, Franca's husband Paolo was always very "willing to help and was never one to demand things or get angry if dinner wasn't ready." Franca pointed out that her own son helped even more by changing diapers and participating in his children's lives. She noted, "Thirty years ago you would never see a man pushing a baby carriage. If you did you would stare and think it was very strange. Now you see men pushing baby carriages all the time."[15] Although Franca approved of this blurring of gender roles, she worried that some women demanded too much of men by asking them to do chores that humiliated them, chores such as ironing and vacuuming: "It's true that my husband can iron, but if he tells me that ironing makes him feel humiliated or he doesn't like it, then I say do something else for me, something that requires more strength, something more masculine."

Speaking with Franca about the roles of men and women within families reminded me of a similar conversation that had taken place during one of my many visits to her house during the spring of 2000.

It was Sunday afternoon and Franca had invited me over to have lunch after church with her entire family—Paolo, Luca, Carla, Regina, and Franca's brother, sister-in-law, and nieces. After a tremendous lunch with multiple courses and many bottles of wine, some of the women began talking about men, women, and marital roles.

It started with Franca telling me the story of how everyone thought Luca and Carla were crazy to get married without owning a house or having any money: "Here [in Parma] you have to have a beautiful house, all the furniture and decorations for each room, a car, and two jobs before people decide to get married. This means people wait and wait and engagements go on forever." At this point in the story, Franca's thirty-two-year-old niece pulled up a chair to join the conversation. Franca put her arm around her and said, "This one likes living at home, she likes having her mom do the cleaning, cooking, and wash and iron her clothes." The niece turned to me and explained that in a few years she would like to move out, but right now she was saving money by living at home and had no time to do the things her mother did. She worked in a bank from 8 AM until 7 PM and came home exhausted.

I tried to ask what she was saving her money for, but she either didn't hear or pretended not to hear my question. I then asked if husbands her age helped out with the household duties. She said that most of her female colleagues who were married had hired help. Carla, who was in another part of the room, overheard my question and pulled up a chair. She explained, "Men help, but there still isn't parity. It's still the woman who has to think of everything." She talked about a number of couples she knew and then said, "Among our friends, I see that there is only one husband who truly takes on some of the responsibility. When he goes to do the food shopping his wife doesn't need to tell him what to get. He goes and gets what they need. He does things independently."

Again teasing her niece, Franca said, "My niece doesn't like men who help in the house, right? You want a man who is a man." The niece nodded, "I'd rather have a nice Filippina come in and do those things." Franca went on to explain that although it is right that men help out in the house, "men and women are different. You can't deny they have physical differences. Paolo is stronger than me. I'd rather have him do the heavier jobs. In front of the children I never wanted to diminish his paternal figure, a father has a different type of authority than a mother."

As Franca spoke I could see Carla shaking her head ever so slightly. She leaned toward me and, knowing my own feminist leanings, whispered, "Don't give in, don't agree. Stand your ground!" Carla seemed annoyed by what her mother-in-law was saying, but other than coaching me she did not express her own thoughts or views. She chose to voice her frustration later in the day, when Franca was not around. We were on our way to the park with another of Franca's nieces. The husbands had gone ahead with the children, which left the three of us to chat as we made our way to the park. Carla brought up her recent mountain vacation with her in-laws. She explained that at first Franca had not wanted to use the dishwasher in the rental apartment because she thought it would be more "poetic" to wash the dishes by hand. Carla explained that she told Franca very clearly, "I'm bringing the detergent for when it's my night to wash dishes. On your night you can do what you want." Then, as an afterthought, Carla muttered under her breath, "And of course it would be too embarrassing to have the men wash the dishes."

Once we arrived at the park, Carla, her cousin-in-law Elsa, and I sat on a bench and chatted while the fathers played with the children on the swings and slides. Elsa brought up the subject of gifts for children and told us how much she disagrees with giving girls gifts of toy irons and toy kitchen sets. Agreeing, Carla shook her head and asked rhetorically, "Would anyone ever give that gift to a boy? My son is going to learn how to make *tortelli*, how to iron, how to do everything!" Elsa added, "How are things ever going to change if we keep on giving our boys cars and our girls irons and pots and pans?" Carla told us that her sister, who had recently had her first child, refused to take a used high chair from a friend because it was blue. Her baby was a girl, so she felt the high chair had to be pink. Carla expressed frustration with her sister's attitude and said that at times her sister lacked *cultura* (culture/sophistication).

Carla and Elsa's discussion of the important role women play in socializing the next generation of Italian men is echoed in Carole Counihan's conversation with a sixty-six-year-old Florentine woman:

Most men in Italy only do the men's chores; they don't do women's chores. . . . But it's something for which we women also bear the guilt. I remember one time when my husband Giorgio was still alive. I was doing some taxing household chore—I don't remember what—when it started to rain. I had the clothes outside drying on the line. So Giorgio said to me, "Don't worry. Continue what you're doing. I'll bring the clothes in off the line; otherwise they'll get soaked." Look, I didn't want him to go out on the terrace to get the clothes and bring them in. I didn't want him to do it, because I thought people might see him from the other apartments and think badly of me for making him do this chore. So you can understand the prejudices about what men should do start from us women. It's our fault as much as theirs. (Counihan 2004:152)

Some of the women I spoke with expressed a desire to change gendered expectations by changing the way they raised their own sons and daughters. Others made a conscious decision not to have children. Elizabeth Krause noted that, for the women she worked with in central Italy, the decision about having children "was not just about rational decision-making; it also involved living life in deeply ambivalent ways" (2005:95). I heard similar expressions of ambivalence in my conversations with women in Parma.

The Blue Ribbon

Veronica was one of the founding board members of Women United. An active member of Udi as well as the Pci (Italian Communist Party), Veronica participated in the political activism of the 1960s and experienced the trajectory of the feminist movement in Parma from the early 1970s through the dissolution of Udi and creation of Women United. With her short hair and trendy outfits, Veronica was known throughout Parma for her youthful sense of style as well as for her activism on behalf of women.

Veronica decided long ago not to have children. When she explained this decision, she remarked that for a woman, giving up motherhood is one of the most difficult things to do. For Veronica it was a decision that stemmed in part from her experience with the feminist movement and in part from her fear of not being able to be a good mother. Although she had many relationships throughout her adult life, she had never married. For many of the men she dated, giving up children would have been too big a sacrifice. As Veronica explained how she came to this critical life decision, she was reminded of a very difficult experience that initially caused her to doubt herself but ultimately enabled her to feel confident she had made the right choice.

VERONICA: One day I found myself near the house of a very good friend, a friend with whom I had shared everything. For a variety of reasons we had lost touch with each other for ten years. Then one day I found myself near her house. She lives in a beautiful house in the countryside, near the Po River where I spent my childhood, and where I return in moments of depression or times when I just want to be alone. One of these times I thought of visiting Katia. Passing by her house, I saw there was a blue ribbon [signaling the birth of a boy] on the front door. Immediately I felt awful. She and I had made plans together, we had decided we would not have children. We had decided to be autonomous women, we could become whatever we wanted, we had big

ideas, big plans. . . . Finding myself outside her front door and seeing that ribbon made me feel she had betrayed me. She hadn't maintained what we had
decided together. She had had a child.

SONJA: You didn't ring the doorbell?

VERONICA: No, I didn't ring the bell. I felt an incredible rage, I cried the whole
way home convincing myself that I hadn't thought enough about my decision not to have children. Up until then, they had been big words, but I hadn't
thought about my decision in a deep or profound way. I went into crisis like a
crazy person. After ten days I went back to Katia's house, and seeing her, hug-
ging her, seeing her baby, convinced me that I had maintained what had been
my desire and my objective. And for a number of reasons, she had decided to
do the opposite. It was one of the most moving moments of my life, one of the
most intense moments of my life. We were both crying like crazy. . . . The blue
ribbon was no longer there because ten days had passed. I rang the bell and
said, "It's Veronica." She said, "Come in, I have something very important to
show you." It was her son. She held him in her arms and said to me, "I didn't
betray you." I told her I had stopped by ten days before and then we hugged. It
is an embrace that I can still picture vividly, like the embrace of my father right
before he died.

Katia's son was more than twenty years old when Veronica told me
this story. More than two decades after the fact, Veronica was still able
to recall many details of this intimate and poignant experience. It is
a memory that represents the culmination of years of discussion, debate, and self-reflection about what it means personally and culturally
to be a woman in Italian society. Italian leftist feminism in the late 1970s
and 1980s drew much from the work of Luce Irigaray, who encouraged
women to stop demanding equality and start working toward the recognition of gender difference. For Irigaray, women must find "a value
in being women and not just in being mothers" (1993:11).

As young women, Veronica and Katia decided to resist the gender
norms that were prevalent in Italian society. Their decision not to have
children marked a departure from the ideology of Catholicism and the
state. They followed the feminist writings of the time and chose to embrace an ideology that sought to liberate women from the role of mother
and housewife. As Veronica put it, "We were two women who were
ready to gobble up the world."

The betrayal Veronica felt initially when she saw the ribbon on
Katia's front door, and the existential crisis that sent her into a tailspin
of self-doubt, are indicative of the pervasive ambivalence about gender
relations that began with the feminist movement and in recent years has
become an important issue in mainstream Italian society. By giving up

motherhood, Veronica resisted the gender norms with which she was raised and challenged the dominant religious and state ideology. When confronted with direct evidence that one of her closest friends, with whom she had discussed many of her ideas about politics and gender, had changed her mind, she felt betrayed and began to question her own decisions. Had she given up an integral part of being a woman? Had she made a huge mistake? As Veronica told me this extremely personal story, I felt my own eyes well up with tears. The emotion with which Veronica had told me her story was palpable. Her verbal intonations and facial expressions reverberated with all the anger, confusion, and love the story represented.

Veronica's story is an ideal site to examine the conflicting demands of tradition and modernity. Her initial decision, the self-doubt that came ten years later, and her re-found confidence, were all shaped by the confluence of interpretations of tradition and modernity that emphasized different understandings of gender, as well as the ideologies of Catholicism, communism, and feminism that helped shape the heuristic divide. The feminist movement in Italy left many women and men wondering how to reconcile new understandings of gender with existing household and kinship demands. As is clear from the stories of the women I worked with, individual responses to this dilemma varied significantly. Some held fast to what they termed an "old-fashioned" division of labor between men and women, while others created personal solutions in accordance with more individualized understandings of gender and personhood. Some of the women who came of age during the Italian feminist movement and charted their own personal courses lamented the fact that they did not leave a clear legacy for future generations of women. The life stories and life decisions of women like Veronica, Luisa, Allegra, Pia, Franca, and others illustrate not only the shaping of individual subjectivities, but how individual women ascribe meaning to the choices they make and the life paths they pursue while negotiating the conflicting demands of locally informed notions of tradition and modernity.

CHAPTER 5

Gender Proficiencies

IN HIS WORK ON MANHOOD AND MASCULINITY in a Cretan village, Herzfeld (1985) alerts us to the importance of performance in studies of masculinity. He argues that often *what* a man does is not as important as *how* he does it. Lancaster (1992), Gutmann (1996), and others build upon Herzfeld's analysis of how the performative aspects of "being a man" often express other tensions and inequalities in society at both the local and national level. For Lancaster, "Machismo's 'finished product' is not only an array of gendered bodies but also a world built around its definition of gender and its allotment of power. Above all else, the operation of this system appears 'natural,' 'normal,' even 'necessary,' and the human products of machismo confront the consciousness prepared by it as inevitable" (Lancaster 1992:20). Lancaster argues that the system of machismo is similar to the hegemony of capitalism when he asserts, "Genders, sexualities, and bodies thus produced also silently, imperceptibly *reproduce* the logic of the system—even when its obvious inequalities are under challenge" (1992:20, original emphasis). What happens, however, when this system and allotment of power is challenged in a way that does not merely reproduce the logic of the system itself, but actually results in some degree of change, however incremental? If the performance of masculinity is at its base a means of securing advantage and power over other men (Herzfeld 1985; Lancaster 1992), then what happens when new ways of envisioning manhood begin to take hold? What happens when "being a good man" as well as "being *good at* being a man" (Herzfeld 1985:16, original emphasis) begins to change?

Individual subjectivities clearly do not shift and transform in uniform or consistent ways. As Gutmann points out in his review of the anthropology of masculinity, "Contrary to the assertion that men are made while women are born (albeit 'in the native's point of view') is the understanding that men are often the defenders of 'nature' and 'the natural order of things,' while women are the ones instigating change in gender relations and much else" (Gutmann 1997a:404). In Italy this has certainly been the case. The women's movement in Italy caught many men off guard. Even men within the Pci, who on a theoretical level advocated gender egalitarianism, were resistant to calls for the restructuring of gender roles inside and outside the home. As Manuela—a founder of Parma's Biblioteca delle Donne (Women's Library)—explained, almost all the women who had been involved with the collective ended up separating from their husbands and partners. As women they had embarked upon a journey toward a radically new way of imagining and interpreting the world, and this new worldview often could not accommodate their previous relationships with men.

Nuccio is an example of a man who says he has been left behind. Although still married to his wife Olivia, Nuccio finds himself lost and confused by his wife's transformation from a *casalinga* (housewife) into a woman with a solid career, new friends, and new activities. I met Nuccio and Olivia through a mutual friend. Although we chatted informally on a number of occasions, it was not until I went over to their house one afternoon to do a life-history interview that we really got to know one another. Because the apartment was small, Olivia went into the bedroom to fold laundry and tidy up while I spoke with Nuccio at the dining room table.

Stretched out casually on a chair, Nuccio told me about his childhood and his life with Olivia in a slow, low-pitched voice, gruff from years of smoking. Nuccio was both self-critical and insightful in telling his life story. Speaking about his marriage to Olivia, he explained that he had always been very jealous. He linked this jealousy to a turbulent and unhappy childhood and explained that though he tried to "stay calm" as a husband, his efforts were in vain. For Nuccio, his own infidelity and recklessness were just cause to suspect the same in the people around him. While Nuccio was having affairs, he constantly suspected Olivia was doing the same. Looking back on the difficult years of their relationship, Nuccio acknowledged that Olivia was always there for him, always helping him. Although he claimed to have always recognized and valued her support, he admitted that his words and thoughts did not "correspond to action." When I asked Nuccio to explain his jealousy, he said it was due to the fact that he grew up insecure and without parental affection. He remembered the first days of school as a young child when he was the only child there without his mother. When I asked Nuccio to explain how his jealousy was expressed in the context of his relationships with others, he responded:

> Most often it was expressed in my relationship with Olivia. In the early years, it also became a form of violence. One time I hit her for no reason. One time she threw a frying pan at me, but she had good reason—thinking back on it I realize she had good reason. It's not normal for a husband to come back home at six in the morning. My behavior was not what it should have been.

To a certain extent, Nuccio's wife accepted the excuse of an unhappy childhood as reason for his infidelity and violence. As with many of the women who came to Women United, any explanation for mistreatment, however plausible, was reason not only to keep going, but to transform their anger and hurt into caring and compassion. Whereas in the past women might have been more likely to blame themselves for a husband's violence (and many still do), the recourse to psychological explanations provides an alternative outlet that is often preferable to accepting that a husband or partner is flawed and incapable of being a supportive mate. What is interesting in the case of Nuccio is that he himself appealed to a particular form of Freudian logic to remove himself partially from blame. Although he acknowledged that his behavior was inappropriate and hurtful, he cited his own childhood and general societal transformations as reasons for his difficulties.

Nuccio spoke about the problems many men of his generation have experienced as a result of the great social transformations of the 1970s, particularly the changes ushered in by the feminist movement. He explained, "Women had an opportunity and I'm convinced that we, as a generation, are the ones who pay the price for this." Nuccio distinguished between the men of his generation who refused to accept the changes in their wives, and the men, like himself, who decided that it was the way things had to be. For Nuccio, however, it was not easy to translate thought into action: "It cost this generation because it's tiring and difficult, it's more tiring than moving furniture, it's psychologically tiring." When his wife Olivia began working at the city tax office, Nuccio was not prepared for the way her personality changed. With a transformed sense of self-esteem, new interests, and new friendships,

Olivia created a new life for herself that no longer revolved around Nuccio and the family.

After hearing from Nuccio that his jealousy would at times turn violent, I asked why he thought men hit their wives. He had a very clear and direct answer:

I believe it is out of insecurity. If you're not able to find success at work, respect your work, or appreciate that your companion is successful at what she does, and cares a bit more about how she looks, and that she does it not for a lover or someone else but for herself, if you're not able to understand this and integrate it with what you do, and you just say, "Oh well, I'm two rungs below, but oh well," then that's that.

Nuccio referred to his own experience and observations of other friends and acquaintances when he explained what had happened to the men of his generation. As he spoke about his own personal failure to find an occupation that he felt proud of or committed to, his regret about not studying at the university level, and his lack of self-fulfillment in his job as a courthouse clerk, he showed a sophisticated command of language. As an intellectually curious and self-reflective individual, Nuccio realized that he had made choices in life that did not allow him to achieve his full potential. When, fifteen years after getting married, his wife entered a *concorso* (competition) for a coveted state job with the local tax office and ended up winning, he found the changes difficult to take, especially in light of his own personal failures. Winning a *concorso* is a great achievement.[1] Entrants must compete against hundreds, if not thousands of other people for a specified number of openings (which these days is quite small) by completing oral and/or written exams. Those who win the competition not only are assured a position with the state but often enjoy job security for many years to come. Nuccio explained:

At first I was at the top of the hierarchy, then slowly [he put out his hands at two different levels and moved one up as the other went down] she arrived here. And if she gets 200 phone calls a day there's nothing I can do. And if before she didn't get any phone calls, not even from relatives, now there are male friends, female friends. Now she is interested in other things. In my opinion men are unprepared for this type of change. I am certain that men are unprepared. First of all, men have little desire to think, because thinking costs too much. . . . If for us in our fifties, up until a short time ago we were like this [gestures with one hand high up and the other low], now we're like this [again shows one hand going down and the other going up]. Now they are above us and we need to accept it . . . in my opinion men were always higher, the woman always had her role and stayed there and didn't say a word, then at a certain point there was an explosion [his hand representing women shoots up in the air].

Nuccio's reflection on his own jealousy and insecurity highlighted the difficulty for the men of his generation who understood that the transformations in their wives were necessary and important, but at the same time were unable to reconcile this conceptual understanding with the turbulence and confusion the changes brought to their everyday lives. Nuccio voiced respect and admiration for his wife but admitted the jealousy and inadequacy he had felt, and to some extent continued to feel, as a result of her transformation. Nuccio connected the violence—both physical and psychological—he directed at Olivia to his own feelings of inadequacy and insecurity.

Nuccio's personal reflections and explanations for intimate-partner violence resonate with what Patrizia Romito recorded during an interview with a thirty-year-old policeman in Trieste in the late 1990s. When asked why male violence against women takes place, the policeman responded:

Many men become violent for this reason, because they will never accept being forced to do something by women, in the raising of children, in the maintenance of the household, and in domestic work. Because then the fights happen for stupid things, the man comes home and doesn't find dinner ready. I've seen men hit women for this reason, to me it's crazy. But maybe finding dinner ready is nothing other than a test that the woman is who the man believes she is. Because the man always needs daily confirmation. Each day that the woman feeds him, he's the man. The day when he doesn't find dinner ready, maybe because he's insecure, I don't know. . . . Many times in our interventions or when I speak with my girlfriend I try to understand why they do it. I'm a man but I don't understand the behavior of many men. If you marry a woman or have a relationship with a woman, one would think you cared for that person, so why humiliate her every day? . . . Parity is not in their mentality, if you ask me, men still don't consider women individuals and equals in all senses. (Romito 2000:106)

The policeman explained that about 80 percent of his work involved intervening in situations of family violence, and that while he was at work he was continuously confronted with "a model of masculinity in which 'he who burps louder, he who hits more women' is more a man; an environment in which his private behavior, specifically the fact that he participates and shares the household work with his girlfriend, was a source of derision" (Romito 2000:106). For Romito, this man's analysis of male violence provided hope and optimism that some men are indeed changing.

Contradictions of the State

Just as local actors negotiate the categories of tradition and modernity in daily social life, at times presenting contradictory understandings of gender and gender proficiency, so is the state engaged in a similar process of negotiation, at times sending mixed messages about the intersection of gender, family, and law.[2]

Throughout the twentieth century, debates over whether the individual, family, or society should be primary in matters of policy and law had a profound impact on many aspects of Italian social life. As David Horn (1994) illustrates in his detailed analysis of fascist and nationalist attempts to control and manage sexual reproduction in Italy during the interwar years (1920s and 1930s), the position of the individual and the family in Italian jurisprudence has affected many aspects of Italian society, including the crafting of social welfare policy, the development of the legal system, and the shaping of individual subjectivities. Fascist policies called for the bodies of women and men to be subordinate to the needs of society as articulated by the state, and codified this view in many of the laws written during the Fascist period.[3] Catholics, however, considered the family to be "a natural institution and therefore substantially beyond the jurisdiction of the state" (Horn 1994:67). Victoria de Grazia points out that many in Italy "regarded the family as the 'mother cell' (*cellula madre*) of society" and felt that "the family, as opposed to the state, best guaranteed the continuity of race and religion through successive generations" (de Grazia 1992:79). Interwar discourses of science and law were at odds with this Catholic understanding of family as a "natural" institution and instead portrayed "the family not only as a legitimate object of surveillance and correction but also as an instrument for the defense of the Italian stock" (Horn 1994:67).

According to Catholic doctrine, which exerted considerable influence before, during, and after Italy's interwar years, it is within the family that "an individual not only is born, but grows and develops and receives the upbringing upon which his future as a man and as a citizen depends" (Antolisei 1992:395). From a Catholic perspective, the state should thus serve to protect and defend the interests of the nuclear family. As Article 29 of the Constitution makes clear, family is understood by the Italian state to be above all "a fact of nature, an expression of social reality that can be neither eliminated nor coerced," that intermediates between the state and the individual (Bonilini 1998:2). As Jeff Pratt points out, the Catholic Church has "consistently stressed the inalienable rights of the family as a 'true society' . . . which no State should restrict" (1996:134).

Until the legal reforms of the 1970s, marriage, gender roles, and sexual relations were legally and socially tied to the rights of the family. Italian law actively supported a man's right to dominate his wife. Divorce was not legal, out of deference to the importance of family unity, and there were laws that endorsed a husband's right to commit adultery and criminalized a wife's adultery, laws that classified sexual violence as a crime against morality while assault and murder were crimes against the person, and laws that explicitly stated a man's position as head of the household. As Sylvia Yanagisako (2002) points out in her work on family silk firms in Como, Italian law supported the rights of men even after death by severely limiting the rights of widows to inherit the wealth and property of their husbands. By safeguarding the rights of the family and the rights of men, the Italian state thus perpetuated the subordination of women and reinforced the power of men to dominate their wives, daughters, and heterosexual partners.

For example, until 1968 the act of adultery called for differential treatment of husbands and wives. Whereas a wife's adultery was considered a crime and represented immediate cause for separation, a husband's adultery was only punishable if he kept a concubine in the marital household or notoriously in another place (Bonilini 1998:20).[1] In addition to the law on adultery, there were other areas of the 1942 Civil Code that clearly asserted the rights and privileges of men, primarily through the institution of marriage.[5] Article 144, titled "Marital Authority," stated, "The husband is the head of the family. The wife follows his civil status, takes his surname (149) and is obliged to accompany him wherever he chooses to establish his residence" (Beltramo et al. 1969:43). Article 145 further established the rights and duties of the husband: "The husband has the duty to protect the wife, keep her with him and furnish her with whatever is required for the necessities of life, in proportion to his means. The wife shall contribute to the maintenance of the husband if he does not have sufficient means" (Beltramo et al. 1969:43).

In 1975, many of these most egregious examples of gender inequality in the legal code were overturned. The marital authority of the husband was repealed and the rights and responsibilities of both spouses were declared to be equal. A revised article, titled "Mutual Rights and Duties of Spouses," asserted,

Through marriage the husband and the wife acquire the same rights and assume the same duties. A mutual obligation to loyalty, moral and material support, cooperation in the interest of the family and cohabitation (146) derives from the marriage. Both spouses are bound, each in relation to his own assets and his own ability for professional or household work, to contribute to the needs of the family. (Beltramo et al. 1996:43)

Even more radical were the changes to the article titled "Marital Authority." The title was changed to "Pattern of Family Life and Residence of the Family," and the content of the article declared that both spouses must "agree between them the pattern of family life and fix the residence of the family according to the requirements of both and to those prevailing for the family. Each of the spouses has the authority to implement the agreed pattern" (Beltramo et al. 1996:43).

Despite such monumental changes to the civil code, intended to create a more egalitarian concept of marriage, there are still a number of examples that highlight the institutionalization of male privilege. For example, during the 1990s women were still prohibited from contracting marriage until 300 days had passed from the "dissolution (149), annulment (117ff.), or cessation of the civil effects (7) of her previous marriage" (Beltramo et al. 1996:27–28). There was no such law for men, and it is interesting to note that the court was able to authorize a marriage before the 300 days were up "when a state of pregnancy is unequivocally excluded" or if it could be demonstrated that "the husband has not lived with the wife during the three hundred days preceding the dissolution, annulment or cessation of civil effects of the marriage" (Beltramo et al. 1996:28).

Another example of the lack of legislative parity in the Italian legal system is visible in the laws governing parental responsibility. Prior to the 1975 revisions, all discussions of parental duties were located in the section of the civil code titled "Paternal Authority." This section (Book IX) of the civil code continually referred to the father, his decision-making power, and his supreme control over the upbringing of children. Although the entire section underwent significant revision in 1975, including a name change from *paternal* to *parental* authority, in the 1990s there was still reference to the father having ultimate authority within the household. Article 316 of the revised civil code stated that authority over a child is to be "exercised by both parents by mutual agreement," but in cases where there is "an incumbent danger of serious prejudice to the child, the father can adopt measures urgent and undeferrable" (Beltramo et al. 1996:87).

Even after extensive reform of family law, the rights of men were still privileged in Italian law. This disparity in rights—and the difficulties often faced by women who resist violence through legal avenues—may also be seen in everyday legal practice. The famous case of *la ragazza in jeans* (the girl in jeans) is one such example.

The Girl in Jeans

In February of 1999, the third penal section of the Supreme Court of Italy overturned the conviction of a forty-five-year-old male driving instructor accused of raping one of his young female students. According to the court decision, the woman could not have been raped because she was wearing jeans at the time of the alleged attack and it is common knowledge that jeans cannot be taken off "not even partially, without the collaboration of the person wearing them" (Castellaneta 1999).

The incident occurred in July of 1992. The first trial ended four years later, in February of 1996, with an acquittal of all charges of sexual violence for lack of evidence, and a sentence—subsequently suspended—of three months in prison for "obscene acts in a public place." The verdict was appealed, and on March 19, 1998, the Court of Appeals handed down a conviction on the charge of sexual violence and sentenced the driving instructor to twenty-six months in jail. The case was subsequently appealed to the Supreme Court, which one year later overturned the Appeals Court ruling with a judgment that declared the driving instructor innocent of all charges of sexual violence (Castellaneta 1999). The ruling sparked outrage in many sectors of Italian society and quickly became known as the case of *la ragazza in jeans*.

Shortly after the ruling, the Italian daily *La Repubblica* published an article with the headline "She Wore Jeans, It Wasn't Rape" and the sidebar "Shock Verdict." The judges of the Supreme Court explained in their ruling that jeans are often very difficult to take off and are impossible to take off if a victim resists her assailant "with all her might." The Court also asserted that "It is illogical to believe that a young woman could supinely endure a rape" just because she was afraid of what could come next. According to the court, the fact that the young woman continued with the driving lesson after being raped and waited until dinner to tell her parents only further proved that the sexual encounter must have been consensual (Castellaneta 1999; Marino 1999).

The Supreme Court's decision in the case of the "girl in jeans" came three years after Parliament passed a new law on sexual violence that revised the law that had been in place since the Fascist penal code, known colloquially as *il Codice Rocco*, was instituted in 1930. Under Italian law, crimes are divided into several broad categories

such as "crimes against the person," "crimes against public morality," "crimes against property," "crimes against the state," and others
(Addis 1989:2). Under the Fascist penal code, sexual violence was classified as a "crime against public morality" and not a "crime against
the person" like assault, murder, and other crimes that inflict bodily
harm. The symbolic implication of this classification is that the crime
of sexual violence—a gendered crime that is almost always committed against women—is a crime against a woman's husband, father, or
brother (as representatives of morality) but is not a violation of the
woman herself (Bassi et al. 1997). There are also important practical
implications of this classification schema. Whereas "crimes against
the person" require mandatory prosecution and proceed regardless
of whether a victim files a report or presses charges, "crimes against
public morality" such as incest and pornography can only be pros-
ecuted if the victim files a police report (Addis 1989:2).

Women's groups first began discussing the need to change the law
on sexual violence in the late 1970s, and in 1977 the Italian Communist Party introduced the first bill aimed at reforming Article 609 of
the Fascist penal code. Nearly two decades of modifications, debates,
and delays ensued. There were disagreements among women's groups
about various aspects of the reform: some wanted the crime of sexual
violence to be prosecutable with or without the consent of the victim,
while others argued for the right of the woman to decide; some favored
a definition of sexual violence that did not distinguish between penetra-
tion and molestation, while others argued for a delineation between
the two. Despite these differences of opinion that tended to divide the
women's movement into separate camps, all supporters of reform were
united in their desire to overturn the existing law and replace it with
one that declared sexual violence to be a crime against the person, with
stringent penalties for those found guilty (Bassi et. al 1997).

In 1996, nineteen years after the first reform bill was introduced, a
new law on sexual violence was finally approved by the Italian Parliament. Three years later, however, the Supreme Court of Italy ruled
that a woman wearing jeans could not possibly be raped if she resisted
"with all her might." As the case of the "girl in jeans" illustrates, despite
the significant changes to the Italian civil and penal codes that have
been instituted over the past thirty years, judicial interpretation is slow
to change, and many judges continue to rule in accordance with the old
legal norms of gender and family.

The legal system itself is based on the principle of law but governed by judicial interpretation. Although new legislation can provide more opportunities for safeguarding the rights of women, it can do little to chip away at the rigid institutional structure of male privilege. When judges rule that it is impossible for a woman to be raped if she is wearing jeans and when women continue to silently endure daily regimes of violence, it is clear that despite many legislative gains, the rights of the individual are still gendered and at the mercy of judicial discretion.

This gendering of law and social life stands in tension with the gains of the Italian feminist movement and late-twentieth-century claims of modernity. The intersection of these conflicting norms can contribute to the multilayered shame that battered women often experience and the difficulties faced by the lawyers who argue cases on their behalf.

A Legal Office in Parma

When I entered Cecilia's law office in downtown Parma for the very first time, I was struck by the beautifully frescoed ceilings, the antique wood desks, and the elegant yet comfortable atmosphere. Cecilia is the daughter of one of Parma's most prominent female lawyers, who is well known throughout the city for the high separation and divorce settlements she is able to obtain.[6] Along with her mother and two other lawyers, Cecilia volunteers her legal services at Women United. Although the consultations are free, in order for a case to be initiated the women must subsequently meet with the lawyers in their offices and, except in extreme circumstances, must pay the usual fee. Most of the legal consultations are with women who are thinking about separating and want to understand the procedures that are involved. From time to time, volunteer lawyers will assist women who intend to press charges against violent husbands or boyfriends, but most of the time the lawyers meet with women to explain the intricacies of legal separation, child custody, and alimony.

After observing a number of Cecilia's legal consultations, I decided to ask for a meeting of my own to discuss some of the questions I had about Italian law. Cecilia was extremely warm and receptive when I went to meet with her at her office. After an informative conversation about the intricacies of the Italian legal system, she asked if I would be interested in spending time in the law office in order to learn about the types of cases they work with on a daily basis. I quickly responded that I would be very interested in such an opportunity, and we made arrangements for me to spend Thursday mornings in her office reading and taking notes on various cases relating to partner and spousal violence.

When I asked Cecilia how many criminal cases of intimate-partner violence her mother's legal office had handled, I was shocked to find that she could count them on one hand. Cecilia explained that the only law that pertains specifically to intimate-partner violence is Article 572 of the penal code, an article titled "Mistreatments in the Family." The law does not refer specifically to intimate-partner violence, as it is a general law that is also used in cases of child abuse and child neglect. The official penalty for mistreatment in the family is one to five years in jail, but there are many aspects of the Italian judicial system that serve to minimize the amount of time a convicted husband might actually serve. According to Italian law, a jail sentence is automatically reduced by a third if the defendant entered a plea bargain or agreed to a trial without witnesses (*rito abbreviato*). The sentence is reduced by another third if there are extenuating circumstances (such as being intoxicated at the time of the act), and the sentence is often further reduced or even suspended if it is a first-time offense. Cecilia added that it is also very difficult to prove the existence of violence in the family. When I asked whether hospital records are used as proof, Cecilia explained that when women go to the emergency room they often say they hurt themselves by falling down the stairs or tripping. According to Cecilia, even if a woman is bold enough to declare it was her partner or husband, once she gets to court people will "still talk about provocation." As for the police, according to Cecilia, when a woman goes to the police station to report her husband she is likely to be told, "Signora, what are you doing? You don't file a report on your own husband." Cecilia shook her head and said, "We're very behind. Italy is dominated by the church. If a woman brings up [in public] the violence she experiences then the family becomes unstable. Our state is based on the family. The family is the first place to deal with problems."

In cases of separation, the fact that one of the spouses was violent may or may not be brought up as a factor. Cecilia pointed out that a judge often will not interpret the violence as mistreatment in the family and will instead see it as "damages." In fact, in order for violence against a spouse or partner to be considered mistreatment in the family, there must be proof that the violence was a repetitive and habitual action. Violence is usually only mentioned in a separation proceeding if the separation is "judicial" (where a judge hands down a sentence) as opposed to "con-sensual" (where both parties agree on a settlement and present it to a judge), and if one or both of the parties is seeking an *addebito* (fault or blame) to be assigned to the other partner. In practical terms, there is no reason to ask for an *addebito* unless the partner asking for the *addebito* thinks he or she will otherwise end up paying alimony to the other spouse. If a judge assigns blame to the spouse who theoretically would receive alimony, then the judge may also reduce the amount of alimony assigned. The reverse is not true. That is, if the spouse who is assigned blame is also the spouse who must pay alimony, the amount of the alimony cannot be increased just because the dissolution of the marriage was his or her fault. This gives women, who usually earn less than their husbands, little incentive, other than the desire for justice, to ask for an *addebito*.

Representations of Gender: Neglect of Wifely Duties

Lidia is an example of a woman who was married to a violent man and pursued a divorce as well as an *addebito* with the help of Cecilia's legal counsel. Cecilia first met Lidia when she came to Women United seeking legal and emotional support. Within a short time Cecilia became Lidia's lawyer in her separation proceedings.[7] Together, Cecilia and Lidia engaged the Italian legal code as well as state-imposed understandings of gender proficiency.

In October of 1999, the lawyer representing Lidia's husband filed the first brief requesting a judicial separation for his client.[8] The brief asserted five facts: the husband was born in 1972 in a town in Calabria; in 1991 the couple was married; in 1991 and 1995 their children were born; living together had become impossible because of the incompatibility of their characters and because of the wife's behavior, including her failure to care properly for the house and the children; and in July of 1999 the wife abandoned the marital household and took the children with her without letting her husband know where they were going.[9] In addition to requesting a judicial separation, the husband's brief asked that an *addebito* be assigned to the wife, that the husband be awarded custody of the children, and that the wife pay £1,000,000 (US$500) in monthly child support.

One month after Lidia's husband filed a brief, Cecilia filed a response on behalf of Lidia. This brief was longer, and provided numerous challenges to the husband's account of the facts. It asserted that the problems in the relationship crystallized when, after five years of living in a small town in the southern region of Calabria, the couple decided to move to Parma:

The majority of their life as a married couple was spent in Calabria, where both spouses have most of their family relations—parents, siblings, etc. Married life was not easy: The wife, who had always been a housewife and always took care of the children in a loving manner, followed her husband in search of work in northern Italy. . . . Perhaps because of the difficult adjustment, perhaps because of the "different customs" with respect to those of the south, the husband began to behave aggressively and violently at home, often hitting his wife in intimate settings as well as in front of the children.

The brief outlined the numerous police reports filed by the wife, as well as official reports filed by the police on the occasions when they had had to intervene to protect Lidia from her husband's violent attacks. These attacks included beatings, insults, and threats with a knife and a gun. At the end of July, after three years of living with violence, Lidia decided to leave her husband and move with her children back to Calabria. The brief noted, "It is impossible to understand how the father can ask for custody of the children when his son, who witnessed numerous instances of violence, no longer wants to see his father." The brief requested a separation with *addebito* assigned to the husband, custody awarded to the wife, and £2,500,000 (US$1,250) in monthly child support.

In December of 1999, at the initial separation hearing, the judge awarded Lidia custody of the children and ordered her husband to pay £1,500,000 (US$750) in child support as an interim measure, until the case could be decided. Following this hearing, the husband's lawyer filed another brief that repeated the items mentioned in the initial brief and described the numerous reasons why it was the wife who did not fulfill the four obligations of marriage: loyalty, collaboration, cohabitation, and contribution.

According to the brief, Lidia had begun going out almost every evening, taking the children with her, and returning after midnight without telling her husband whom she was seeing and where she was going. In addition, Lidia did not demonstrate "a physical and spiritual dedication to her husband, whom she considered not a spouse but a provider of income." The brief went on to state that in addition to not collaborating in the maintenance of family unity, Lidia did not satisfy her obligation to contribute to the family, "not because she has never worked outside the house but because at least since 1998 she has neglected her housework by not adequately caring for the children or the marital household." Finally, the brief accused Lidia of provoking her husband's behavior: "One cannot keep quiet the fact that it was the wife's behavior that caused her husband to react in ways that ignited the episodes that signaled the dissolution of the marriage."

The last brief filed in the case was Cecilia's fiery reply, which referred once again to the numerous police reports and asserted that violent behavior "is not in any way justifiable." In the brief, Cecilia pointed to the fact that the husband himself did not deny the violent episodes, but instead tried to justify them as reactions to his wife's behavior. The brief went on to refute each of the husband's accusations, and concluded that Lidia never neglected her duties as a mother and a wife, and had in fact been forced by her husband's behavior to leave the house and move back to Calabria to live with her parents.

In April of 2000, a year and a half after the first brief had been filed in Lidia's separation case, her husband finally agreed to a consensual separation that would give Lidia custody of the children and £900,000 (US $450) per month in child support.[10] The briefs filed on either side of this case illustrate how lawyers construct their cases to appeal to the models of gender instituted by the state. Although the language of the post-1975 Article 143, "Mutual Rights and Duties of Spouses," is gender-neutral, the content is often used by lawyers representing husbands in separation proceedings to accuse wives of neglecting their household and marital responsibilities. Because both spouses are "bound, each in relation to his own assets and his own ability for professional or household work, to contribute to the needs of the family," the neglect of household duties becomes a frequent accusation by husbands. Lawyers can thus mobilize the discourse of tradition as well as that of modernity to help construct understandings of gender that best suit a particular client's needs.

Although women are increasingly working outside the home in Parma and throughout Italy, if one partner stays home or works part-time it is almost always the woman. Although in some ways the duties of marriage outlined by Article 143 might seem to be emancipatory, the interpretations of these duties often result in legal arguments that only reestablish men's power as husbands. When a woman does not work outside the home she is still bound by law to "contribute to the needs of the family," a requirement that is amorphous and difficult to define. Whereas a spouse working outside the home need only bring home a paycheck to contribute to the needs of the family, a spouse working inside the home may always be criticized for his or her failure to contribute adequately to the household. When a wife works at home to care for the household and the children, she is legally and morally bound to do her work in a manner that is beyond reproach. If she does not, her identity as a wife, as a woman, and as a *casalinga* (housewife) may be in jeopardy. Many of the women I met with at Women United explained that they continued to cook, clean, iron, and care for the house, even though their husbands routinely beat them, because they never wanted to be accused (by family, friends, or the legal system) of neglecting their household duties.

In the case of Lidia's separation, the briefs filed on behalf of the husband attempted to portray Lidia as a woman who failed in her wifely duties, and through this failure provoked her husband's violence. The briefs filed on behalf of Lidia, on the other hand, pointed to the husband's violence, and stated that at various times during the marriage he failed to provide for the sustenance of his wife and children. There is a tacit acknowledgment within the two sets of briefs of particular marital roles. The argument underlying both sets of briefs is that the other spouse failed to comply with the rules of conduct outlined by society and the legal system. Despite the revisions passed in 1975 that sought to make the civil code more gender-neutral and egalitarian, there are still implicit codes of conduct for both husbands and wives that continue to shape local models of gender and family.

Crimes of Maltreatment

Violence against family members can be subject to a number of different laws under the Italian Penal Code. The two most serious crimes are *maltrattamenti in famiglia o verso i fanciulli* (mistreatments in the family or of the children) and *abuso dei mezzi di correzione e di disciplina* (abuse of means of punishment and discipline), both of which are classified as "crimes against family assistance."[11] There are other, more general crimes, into which family violence can also fall. These include: *percosse* (blows), *lesioni* (damages), *ingiurie* (injuries), *violenza privata* (private violence), and *violenza sessuale* (sexual violence).

According to Article 571 of the penal code, the crime of "abuse of means of punishment and discipline" occurs when "anyone abuses the means of punishment or discipline and damages a person under his authority." In many respects, this crime is an anachronism of the Fascist code, as it implicitly legitimizes physical violence as a method of punishment for educational or training purposes (Terragni 1997b:186). Over time the law has come to refer primarily to parent-child relations, but in its original formulation it applied to a wider range of hierarchical relations, including the relationship between husband and wife. Only with the 1975 reform of family law did the husband lose his position as head of the family with legal power over both his wife and children.

Mistreatment in the family, on the other hand, is a crime that can be imputed to anyone who mistreats a family member in a systematic and repetitive fashion. According to Article 572 of the penal code, mistreatment in the family occurs when someone "mistreats a member of the family, or a minor under the age of 14, or an individual under one's authority." It is important to note that the article very clearly specifies that mistreatment is not represented by a single offending action, but by a series of actions. Individual actions may still be considered crimes, but they are not prosecutable as mistreatment in the family. Although mistreatment in the family carries a penalty of one to five—and in extreme cases up to twenty—years in jail the penalties are rarely applied because more often than not the incident or incidents in question do not qualify as mistreatment in the family. Instead, they qualify as crimes such as *percosse, lesioni, ingiurie,* and/or *minacce* (threats), all of which carry more lenient penalties and often go unreported.

Intrigued by the definition of mistreatment in the family, I researched Article 572 in the University of Parma's legal library and found a number of judicial interpretations by Italy's Supreme Court. In a 1987 sentence, the court ruled that "the crime of mistreatment is a habitual crime because it is characterized by the existence of a series of events that when isolated might not be considered crimes." The court went on to explain that only when acts of mistreatment are committed for a prolonged period of time and perpetuated with some form of intent can they be classified as *maltrattamenti in famiglia o verso fanciulli*. Given these strict guidelines, it is no surprise that the crime "is consummated with the last in the list of events."[12]

In another sentence, handed down by the Supreme Court in 1996, the court ruled that it is the judge who has the responsibility of determining whether or not in the relationship in question there truly exists a "system of life that is customarily painful and humiliating, knowingly instituted by the accused."[13]

Although it is up to judges to rule as they see fit, the interpretations of the Supreme Court certainly serve as a guide for future rulings. The requirement of recurrence, and the fact that the mistreatment must be a way of life for both aggressor and victim, make the crime of mistreatment in the family extremely difficult to prove. Not only does a prosecutor need evidence of blows, injuries, damages, and/or threats (crimes that often occur without witnesses, in the seclusion of the home), but a prosecutor also needs to prove that these acts were habitual and committed with intent. Whether violence must take place once a month or every day to qualify as a "system of life" is left entirely to judicial discretion. Tina Lagostena Bassi found the following wording in a ruling (Foggia, Corte D'Assise, May 30, 1986) that absolved a husband's violence: "As is known, Article 572 of the Penal Code punishes the person who maltreats a member of his or her family for purposes other than those of correction and discipline. . . . It is evident, therefore, that mere quarrels and acts of loutishness do not in themselves constitute maltreatment. The male's preeminent role in the family and his authority over its other members is a normal, accepted fact and cannot in itself constitute maltreatment" (1993:202). Despite the many legal changes of the late twentieth century, such interpretations of the law only reinforce the legacy of earlier legal codes that outlined the rights and duties of husbands and wives and emphasized the power and authority of men through the presumption of paternal authority.

Making Sense of Change

As inequalities of the sex/gender system begin to shift, and large-scale socioeconomic transformations begin to take place, gender relations and models of what it is to be a man or a woman also begin to change. Many of the large-scale transformations taking place in Italy are unfolding in similar ways around the world. When Mathew Gutmann (1996) argues that "the fact that the ground is shifting under the feet of many men in Mexico is due . . . to large-scale socioeconomic transformations generally involving women at first, or at least initially attracting their attention," he could just as easily be talking about Parma. The changes he cites—"greater numbers of women working outside the home for money; parity of girls and boys through junior high school; a sharp fall in the number of children women have been having in the past 20 years; [and] the feminist movement" (Gutmann 1996:24)—are the very same ones taking place in northern Italy.

Toward the end of my fieldwork, I spoke with a reporter for the *Gazzetta di Parma*—the conservative-leaning local daily that many local intellectuals disdain for its sensationalism and tendency toward gossip—about an article she had written about spousal and partner violence. When I asked her to tell me what she thought about intimate-partner violence, she first told me that it was difficult to "get inside someone's head" in order to understand why he or she might do a particular thing. She suggested that many men might be violent because they have problems and perhaps had a difficult childhood: "I don't think it could ever just happen, there has to be some history of difficulty. Probably they already had the character of being a bit this way and then something happened to push them to do this." The reporter went on to explain that in her view men must take a big step forward:

They always have the feeling of being superior, of being *il padrone*. Just look at the big men, the big managers. What kind of women do they have? Women with chicken brains, women who are statues, beautiful, but don't ever question or challenge, they never enter the man's role as man, as manager. I'm me and you're you. All the big managers are like this. They could have women with whom they could have interesting dialogue, but this would challenge their position—their ego has to remain unchallenged. I have friends like this. They have two degrees, big important jobs, are always right, and their women have to stay in the house, raise the children, and never contradict them.

The connection between a man controlling his wife—either physically or symbolically—and the performance of his role as *padrone* is similar to the link Gutmann (1996) found that the people of Colonia Santo Domingo, Mexico, sometimes made between male violence and being macho. As in Santo Domingo, daily social life in Parma has been affected by recent large-scale political and socioeconomic shifts. In Italy these shifts were shaped by the activism of the 1960s, the Italian feminist movement, changes to family law, increased educational and work opportunities for women, the economic necessity of a dual-income family, the delaying of marriage, the fall in the birthrate, and the dissolution of once well-defined political identities. For many, the result has been ambivalence and confusion about gender roles and what it means to be a mother, father, wife, husband, woman, or man. This is not to say, however, that gender proficiencies have not always been in flux. This is precisely the trap of the tradition/modernity dichotomy. What is classified as "modern" or "new" is often set in contrast to a vision of fixity and immutability that extends to encompass nearly all of what existed in the "traditional past."

Handler and Linnekin (1984), Coontz (1992), Argyrou (1996), Collier (1997), Sutton (1998), and others alert us to the ongoing construction of tradition. At the same time, however, there is a continual re-construction of modernity. For proponents of the "old-fashioned" style of gender relations, monolithic interpretations of the past are a form of what Herzfeld has termed structural nostalgia, or a longing, repeated from generation to generation, for a pristine time when "the balanced perfection of social relations has not yet suffered the decay that affects everything human" (Herzfeld 1997:109). For proponents of "modern" forms of gender relations, such interpretations of the past are a form of what I term structural disdain—a contempt for particular aspects of the past that is perpetuated to champion the merits of modernity.

It is for this reason that we must question local explanations of violence—both that it is a remnant of "traditional" gender relations and that it is a product of the transition to "modernity." It might be easy to assume that intimate-partner violence was more pronounced in the past or is more pronounced among couples that embrace a more "traditional" understanding of gender, but such displacement of violence essentializes violence itself as something bound to the category of what we construct or construe as "tradition." The question of why violence against intimates occurs is one that must be explored through the particularities of daily life. It cannot be answered with overarching statements that mask the complexity of what is at stake. While some scholars suggest that violence intensifies as women begin to be successful outside the home (clearly the theory endorsed by Nuccio and other men I spoke with), others suggest that violence is most pronounced in areas of the world where women have limited access to economic and social power.[14]

Collier (1997), Counihan (2004), and Del Negro (2004) write against this trend by introducing us to alternate understandings of modernity and tradition that are located in the cultural specificities of daily life. The diversity of responses to the large-scale transformations taking place in Italian society not only alerts us to the multiple and contested expressions of gender, but also confirms the anthropological conviction that what it means to "be a man" and "be a woman" in different societies can never be universally defined. Gender is a fluid concept that shifts according to time and context, and is constantly in a state of transformation. Though we speak of the past versus the present, tradition versus modernity, and old versus new, the distinctions themselves represent an "interpretive process that embodies both continuity and discontinuity" (Handler and Linnekin 1984:273). It is this interpretive process that we must address if we are to understand how individuals negotiate social change and incorporate it into their everyday lives.

Adjustments and Realizations:
The First Years of Marriage

In presenting the generational and individual diversity of understandings of gender and gender relations, I intend to illustrate the range of subjectivities, or representations, of "particular forms of thinking, feeling, and desiring" that, as Begoña Aretxaga (1997) argues, are always subject to transformation through the actions and discourses of everyday life. During my year in Parma, I found myself continually meeting young singles—through contacts at Women United and Family Aid and through friends at the University of Parma—but I rarely met young married couples. Whether this was a function of my particular networks or of the declining marriage rates is impossible to say, but during the later part of my fieldwork I made a concerted effort to find young married men and women to speak with and get to know.

One evening at a couples' meeting held monthly by don Bernardo of the Rocco di Marco parish, I met three young couples, all of whom had been married less than six months and had started attending the couples' group as a way of meeting more people in the church community. I spoke to them about my research and mentioned my interest in talking to them about their lives and thoughts on marriage. They were enthusiastic about my project and suggested that we choose a night when all three couples were free. I was surprised at their suggestion of a group meeting, and although I was unsure how effective a group interview could be, I was also intrigued. We traded phone numbers and decided to meet up a few weeks later.

When I arrived at Elena and Carlo's home, I still had not decided how I would structure the evening, but I had a feeling that it would work better to separate the women from the men and conduct two sessions. Elena and Carlo lived in a modest apartment owned by Carlo's parents. They were living rent-free, right above Carlo's parents, until their new apartment was ready. Elena and Carlo met in the parish when they were both fifteen. Every Sunday during mass, Elena sang and Carlo played the guitar. They started dating when they were sixteen years old and remained *fidanzati* (boyfriend and girlfriend) for twelve years.[15] Although Carlo started working right after high school, Elena went on to study at the University of Bologna. They decided to get married when they had both found good jobs and had managed to save enough money to buy an apartment.

When the other two couples arrived, I explained that I wanted to do two interviews, one with the women and the other with the men. I had noticed at the couples' group that the men tended to talk with the men and the women with the women. The men were only too happy to go downstairs and chat. As they walked out of the room, the women teased them about all the secrets they were going to tell in their absence.

All three couples had been *fidanzati* for many years and had lived with their respective parents until their wedding day. Elena and Bena, both twenty-nine, described the first few months as idyllic. They were thrilled to have their own home and create their own rhythm and lifestyle. For Anita, who was a bit younger, it was more difficult, as she had left all her family and friends and moved sixty miles away to Parma, where her husband had found a good job working for Parmalat, the multinational dairy corporation.

Elena explained that when she was engaged people would say to her, "When you get married you'll see the difference, you'll have to cook, clean, do all these things," but she did not see it this way. In fact, she felt freer as a married woman than she had as a single person living at home. If she and Carlo wanted to stay out late shopping and grab a bite to eat, there was no one they needed to call, no one they had to worry about offending. She and Carlo had tried to divide the household responsibilities evenly. Although they did not have a precise division of duties, they did make an effort to share various tasks. In the morning they would decide together what to cook for dinner. Then whoever got home first started preparing dinner. Usually Elena ended up doing the cooking because Carlo had less experience, but he would set and clear the table, and they did much of the cleaning together. "For the moment, ironing is my responsibility because Carlo doesn't like doing it," Elena said, "but for the other things, whoever arrives first does it."

Smiling sheepishly, Bena explained that in her marriage most of the household duties fell to her. "He'll lend me a hand when I start complaining, but no, the household duties aren't divided, there's little to say. The only thing I demand is that when we finish eating we do the dishes together. I don't like to see him watching TV while I have to work." Bena said she did not mind doing the cooking, cleaning, and laundry. She had a small house and said it was simply a matter of being organized:

It was worse before, when there were certain fixed hours, when you had to eat lunch, when you had to eat dinner. Now we're much more free in the sense that we go out when we want, eat when we want, if we're tired we'll go out and buy *torta fritta* and eat dinner while watching a movie. . . . I don't find the housework particularly difficult since I always did a bit while living at home. . . . I like cooking. And for the rest, I ironed my own clothes before, so ironing for two people instead of one isn't too different. In the beginning I could have organized myself a bit better because I was always behind with the laundry.

Elena agreed that organization is important, but pointed out that after a few months of marriage, she realized that even if she didn't organize everything, things would still work out. Bena added, "You're more organized in the beginning because you want to *fare una bella figura*, you don't want him to complain!" All three laughed and agreed that at the beginning you were still getting to know one another and trying not to show your faults.

Anita explained that dividing the household duties came naturally to her husband. Both of his parents worked, and he was used to washing dishes and doing other household tasks. For Anita, this was difficult to get used to. She had seen her mother serve her father's every need, even bring him his clothes while he was taking a bath, and Anita had always assumed she would do the same. "I thought I would do everything, *fare bella figura*, most of all because I was in the house and didn't have anything else to do." Now both Anita and her husband work, and they divide all the household tasks. She will vacuum while he dusts, and they take turns washing the dishes. The only task that is solely Anita's responsibility is the ironing. Her husband told her right after they got married, "Ask me to do anything, but please don't ask me to iron."

Anita, Bena, and Elena all agreed that the men of their generation do more household tasks than men of their fathers' generation. Their fathers arrived home at lunch and dinnertime to find everything on the table, ready to eat. After meals they would retire to the living room to read or watch television while their wives did the dishes and cleaned up. It was seen as shameful for men to do certain chores. Even taking out the trash was embarrassing for some men. Every morning their wives laid out their clothing and shoes for the day and prepared breakfast. Elena's father would shout out from the shower, "How are you dressing me today?" According to Elena, her mother's work in the home was hardly an imposition. It came naturally for her mother to attend to all the household work. Her father did not demand things in a mean or spiteful way. It was simply the way things were.

When I spoke with Bena, Elena, and Anita, they were all working with their husbands to negotiate the household space and formulate their own divisions of labor. The women agreed about the need for equal rights, but argued that men and women are different and should thus occupy different roles within society. Bena explained, "There should be more collaboration between men and women with household tasks, but without taking away that which is feminine and that which is masculine, in the good sense of the terms. At the end of the day, we, as women, have a different sensibility than men."

Carole Counihan (2004) describes a similar tension between the naturalization of certain duties as masculine and feminine and the understanding that much of the division of labor stems from the socialization of girls and boys. One of Counihan's informants, Piera, explained that her brother did absolutely nothing in the house, and placed the blame both on the way her brother was raised and on the "natural" tendencies of men and women:

It's different with me. I'm not saying this out of jealousy, but for me it's different, because I'm a girl, I'm a woman. If I see something out of place, I am supposed to put it away. But instead, if Piero finds something out of place, it is not important for him to put it away, because there is always my mother and I to do it. In Italy we think that it's the women's job to do the housework, and so my parents raised me to help at an early age. I would feel badly if I didn't know how to do the housework. It's always good to know how to do it. In fact, I think that it is an instinct we women have—when we see disorder, we straighten it up. It always comes back to the fact that we do it. We don't give it a lot of weight. We don't push very hard against it—we're not there yet. We might think about protesting our burden, but then the idea passes and we do what we have to do. (Counihan 2004:168)

The conflation of essentialized notions of gender with an understanding of the power of socialization emerged in many of my interviews with women and men of varying ages and backgrounds. Some of the younger women, like Carla, emphasized the importance of raising sons and daughters with the same understanding of domestic labor; others, like Bena and Anita, entered marriage with a set of assumptions about what their roles as wives and mothers would be. Although all the young married women I spoke with worked outside the home, some willingly accepted a greater share of domestic labor whereas others struggled to reconcile their desire for parity with the realization of what they could and could not expect from their husbands in the way of household and family chores.

Men in Transition

When I interviewed young married men, such as Elena's husband Carlo, many spoke enthusiastically about marriage and the freedom it had brought them—freedom to follow their own schedules as couples.

Carlo, who met and started dating Elena when he was fifteen, explained that he would have liked to marry earlier, but there were practical issues to consider. Elena needed to finish her studies at the university and find a job, and together they needed to start saving money to buy a home.[16] According to Carlo, they "made a sacrifice" and decided they would not marry until they had enough money to buy their own home. They wanted to start off on the right foot without debts and other difficulties. Bena and Gino made the same decision. Although they started dating when they were in their early twenties, they did not marry until seven years later, when they were on more firm financial footing.

As I explained earlier, the expectation in Parma, as in much of Italy, is that a newly married couple will move into a home that either they purchased themselves or was purchased for them by one or both sets of parents. Not only must the couple have a home, but the home must be outfitted with all the furniture and decorations needed to start off their married lives together. Preparation of the house and all its trimmings is seen as an important prerequisite of marriage. Wealthy parents will often purchase apartments when their children are young and rent them out, with the expectation that once their children are of marrying age, one of them will move into the apartment with a spouse. For people who do not come from wealthy families, the cultural expectations surrounding *la casa* can result in lengthy engagement periods and postponement of marriage.

Rather than take any risks, Carlo and Elena decided to play it safe and live at home with their parents until they had saved enough money to purchase a home. When I asked Carlo how his life changed when he left the home of his parents to start a new life with Elena, he told me that he didn't think he experienced any type of trauma.[17] Smiling, he explained that he used the word "trauma" because he played on a soccer team with many men who were older than him. Almost all of them were married, and when they heard he was planning to get married, they teased him and asked why he would want to do such a thing; that once married he would never be able to go out, his wife would try to prevent him from playing soccer, and his life would never be the same. For Carlo, marrying Elena meant expanding rather than limiting his freedom. Now that they were married, they were able to manage their own lives and their own schedules. Rather than having to eat with their parents at a specified time every day, they could eat when they wanted and go out when they wanted. Usually, whoever returned home first would start dinner, and although Elena usually did the cooking and always did the ironing, they divided many of the other household tasks evenly. When they wanted to eat at home, they would eat at home, and when they wanted to go out, they would go out. As Carlo explained, "We are able to manage our own time, our own things, we feel more free, and perhaps have become more responsible in the process. It gives you more energy, more force. Before we were at home with our families where the father decides, the mother decides, you're there and you endure their rules, you follow their decisions . . . now we're on our own and we have more responsibility. I might say this is the best period of our lives."

In stark contrast to Carlo's description of marriage as a partnership between two people was the conversation I had on a different occasion with Leonardo, a young man who told me he was disturbed by the blurring of gender roles. I met Leonardo, a university student who lived with his parents, one afternoon when I was over at my friend Paola's house. Paola, who was in her mid-fifties and is married with a daughter in high school, had invited me and her friend Mariella to stop by for afternoon tea. What I had thought was going to be a quiet chat with Paola and Mariella turned into a lively conversation about gender, marriage, and family when Leonardo (a family friend of Paola's) came by for an impromptu visit.

Leonardo had clear opinions on the roles of men and women and society and did not hesitate to state them bluntly. He explained that he wanted to find an "old-fashioned" woman, one who was not too intelligent or ambitious and who would depend on him both emotionally and financially. As he put it, "Women who swear or who go on vacations to Greece to escape the taboos of our society, forget them.[18] A woman can have a job, but not one that takes her away from me too much. I want her to be there when I come home at the end of the day."

Paola and Mariella agreed with many of Leonardo's statements and added their own opinions on the importance of clearly demarcated roles for men and women. Paola explained that a woman "needs to be feminine but also needs her own economic independence," and that while a man could be great in the house and could be a great cook, "he can never have the affinity or sensibility of a woman with the house and with the children." She added that it was also important for the woman to "see a man as a man" and that doing housework could cause a man to "lose his masculinity."

Mariella agreed and said that a man "needs to feel he is in command." She went on to explain that in today's society men were in "crisis." They

no longer had their role in the family, and as a result they found themselves lost and confused. Mariella revealed her own feelings of betrayal
and disillusionment when she confessed that she had been an active
feminist in her younger years, but had grown increasingly critical of the
movement's call for the sexual liberation of women:

> When it came time for the men of my generation to choose wives, they chose the
> women who were a bit less sophisticated, a bit more subservient. The women
> who were more forward, like me, weren't chosen. . . . We worked well for
> friendship and dialogue, for intellectual stimulation, but when it came time for
> marriage they chose the others. This is how Italian men are.

My conversation with Paola, Mariella, and Leonardo about gender in
Italian society and their discomfort with "new" interpretations of what
it means to be a man and what it means to be a woman echoes much of
what Roger Lancaster (1992) describes in his study of machismo and
masculinity in Nicaragua. As one of his informants explained, there is
a difference between the "new" and "old" ideals of what makes a good
man: "The new idea of a good man—that is, the revolutionary New
Man—is someone who studies to improve himself and his country, who
works hard, who is responsible toward his compañera, his children, and
is generous with those around him," whereas the old idea of a good man
was "someone who could drink, fight, gamble, and have a large number
of sexual conquests" (Lancaster 1992:175). Although there are many differences between Italian and Nicaraguan ideals of masculinity, the distinction Lancaster draws between "old" and "new" understandings of
manhood is very similar to the distinctions I noticed in Italy. In Italy, as
in Nicaragua, there is a disjuncture between theory and practice. In daily
life, ideals can often become blurred. As one of Lancaster's informants
pointed out, "Today, I think, young men are apt to be a bit confused by
the transition. They don't always know quite what's expected of them.
Maybe their father behaves one way, and their older brother behaves
another, so they have two conflicting models" (Lancaster 1992:175).

For Lancaster, machismo is a system, "a field of productive relations" under which "relations between men, women, and children are
structured in certain standard ways" (Lancaster 1992:19–20). When I
asked people in Parma to tell me about the fathers of previous generations, they often spoke of the *padre padrone* (master father), a phrase that
conveys the image of a man who governs with an iron fist, and treats
his household as an estate and his family as his indentured servants.[19]
People also spoke to me about men who spent all their free time in bars

or street corners, socializing with other men. The ability to produce a son was yet another sign of "old-style" virility and manhood.

When I asked about the "new-style" fathers of today, people spoke of a more even distribution of household tasks and of fathers becoming involved in their children's lives. Whereas everything in a child's life, from changing diapers and feeding to doctor's appointments and meetings with teachers, used to be the mother's domain, by the late 1990s many fathers were taking their children to school and getting them dressed in the morning. Although some people expressed structural nostalgia (Herzfeld 1997) for the golden era of tradition and longed to return to what was remembered as a pristine time, others expressed structural disdain and emphasized the way in which society had "progressed" from an earlier time of inequality and exploitation. Ascertaining the relative "truth" of such monolithic recollections of the past would be a fruitless endeavor,[20] but we *can* ask how individual social actors use such interpretations as rhetorical devices to bolster particular claims about how Italian society is changing and about particular strategies for resisting or accelerating that change.

Feminist Politics and the State

In her well-known and controversial work on feminist politics and the state, Catharine MacKinnon (1989) suggests that the effectiveness of male dominance in society ensures that the state, by adopting a policy of "negative freedom" (non-interference) in law, while men are granted "positive freedom" (ability to control or determine) in society, only perpetuates the subordination of women:

> Rape law assumes that consent to sex is as real for women as it is for men. Privacy law assumes that women in private have the same privacy men do. Obscenity law assumes that women have the access to speech men have. Equality law assumes that women are already socially equal to men. . . . These laws are . . . integral to sexual politics because the state, through law, institutionalizes male power over women through institutionalizing the male point of view in law. Its first state act is to see women from the standpoint of male dominance; its next act is to treat them that way. (MacKinnon 1989:169)

According to MacKinnon, the masculinity of the state, perpetuated by a legal system that does not safeguard the rights of marginalized groups, such as women, will only reinforce the subordination of such groups in daily social life. The remedy she suggests is thus a "feminist jurisprudence" that uses law to confront the subordinate status of women. MacKinnon recognizes that critics will suggest that "feminist law is special pleading for a particular group" but responds that "existing law is already special pleading for a particular group" (MacKinnon 1989:249).

The problem with this approach to feminist politics, as Wendy Brown points out, is that such remedies do not question "whether legal 'protection' for a certain injury-forming identity discursively entrenches the injury–identity connection it denounces" (Brown 1995:21). Brown goes on to ask, "Might such protection codify within the law the very powerlessness it aims to redress? Might it discursively collude with the conversion of attribute into identity, of a historical effect of power into a presumed cause of liberation?" (21). In other words, what gains can possibly be made by working within the very structures of power that produce and reproduce subordination and oppression? For Brown, the state is masculinist, but it is also racist and classist and "does not harbor and deploy only one kind of political power" (1995:175). Each type of power must thus be examined in relation with other forms of power, but also in its own particular historical, political, and social context.

MacKinnon's theory of the state, although static and reductive in its definition of gender, does make some sense in the context of Italian law. Within Italy, the powers of the state, as expressed through law, reinscribe both the power of men and the power of the Catholic Church. Through history, these two powers have colluded in law and daily practice to perpetuate the subordination of women in Italian society. The problem faced by feminists and other progressives in Italy—what to do about the masculinity of the state—is one on which MacKinnon and Brown would fundamentally disagree. For MacKinnon, equality requires "a new jurisprudence, a new relation between life and law" (1989:249) that recognizes the inequality between the sexes and the pervasiveness of male power. MacKinnon argues that we must "recognize that male forms of power over women are affirmatively embodied as individual rights in law" (244) and that laws that are seemingly gender-neutral actually perpetuate the subordination of women: "When it [the state] is most ruthlessly neutral, it is most male; when it is most sex blind, it is most blind to the sex of the standard being applied" (245).

Brown, on the other hand, challenges MacKinnon's proposal of a feminist jurisprudence. In response to calls for legislation against such issues as pornography and prostitution, Brown questions the wisdom of "legally codifying and thereby ontologizing a cultural construction of male sexual rapaciousness and female powerlessness" (1995:170). She argues that to do so would mean seeking protection from precisely the same power "whose violation one fears" and perpetuating "the very modality of dependence and powerlessness marking much of women's experience across widely diverse cultures and epochs" (170). Although Brown's argument is convincing, and illuminates serious flaws in MacKinnon's call for a feminist jurisprudence, it remains unclear from Brown's analysis what women, on a practical level, can do when they find themselves trapped in a legal system that continually privileges the rights of men.

New-left Italian feminists faced the very same dilemma in their critique of nationally organized demands for equal rights. As the women of the influential Milan Women's Bookstore Collective argued,

When women try to make laws or ask Parliament to resolve some of the social conflicts in which they are implicated, they do damage to their own sex. . . . Besides being ambiguously formulated (women are made equal to men as if man were the measure of what is best for woman), these laws do not say anything about the relations between the sexes. . . . Contrary to what some women seem to believe, there are no laws which can give value to female sexuality if such value is not already socially recognized. (Milan Women's Bookstore Collective 1990:67)

The women of the Bookstore Collective go on to argue, in a theory similar to Brown's, that the category of women is neither homogeneous nor uniformly oppressed, and that when women rely on the law, they rely on an institution created and controlled by men. For the women of the Bookstore Collective, the law cannot take into account the diverse experiences and choices women have, because

the law necessarily anticipates what is going to happen only in an abstract, general way. . . . This levels the condition of women to their least common denominator, keeps people from perceiving women's different choices as well as the real opportunities they have to improve situations for themselves, and thus denies the existence of the female gender—only a "female condition" exists, with which probably no one really identifies. (Milan Women's Bookstore Collective 1990:67–68)

As with Brown's ideas, the theories of the Milan Bookstore Collective become problematic when examined in light of laws that are not gender-neutral, but actively endorse and support the power of men. Although seeking protection from an institution controlled by the very same group whose power one seeks to displace is indeed problematic, so is it problematic to try to work outside a domain that is as pervasive and all-encompassing as the state. As Brown argues, rather than being an institution or bounded entity, the state is "a significantly unbounded terrain of powers and techniques, an ensemble of discourses, rules, and practices" (1995:174). It is a domain that extends into nearly every aspect of social life.

The question activists must face is how to disrupt society's passive acceptance of intimate-partner violence without reinscribing the subordination of women. Accomplishing this goal requires moving beyond the question of working inside or outside existing structures of power. In Italy, and elsewhere, it requires disrupting the discourses that perpetuate the layers of shame that can prevent women from seeking help and vocalizing their experiences. Such discourses do not exist only in explicitly state-controlled spaces, but permeate much of society itself, even the very institutions dedicated to helping women overcome subordination and oppression.

CHAPTER 6

Engendering Resistance

THROUGHOUT MY FIRST FEW MONTHS IN PARMA, I spent most of each day listening, watching, and taking copious notes at Women United and Family Aid. My dual role as both volunteer and anthropologist enabled me to at times be intimately involved in the daily running of the organizations and at other moments move off to the sidelines. Despite my privileged position as a participant observer, many of my early discussions with colleagues focused on the organizations' internal tensions rather than on the stories of violence we had been privy to throughout the day.

When I went home to my apartment in the evenings and wrote up the notes I had amassed during the course of the day, I would try, often without much success, to make sense of what I was observing. I thought about the neat and organized project I had envisioned and outlined back home and wondered how I could get my colleagues to talk to me about the issues that were relevant to my research—partner violence, gender relations, and community recognition of domestic violence.

After a few months of volunteering at Women United and Family Aid, I began to grow tired of hearing about internal disagreements and friction. I wanted to know how the city of Parma was responding to intimate-partner violence. I was not interested in studying what seemed to be an exaggerated version of the office politics I had experienced in my own society. Night after night I struggled to organize and understand my findings. Then one day I realized that in the process of continually looking for ways to get at what mattered to me, I was discounting what mattered to the women I was working with. I was not paying attention to what was *at stake* (Kleinman 1995) for the women of Women United and Family Aid. Once I decided to let go of the orderly and schematic project I had outlined before arriving in Parma, I began to realize that it was a mistake to discount the daily tensions and conflicts I was observing as routine organizational tensions. I realized that office politics, no matter how ordinary and common they may seem, take shape in particular ways and can provide a window into larger cultural tensions. In the case of Women United and Family Aid, the daily disagreements and conflicts actually reproduced the same gender tensions I was noting in the larger society. Although I didn't realize it at the time, in my frustration to record conversations I deemed "useful," I was ignoring key sites of resistance against dominant gender norms.

The internal dynamics of Women United and Family Aid reveal that in a social context where there are no men, power can still be profoundly gendered. Within both organizations, hierarchical relationships mirrored relations between men and women in the larger society. In writing about his work in a Boston homeless shelter, Robert Desjarlais (1997) points out that while the study of cultural discourses is important, such studies

seldom consider how the stuff of personhood is built out of the events and doings of everyday life. They also tend to neglect the plurality of forces that occasion diverse ways of being at any moment within a society. To rectify this tendency we need to examine how patterns of sensation, forms of agency, or a sense of personhood come about in specific social interactions. Such a study requires not only a reading of broader cultural "discourses" in the Foucaultian sense of the word, but an ear toward mundane utterances, conversational exchanges, and day-to-day contingencies. (Desjarlais 1997:28)

By deciding to focus on the day-to-day micropolitics within Women United and Family Aid, I was able to move beyond the broader cultural significance of the two organizations and examine the mundane aspects of everyday practice. Once I began paying attention to what at first glance appeared to be routine office politics, I was able to notice internal gendered hierarchies as well as subtle but discernable tides of resistance. As microcosms of society at large, and symbols of the opposition between communism and Catholicism, the two organizations revealed how gendered hierarchies can take shape and how they can and are resisted through subtle acts of parody and play as well as through bold, courageous moments of defiance. Despite the vast ideological differences between the women of Women United and Family Aid, their daily lives revealed similar processes of reproduction and resistance.

In the Name of Motherhood

One of the first things I noticed when I began volunteering at Family Aid was the continual emphasis on familial idioms. Despite the fact that men were not involved with day-to-day activities within the organization, structural "fathers" and "mothers" still emerged within the organization's hierarchy in ways that mirrored the role divisions endorsed by Catholicism and the Catholic Church. Although papal edicts regarding women and their position in society have changed over the last century, the Catholic Church still identifies the production of children and the maintenance of family ties as the most important role women have in society. In his 1995 letter to women on the occasion of the United Nations' Fourth World Conference on Women held in Beijing, Pope John Paul II explained the role of woman as that of "helper" and complement to man:

We are then told that, from the very beginning, man has been created "male and female" (*Gen* 1:27). Scripture itself provides the interpretation of this fact: Even though man is surrounded by the innumerable creatures of the created world, he realizes that *he is alone* (cf. *Gen* 2:20). God intervenes in order to help him escape from this situation of solitude: "*It is not good that the man should be alone; I will make him a helper fit for him*" (*Gen* 2:18). The creation of woman is thus marked from the outset by *the principle of help*: a help which is not one sided but *mutual*. Woman complements man, just as man complements woman: men and women are *complementary*. Womanhood expresses the "human" as much as manhood does, but in a different and complementary way. (John Paul II 1995a, original emphases)

In this letter, Pope John Paul II proclaims the importance of "universal recognition of the dignity of women" and posits Mary as the "highest expression of the 'feminine genius'" because of her obedience to God and acceptance of her role as wife and mother of the holy family. For Pope John Paul II, women "reveal the gift of their womanhood by placing themselves at the service of others in their everyday lives." In a General Audience speech titled "Mary Sheds Light on Role of Women," the Pope explained how the Virgin Mary, who selflessly devoted herself to her mission, exemplifies this service:

With regard to the angel's message, the Virgin makes no proud demands nor does she seek to satisfy personal ambitions. Luke presents her to us as wanting only to offer her humble service with total and trusting acceptance of the divine plan of salvation. This is the meaning of her response: "Behold, I am the hand-maiden of the Lord; let it be done to me according to your word" (*Lk* 1:38). (John Paul II 1995b)

When I spoke with don Bernardo, priest of the Rocco di Marco parish, he explained that according to Catholicism, husbands and wives possess the same dignity but play different roles in society: "One is a wife and the other is a husband. They don't do the same things. . . . The wife is the custodian of life and the raiser of children; she is the one who creates the atmosphere of the family." For don Bernardo, the husband's role is "to provide the things that are necessary for the family, to be present in family life, to be interested in the children, and to promote a certain atmosphere in the family, even if it is more the woman who does this, and to show his collaboration and his willingness to help."

In my conversations with don Bernardo, he spoke openly about the feminist movement in Italy. He expressed support for parity between men and women in the workplace, but was firm in his conviction that feminism must promote respect for women as mothers and educators. Don Bernardo explained that the distinction between men and women was challenged in the 1970s, but that in recent years feminists have changed their focus and are speaking more about the need to distinguish between parity and sameness. "It is our anatomy that tells us we are different," according to don Bernardo. This focus on biology and separation of roles is codified in Pope John Paul II's letter to women. He writes: "In this perspective of 'service'—which, when it is carried out with freedom, reciprocity and love, expresses the truly "royal" nature of mankind—one can also appreciate that the presence *of a certain diversity of roles* is in no way prejudicial to women, provided that this diversity is not the result of an arbitrary imposition, but is rather an expression of what is specific to being male and female" (John Paul II 1995a, original emphasis).

When I asked don Bernardo what he thought about the prohibition against the ordination of women, his answer reflected the position of the Vatican but also spoke to the parallels between the organization of the Catholic Church and its vision of the family.

SONJA: But women are not permitted to be ordained?

DON BERNARDO: And I respond that I cannot become a nun, a great injustice. A man cannot become a wife and a wife cannot become a husband, a great injustice. Saint Joseph wanted to have a child but God chose Mary to have Jesus. Unfortunately, women are different from men. Jesus is not against women, on the contrary. . . . He saved prostitutes, spoke with women, and broke with many of the conventions and prejudices of his day that were against women, but he understands that they have different roles. The Church has always been the first to help women. The Church, however, is faithful to the occupations that God chose for Adam and Eve.

These occupations—woman as nurturer and man as provider—are embraced by the Church, both in its own internal hierarchy of nuns and priests and in the vision of family it promotes throughout the world. My conversations with don Bernardo and his interpretation of a gendered division of labor within the family echoed much of what I observed while working as a volunteer at Family Aid.

Reproducing Family

Given that a central goal of Family Aid was to promote motherhood, it is not surprising that both the workers and volunteers imagined the organization itself to be a family. The women who came in for help were referred to as *mamme* (moms), the shelters were treated as households, shelter supervisors were encouraged to act as surrogate mothers, office workers were called in as "fathers" to make important decisions, and the "moms" living in the shelters were viewed as children in need of training and guidance. During my months as a volunteer, there was continual tension between the women working in the shelters and the women working in the office, and nearly all issues and problems were refracted through a particularly Catholic model of family that emphasized the leadership and decision-making role of "fathers" and the *lavoro di cura* of "mothers."

When Monica, the woman who moved from a shelter run by Women United to a shelter run by Family Aid, broke curfew one evening, the supervisors and the social workers in the main office were both angry. According to Sara, a social worker in her early twenties, it was important to "give meaning to the rule" and explain why the rule exists. In an explanation to one of the other residents who did not understand why coming home at midnight was such a serious violation, Sara told her: "When your daughter grows up and is eighteen, and one night she is supposed to come home at 10 PM but by 11 PM she still isn't home, don't tell me you wouldn't call the police. The rule is important because we were worried about Monica." In this explanation, Sara emphasized the mother/daughter relationship that is cultivated between the women working or volunteering at the shelter and the women living in the shelter.

A few months later, when Sofia, a mom living in one of Family Aid's first-stage shelters, wanted to quit the sewing class she was taking as part of a job-training program organized by a cooperative affiliated with Family Aid, there was a long discussion in the weekly *équipe* (team) meeting over whether to allow her to quit or force her to continue.[1] A few of the shelter supervisors had already tried to convince her to continue with the course, but Sofia seemed determined to quit. At one point she blew up at one of the supervisors and shouted, "You (referring to the women of Family Aid) always want me to do what you want!"

In the process of discussing how to handle the situation, many of the supervisors said they thought it was important for Sofia to finish the course but that the decision was ultimately hers to make. The psychologist hired to facilitate discussion and lead the *équipe* meetings urged the supervisors to rethink their position: "You're all saying she needs to make the decision herself but I'm thinking, if we had an eight-year-old child who didn't want to go to school would we just let her quit? No. It's true she's a woman, but I see a young girl . . . she is using her children as an excuse, saying she needs to stay home with them." The president agreed and added: "It's like a child who wants to separate but every time she wants to come back to her mother's arms." The *équipe* psychologist continued: "But if we let her come back and say, poor Sofia, come here, we are really saying, yes, it's true that you can't make it on your own. It's like a child who is learning to walk. First you give your hand, then your finger, and then you take the finger away and the baby sees she can walk on her own."

References to mother/daughter relationships repeatedly came up as examples during discussions and *équipe* meetings. Not only were the women in the shelters often represented as children in need of guidance and nurturance, but the women working and volunteering were also slotted into familial roles according to a gendered division of labor. The women who worked as day and night supervisors within the shelters were charged with organizing and running the shelters as if they were households. The supervisors planned the weekly menu, made the weekly shopping list, ensured the kitchen and common areas were kept clean and tidy, and organized childcare for the women who worked or attended school. The women who were based in the Family Aid headquarters (two social workers, the president, and vice president) were responsible for making all of the major decisions regarding the shelters and the "plans" for the women living in the shelters.

As Alessandra, one of the office social workers, explained, "The role of the shelter supervisor is to take on the role of the mom when she [the biological mom] is not present, either physically or psychologically." The role of the social workers, on the other hand, is to help the moms with the plans that were created for them. For some moms this means help in finding steady work; for others it means job training or learning parenting skills. As a volunteer I observed that the friction between the "houses" (shelters) and the "office" (central headquarters) often surfaced in weekly *équipe* meetings, and that family idioms were continually used to describe situations and conflicts within the organization.

One morning Alessandra complained in *équipe* that she was tired of constantly having to go over to the shelter to intervene and settle disputes. The president reminded her that it was sometimes necessary to have someone from the office go over to settle disputes because coming from the office lends a sense of seriousness to the issue at hand. The *équipe* psychologist pointed out that the office seems to take on the role of *babbo* (dad), while the supervisors who are in the house all day with the mothers and children take on the role of *mamma*. In a similar exchange, one of the shelter supervisors complained that she was made to feel like the evil mother when she spoke harshly to Sofia one morning, then found out that later in the day Alessandra had invited Sofia to a meeting and ended up taking her to lunch. She explained, "I felt like the bad mother who yelled at her and then Alessandra came in like the good father."

Tensions between the women working in the office and the women working in the shelters were shaped by the gendered distinctions in their roles. The shelter supervisors often told me that the women of the office "just don't understand" what goes on in the shelter on a daily basis. They resented it when the women of the office came to the shelter and commented on a less than immaculate kitchen floor or toys and games spread out in the living room.

One afternoon when I arrived for a shift at one of the shelters, I found Maria, one of the shelter supervisors, busy scrubbing the kitchen and common areas. When one of the moms asked why she was working so hard, Maria responded that the president was coming later in the afternoon and she didn't want to hear any comments about the house not being clean enough. Later in the day when I asked Maria why she was so intent on making sure the house was immaculate, she explained, "I try to avoid having to hear any comments because whoever is not here on a daily basis just cannot understand." Many of the supervisors commented to me that the women who worked in the office (president, vice president, and social workers) could never understand the continual crises and chaos supervisors had to deal with on a daily basis.

In one meeting, the *équipe* psychologist noted tension and a lack of trust among the women working in the organization. She questioned the president about the division of responsibility among the women who work as supervisors in the "houses" and the women who work in the "office." The psychologist wondered how the supervisors could help women become independent when the supervisors themselves were not independent. She asked: "Why do they always need to call [the office] when there's a problem. . . . Don't you think you are depriving the supervisors of their own power?" The psychologist pointed out that the supervisors were confused about their role within the organization because they spent nearly all their time cooking, cleaning, and organizing the shelter instead of working substantively with the women to achieve certain specified goals.

The role of shelter supervisors was thus a problematic one. Although hired as "educators" to work with the women on a daily basis, in effect they became the mothers of the shelter, and fulfilled the role of household manager and nurturer. They spent their shifts cleaning, cooking, and caring for children. Although the moms living in the shelters had evening chores, they were often out all day attending classes or working, and it was the shelter supervisors who took up the slack. The supervisors worked in the shelter all day long and assumed many of the household duties. But they were not given the authority to make important decisions for either the shelter or the moms, and had to constantly consult with the women in the central office. The hierarchy of roles and duties within the organization thus mirrored those of men who take on the role of breadwinner and provider and women who take on the role of household manager and nurturer.

Pregnancy Is Not Always a Beautiful Thing

When I first met Claudia, she had been a shelter supervisor at Family Aid for five years. After more than fifteen years as an office worker, she had decided to make a life change, and at the age of thirty-eight she began working at Family Aid. She came to the organization out of a desire to help people in need. When she first began working as a shelter supervisor many of the moms were young Italian girls who were pregnant and in need of food and shelter. Some had been sent away by their families in order to avoid the stigma of an extramarital pregnancy;

others came of their own accord. Shortly after Claudia arrived, how-ever, the clientele began to change. The number of pregnant girls seek-ing shelter had been in decline for a number of years, and the election of a new board brought a change in the shelter-admission policies. Family Aid grew quickly as it reached out to new categories of women, many of whom were older and already had two or three children. These moms often arrived with violent pasts that included abusive partners, poverty, and at times forced prostitution. The number of immigrant women liv-ing in the shelters also rose significantly during this period.

When I interviewed Claudia, she told me it was very difficult for her to tell a woman who was thirty-five years old how to wash dishes. Claudia explained that she "can't and shouldn't" try to change these women. Rather, her responsibility as a shelter supervisor should be to facilitate group living. For Claudia, when there were young girls in the house the path toward autonomy was much clearer, as the girls were eager to learn how to cook, clean, raise children, and maintain a house-hold. Given the decision to expand Family Aid's clientele to include both immigrant and older women, Claudia felt it was imperative that the organization change its methodology as well.

I continue to say we either need to change the way we do things or we will al-ways be frustrated. The clients change but we never change? That means some-thing is not right. What do we do? We change the structure of the shelter—we build a bigger kitchen—but we don't change mentally, we don't change our expectations. We need to have the moms sign a contract that is clear, one they understand. We have women who barely speak Italian. They sign that they ac-cept the rules because they have nowhere else to go.

In addition to expressing her frustrations with the methodology, Claudia also admitted that on a personal level there were many issues she did not feel comfortable raising at *équipe* meetings or with the other women of Family Aid. She told me she could understand why a woman would want to get an abortion, and confessed that she personally had experienced the difficulty of an unplanned pregnancy.

I'm not convinced a pregnancy is always a beautiful thing, a gift. I think it is possible that for many women being pregnant and having a child is not all roses and flowers, and I'm not just talking about the difficulty of raising a child, I'm talking about the woman's mental state. . . . At a certain point I had to face this as well. I had never had a relationship with a man before. I had lived my life going to church, working, and doing volunteer work, and then I found myself preg-nant and unmarried. It changed my life completely. It meant I had to face the judgment of everyone, it meant something very serious and facing the idea of an abortion, at a concrete level, seemed like the perfect solution, something that

could take this huge weight off your shoulders. In reality it's the complete opposite because then you end up carrying the weight of an abortion your whole
life, but if I hadn't had all the support I did, most of all psychological, I couldn't
have done it. I'm not surprised at all that many women end up aborting. But
unfortunately, the people I know who have had abortions carry it with them
forever.

For Claudia, it was an outrage that the issue of abortion was never
discussed at Family Aid: "An organization founded in opposition to
abortion never talks about it again? Are we kidding? We don't even
know what the volunteers think about abortion. We can't be scared to
find out what people think." For many months Claudia herself hid the
fact she was pregnant and to this day hides the fact that she lives with
her companion and their daughter.

Now I live with my companion, something I can't even talk about because at
work many people don't know. If they did, who knows what would happen.
The nuns don't know, they think I am still at home with my parents. For many
months now I've been living with my companion. It's not something I'm proud
of but it's a decision I made. I don't need anyone's opinion; it's a decision I made
for myself.

Claudia's experiences as a shelter supervisor—her frustration with
Family Aid's static methodology, and the refusal of many of the workers
and volunteers to discuss alternative points of view on pregnancy and
motherhood—speak to the rigidity of the models of gender and family
upon which the organization was funded and within which it operated. Other volunteers and supervisors I spoke with expressed similar
frustrations. As one active volunteer confessed during an interview:
"I'll tell you, I'm a bit of a rebel. I don't like it when I feel certain things
are too rigid. I too was a bit of a feminist back in the old days, not like
the ones you see around, but I supported the rights of women." She
went on to tell me that although she could never voice her true opinion
at Family Aid, she supported a woman's right to choose and felt that in
some cases, abortion could be a woman's only option.

Although there were murmurings of disagreement, and subtle acts of
resistance through the choices women made in their personal lives, at no
point during my time with Family Aid did I observe a significant challenge to the status quo. The supervisors went on with their jobs—they
cooked, cleaned, and sometimes grumbled—and the women in the central office continued to work with the moms to help them on their individual paths toward self-sufficiency. The rigidity of the organization's

ideology and structure and its parallels with the hierarchy of the Catholic Church were impressed on me one Sunday when I was working as a supervisor in one of the shelters.

Sister Anna

When I arrived that Sunday morning to begin my shift, the night supervisor told me on her way out that the moms had recently thrown out six kilos of "perfectly good meat" insisting it had gone bad. For that reason a new rule had been instituted by the central office. The women would have to plan ahead and ask the Saturday supervisor to bring up all the food they needed for the weekend. Sunday and evening supervisors would not be given access to the *cantina* (basement), where additional food was stored, and the moms would have to live with the consequences of their actions. If they threw out food during the day, there would be nothing to eat at night. If they threw out food on Saturday, there would be nothing left to eat on Sunday.

Shortly before I began my afternoon shift, the moms began complaining to me that the refrigerator was bare and there was nothing to make for lunch. As a Sunday supervisor, I was in the difficult position of having no choice but to enforce the new rule that had been set up by the central office. Without keys to the basement, even if I wanted to bring up extra food, there was no way for me to do so. Feeling somewhat limited by my position as a Sunday supervisor, I encouraged the moms to make a *frittata* (omelet) with the eggs that were left in the refrigerator. They balked and complained that at the very minimum they needed some *grana* (a type of cheese), and begged me to go next door and ask the nuns if we could borrow some.

Unsure of the best way to handle the situation, I agreed to go next door. When I rang the doorbell of the nunnery, I was met by Sister Anna. As usual she greeted me with her warm and engaging smile. Although in her mid-seventies and beginning to feel the frailty of her age, Anna was always cheerful and ready to chat with everyone coming in and out of the nunnery. Sister Anna asked me what I needed and I explained the situation. I told her that we were low on food over at the shelter. I told her the women were upset, and there was nothing I could do since I did not have access to the basement. I then asked if it would be possible for us to borrow a bit of cheese. Sister Anna told me that she was very sorry but Sister Carmela, the mother superior, was out for the day and there was no one else who had permission to give out food. I thanked her and told her I understood. As I turned to leave, Sister Anna gave me a big smile, patted me on the arm, and told me we were "the same."

At first I didn't quite understand what Sister Anna was trying to tell me. During my short walk back to the shelter I thought about our conversation and realized that with her knowing smile, Sister Anna was alluding to the fact that we were both caught in the hierarchy of the structures in which we were both enmeshed—she as a nun who must defer to the rules of the nunnery and I as a shelter volunteer who must defer to the rules of the organization. The moms were low on food, and though there would be enough to scrape by for lunch, the moms and children would be forced to go without cheese, and there was nothing either of us could do about it.

Organizational Fairy Tales

The one time I observed a direct challenge to the methodology and authority at Family Aid was during a training meeting that brought volunteers, shelter supervisors, and social workers together in one room to discuss the goals and structure of the organization. The meeting was led by a psychologist with a specialty in the management of organizations. She had been hired to help clarify Family Aid's objectives and look for ways to manage its recent growth in personnel and services.

Midway through the meeting, the management psychologist divided us into groups according to our roles within the organization. There was a group for the board of directors (including the president and vice president), a group for the volunteer coordinators, a group for the office social workers, and a group for the shelter supervisors. Our assignment was to create "a fairy tale of our service" that included identifying the hero, the villain, the goals, the obstacles, and the magic objects. The stories created by each group revealed the similarities and differences in the way each group interpreted the goals and methodology of Family Aid. The final story, created by the shelter supervisors (the paid employees of the organization) can be interpreted as a subtle act of resistance against the methodology of the organization. Each group had about fifteen minutes to create its fairy tale; we then went around in a circle and the groups read their stories aloud.

The board members were the first to share their story. They told a fairy tale about a mom who once upon a time becomes pregnant and has no home and nowhere to go. After wandering in the woods with a friend she eventually sees a house in the distance that is all lit up.

The friend encourages her to knock at the front door. When she does she finds a family seated around a big table. The family welcomes her and invites her to sit down. The mom stays with this family and learns how to work. When she gives birth to her child, the older children in the family help out by taking care of the baby during the day while she is working. At the end of their story, the board members identified the mom as the hero, the rejection she experiences before finding the house as the villain, and the family that welcomes her as the magic object. This story underscores the board's efforts to make Family Aid feel like a family for the moms they shelter. It also has religious undertones that draw from Catholic values of self-sacrifice and service toward others.

The volunteer-coordinator group went next. They told the story of a young pregnant girl abandoned in the midst of tranquility and well-being. While the young girl is sitting alone on a bench, a woman comes up and joins her. The woman takes a magic object out of her bag. It is a cell phone that she uses to call many other good witches who come to help. They make a hot meal and help the young girl find shelter. In this story, the hero was the mom, the villain was the person who rejected her, the goal was successful maternity, and the magic objects were Family Aid and love of life. Rather than emphasize family, the volunteer coordinator group underscored the importance of solidarity among women. Although the goal was still successful maternity, the means to attain that goal were slightly different from the story told by the board of directors.

The social-worker group told a story that was very similar to that of the volunteer coordinators, but added professionalism, training, and methodology to the collection of magic objects. It was clear that the social workers, as the only trained professionals within the organization, valued training and methodology as important aspects of their position.

The last group to tell its story was the one made up of shelter supervisors. Their narrative was strikingly different from the other three fairy tales. They told the story of a group of wild horses that were once free to wander and play in the fields. One day, out of the blue, the horses are captured and put into stalls. They are cleaned and fed and at a certain point they are forced to enter a competition that requires them to overcome obstacles like bars, walls, and streams. Some horses pass these obstacles while others do not. During the competition some horses are able to continue while others must return to the stables. Then out of nowhere a big storm arrives and creates further problems for the horses. Eventually a few of the horses cross the finish line. In this story the heroes were the moms (symbolized by the horses), the villains were the moms' personal stories and the people who made the challenges too difficult, the obstacles were the other moms and unexpected occurrences, and the magic objects were the supervisors and their strategies.

The story of the supervisor group clearly deviated the most from the dominant narrative of motherhood and the sanctity of life. There was no mention of family or maternity in the supervisors' fairy tale. Their story of captured horses (the moms they must help) forced to compete for an often unattainable goal reflected the difficulties the supervisors encountered in their work and the frustration they sometimes felt with the goals and practices of the organization. The supervisors are paid employees and work with the mothers on a daily—and nightly—basis. Theirs was a story not of faith and good works but of a challenging, and often frustrating, path toward freedom and self-sufficiency. Although the story they told was a subtle act of resistance against the clearly identified ideals of Family Aid, their frustration did not lead toward any fundamental structural change during the time I worked with the organization.

More Male than Men

Within Women United I noted a similar frustration among the paid employees, but unlike the Family Aid supervisors, the caseworkers of Women United eventually escalated their subtle acts of resistance into a bold defiance of the hierarchy within the organization. When I first arrived at Women United in September of 1999, it was a period of intense conflict, frustration, and tension for the organization. In an interview with a caseworker at Women United, I asked why there was such conflict and tension between the women who worked for the organization as volunteers (board members) and the women who worked for the organization as paid employees (caseworkers). According to the caseworker, the answer was simple: it was all a question of power.

In my opinion it has to do with a power dynamic. The women on the board like Carlotta and Martina are part of the organization because it gives them a position of power. These women worked harder than men to achieve their positions of power—Martina was the first female doctor in Parma, she built up her own career. These women became worse than the men in positions of power, these women worked harder and became more aggressive toward the people under them.

From daily conversations with caseworkers and board members at Women United, I learned that many of the conflicts and tensions within the organization were connected to the performance of gender and societal norms for masculinity and femininity. Ironically, throughout my fourteen months of ethnographic fieldwork, the explanations my friends and colleagues provided for the conflicts within the organization echoed many of the gender norms and stereotypes the organization was dedicated to overturning in the larger society.

The idea that egalitarian groups produce their own internal hierarchies, or that the theoretical ideals of an organization or social movement can be at odds with daily practice, is nothing new for anthropology. What does lend new insight, however, is the extent to which the women of Women United categorized themselves along gendered lines in an environment populated exclusively by women. In what could be described as a classic example of hegemony, I found that the women of Women United were reproducing the very same gender system they were trying to fight against. What distinguishes this example of hegemony from static notions of structure, however, is that the "women" within the organization—the caseworkers who were marginalized from decision making and deprived of agency to maneuver within the organization—were not completely complicit in their domination. Although their resistance began with small acts of parody and play, the tide eventually turned, and through the bold actions of several caseworkers the structure of the organization was transformed.

At Women United, caseworkers were considered to be employees and did not have voting rights within the organization. Although generally speaking there was an age discrepancy between board members, who were volunteers, and caseworkers, who were paid on an hourly basis (board members were generally in their fifties and sixties, and caseworkers were generally in their twenties and thirties), I did not observe any evident class distinctions between caseworkers and board members. For the most part, all of the women associated in a volunteer or employee capacity with Women United came from a professional or upper-middle-class background. Except for one, who worked in the service industry, nearly all the board members had careers as teachers, professors, lawyers, doctors, therapists, or some other professional occupation. Of the caseworkers, almost all came from families where one or both parents were professionals. By far the most distinguishing characteristics that separated caseworkers and board members were age and the fact that caseworkers were paid for their time and board members were not.

As a frequent participant in the organization's activities during the fall of 1999, I noticed that the president of Women United would often speak angrily to the caseworkers and would frequently use disparaging language and insults to get her point across. Surprised to see this type of behavior taking place within the organization, I wondered why no one on the board was doing anything to intervene. When I spoke with the caseworkers about the issue, they told me that the president frequently berated them in what they termed a "masculine" way. They explained that she was "worse than a man" and would often insult people inside and outside the organization by calling them "stupid" or "dumb," and would even tell people to "screw off." In an interview with Cinzia, a thirty-year-old caseworker, I asked why the board had not yet intervened. Cinzia explained:

Look, the fact is this, with Emanuela and Amalia [board members] Carlotta's [the president's] true identity came out. Amalia witnessed an episode of violence against me that brought me to tears, she attacked me in a way that I had the sensation she wanted to strangle me, physically strangle me . . . her eyes were almost bloody, red, I mean they were violent. I was shaken, I have never in my life witnessed such a violent scene like the ones you see in movies, for me it was a very disturbing experience. . . . But the others don't have any idea what we mean when we say she is a very aggressive person. Even Emanuela, last year, told me, "Look Cinzia, every workplace has its problems." Yes, that's unfortunate, but here it's not the same thing, she [Emanuela] didn't really understand what I was saying. Then, after their disagreement, when they got into an argument, then she understood what we had been trying to say all along. At that point she really understood.

The conflict between the president and the caseworkers was just one example of a larger systemic conflict between the caseworkers and the board. The board ignored caseworker complaints about the president, which gave the caseworkers no recourse other than resigning from their positions. Within the organization there was an imbalance of power and a hierarchical relationship between the board and caseworkers that reproduced precisely the type of hierarchical relations that communist and feminist groups ordinarily work to subvert.

According to Isabella, a caseworker who eventually decided to leave the organization, "It's always been this way, even when there was a different president, a different board, and all different workers, we had the same problems. It has to do with the way the organization is structured." Cinzia had a similar analysis and explained that there were similar problems under the previous president, who although bureaucratic, had been a very effective president. Throughout 1997, tensions had been high, and there were many internal disputes that had led the president to resign and all but one of the caseworkers to quit. Cinzia later found in the computer a resignation letter that had been written by the caseworkers during this period of crisis. She told me that it read, "as if it had been written by me or Isabella . . . she [the caseworker] said that culturally she can't accept, as a woman she can no longer accept, certain things that are happening within the organization."

I later obtained a copy of this 1997 letter, and it did indeed reflect many of the sentiments voiced to me by the organization caseworkers I had gotten to know:

We have chosen to resign after a long and difficult period of individual suffering for in our opinion the situation inside the organization has degraded to a point of no return . . . just three months ago, four other caseworkers submitted their resignations and to this day there has been no reflection on the reasons behind these resignations. It is clear that the way of relating inside the organization is characterized by authoritarian behavior and is based on the denial of problems, and the marginalization and expulsion of those who disagree. We believe that in order to achieve the primary objective of an association that wants to bring solidarity to women who are suffering, the relationships among the women who work within the association must be based on mutual respect . . . it is impossible to bring solidarity to people outside the organization if it has not yet been proven to work inside the organization. It is for these reasons we believe that the board of directors has, not only recently, pursued a path of no return. For example, there has never been a discussion of women or cases at board meetings, it is as if these issues pertain only to caseworkers; caseworkers have never been invited to share their training and experience with the other members of the association as there is no opportunity for the sharing of knowledge and experience; and there has never been an effort to support a supervision meeting for caseworkers nor an effort to create another way to help the caseworkers and the entire association grow and expand in experience and knowledge. . . . At this point, our responsibility toward the women and other institutions of Parma forces us to give a clear and definite signal regarding the incapacity of Women United to constructively face its own chronic problems.

Although I spent the majority of my time at Women United with the caseworkers in the administrative office and shelter, I also had regular interactions with a number of board members, which gave me an opportunity to discuss their perspectives on the conflict. In an interview with Emanuela, who was often sympathetic to the caseworkers' concerns, I asked what had happened during the "period of crisis" in 1997 when the president resigned and close to three-quarters of the board and caseworkers decided to leave.

EMANUELA: Look, I'm not really sure what happened, but I see that in this organization there will always be this misunderstanding between volunteers and employees [caseworkers]. I suppose that it will always be like this because in Women

United, and I think in all organizations like this one, there are employees and volunteers and there is a power that the volunteers call their own, they want this power for themselves. The employees have certain skills and they too want to be recognized. But the volunteers feel very frustrated with respect to the employees because the volunteers don't have the skills of the employees. If the employees are professionals then the volunteers are afraid they will lose . . . lose . . .

SONJA: Power?

EMANUELA: Their role, not power, their role. They look to increase their power in order to prevent losing their role because in fact they don't have a role. The employees don't handle this very well. It is difficult for them to understand that the volunteers give their time for free and that certain things must be done to make things easy for the volunteers. . . . When the employees rebel because they have to go to the station to buy train tickets for the volunteers, what they don't understand is that the volunteers may lose one or two days of work, and often forfeit pay, to go do something that will benefit the employees as well. They don't understand that they're going to buy the train tickets for the organization and not for the volunteers. . . . They say they're being treated as secretaries, but unfortunately sometimes someone has to do these things.

The caseworkers were an essential component of Women United, but they were paid, and therefore were not afforded the same status as women who volunteered their time. The caseworkers expressed to me many times their belief that the board did not respect them, and that they were treated as "secretaries." On the other hand, on numerous occasions I heard the president and other board members commenting that the caseworkers could not possibly be as dedicated as the volunteers. The president once explained to me that for the caseworkers, the organization represents a job instead of an ideological cause. While many of the board members continually emphasized the importance of dedication, volunteerism, and solidarity among women, the caseworkers often discussed the need for increased professionalism and training. They pointed out that the needs of the organization had changed and that merely being a woman did not qualify one to provide help to women living with violence.

One quiet afternoon, a few weeks into my research, I was sitting in the office with two caseworkers, Ghita and Isabella, when the topic of professionalism came up. Strangely enough, the telephone was not ringing, there were no scheduled meetings, and there were no urgent letters to be sent out. We were all quietly working on our own projects when Isabella picked up one of the documents Women United routinely includes as part of its public relations package, a document titled "Chi Siamo, Cosa Facciamo" (Who We Are, What We Do), and started reading it aloud. Isabella, Ghita, and I had all seen this bulleted list of questions and answers about Women United hundreds of times, but that afternoon Isabella decided to give it a second look. She started reading, "Who we are, what we do. We help women regain a sense of freedom and self-confidence. We create a plan with each woman to help her leave her violent situation." Then she paused, looked up from the sheet of paper, and said to Ghita and me, "But that's not what happens. We don't have the skills to help women regain a sense of autonomy. Not one of us has been trained to do that." Ghita, who had stopped what she was doing to listen to Isabella, nodded and added:

I'm embarrassed to tell people what the organization does for women. We just listen and make suggestions as to where to go for more help. . . . Dignity, freedom, these are all very beautiful words but when the woman goes home, then what? How many of these women come back for a second meeting with us? Not a second meeting with one of the lawyers or psychologists but a second meeting with us? Very few.

Isabella continued:

The board decided that our job was to point the women in the right direction, to direct them to other services, not to continue seeing each woman multiple times. This means we are an information booth. They [the board] think just because you're a woman and you're on the left you're capable of helping other women. The women who come stay in the safe house, what is passed on to them? Does this ideal of solidarity among women pass on to the women themselves? No. Do the women feel part of something? Understand what Women United is all about? No. At the Catholic organizations there is a fundamental philosophy that the women all know about from the minute they arrive.

When I asked Isabella and Ghita why they had not raised their concerns with the board of directors, they both scoffed at the idea and said the board took weeks to decide anything. The very same issue came up a few days later in the caseworkers' weekly supervision meeting.[2] Ghita, clearly frustrated with the organization's methodology, voiced her concern that Women United was not living up to its goals, and asked the group why women were not coming back for second, let alone third and fourth, meetings with caseworkers. The other caseworkers agreed with Ghita's assessment, but when someone suggested that they sign each woman up right away for three meetings so as to create a *percorso* (journey or path) for each woman, similar to how other women's centers work, the others disagreed. They said that the board took forever to decide anything, and that, furthermore, the board had decided a while back that the role of the organization should be simply to direct women to the appropriate services. Maura confessed that she had lost all desire to fight back and had decided to just accept the decisions of the president and board, even if she disagreed. Isabella noted that the caseworkers had lost their sense of autonomy, just like the women they try to help. As the conversation continued, and frustrations were met with resigned acceptance of the situation at hand, the psychologist pointed out that the caseworkers were going through steps similar to those that women with violent partners go through.

Seeing the caseworkers—my friends and colleagues—frustrated and unwilling to try to find a solution or work toward change began to make me angry. Without thinking I blurted out, "Why can't you just go ahead and start signing women up for three meetings? There doesn't seem to be a rule against that, right? It seems like you don't have any power but that's not true, why can't you just change things yourselves without going through the board?" As soon as the words tumbled out of my mouth I worried I had overstepped my bounds, both as an anthropologist and as a new volunteer at the organization. The caseworkers looked at me without saying a word. I think they were surprised to hear me say anything, as I was usually silent during supervision meetings. After a discernible pause, the psychologist said, "She's right, there are some things you can change on your own," and the meeting continued without further reference to my outburst. The meeting eventually ended with an agreement among everyone at the table to start changing the way meetings with women were handled. It was agreed that the first thing to change would be the procedure for follow-up appointments. Instead of waiting for women to call back, the caseworkers would set up three successive appointments for each new woman who came in for an initial meeting.

Over the next few months, the caseworkers continued to meet with women and take care of business, and the board continued to meet every Tuesday night to oversee the organization. The situation with the president grew worse as her personality grew increasingly volatile. One afternoon in November, I was working on a data collection project for Women United when I, along with one of the interns, became the object of the president's rage. She yelled that we hadn't understood a word she had said, that we were doing everything wrong, and that she herself could have finished the project in a single day. Both the intern and I stood and listened to the verbal beating, shocked by what we were hearing. The intern later told me she had never been treated so poorly in her entire life. Of the three people who had witnessed the incident—Rosaria (vice president), Maria Angela (volunteer), and Amalia (board member)—only Amalia tried to stand up for us, but there was little she could do to intervene.

As the weeks went on, complaints about the president and members of the board continued to circulate among the organization's caseworkers and a few volunteers. During this time I noticed the expressions of anger and frustration had a gendered tone that both questioned and played with aspects of Women United's ideology. Three caseworkers and two volunteers, on separate occasions, told me stories illustrating how Carlotta, the president, "hated women" and had the characteristics of a man. Amalia told me about a time when a female journalist reported on a legal case with which the organization had been involved. Amalia explained that the journalist had made some mistakes in reporting the facts of the case but that the president had been excessive in her condemnation:

Carlotta called her a *puttana*.[3] If she had called her stupid, okay, incapable, okay, but a *puttana*? That's what men use to insult women. The lowest types of men call women prostitutes. I can go work for a trucking company and hear men insulting women like this. Okay, but I can talk to them, explain to them, but a woman? The president of Women United, calling another woman a *puttana*?

By excluding the president from the category of "women" and conflating her aggression, violence, and misogyny with the category of "men," the caseworkers and volunteers were able on the one hand to reproduce the organization's ideological precept of providing solidarity and support for all women, and on the other hand to expose the organization's disjuncture between theory and practice and thus challenge the system itself.

The caseworkers spoke to one another frequently about the president and told stories that enabled them to bond together and provide support and solidarity for each other against her actions. The caseworkers expressed similar sentiments whenever the name of another board member, Gaia, would come up in conversation. The only difference was that with Gaia, it was not her gender that was called into question, but her class.

According to the caseworkers, Gaia also "hated women." One story they used to bolster this claim occurred at a meeting to discuss the women living in the safe house. One of the residents—a young immigrant woman who had been forced into organized sex work but was eventually able to escape—was being housed there for safety purposes.

After a few months had passed and she was out of immediate danger, she decided she wanted to start looking for a job that she could do in a nonpublic place. Her only request was that it not be a job that required bathing elderly people (working as assistants to the elderly is a relatively common job for recent immigrants in Parma). According to the caseworkers who attended the meeting, when Gaia heard this request, she said, "Why should she care? She's had sex with eighty-five-year-old men—what's the big deal if she has to wash them?"

That this board member routinely made such comments about the women in the safe house—in effect reproducing the attitudes and values the organization works to fight against—was confirmed by a conversation I had with a volunteer. Rita, a woman in her late twenties who volunteered at the organization once a week, recounted a story about a woman from a region in southern Italy who came to Women United after experiencing extreme violence at the hands of her husband and father, and was "treated terribly" by Women United. According to Rita, the woman was "difficult to tolerate because she lacked *cultura* (general sophistication and worldliness) and was very feminine, with tight clothes." At one point Gaia reportedly said about the woman, "That girl, all she wants to do is have sex"—a comment that stands in complete opposition to the organization's professed ideology of female solidarity and the freedom to dress, think, and act independently as women. As with the immigrant woman who was looking for a job without intimate contact, the woman in Rita's story was from a region in the south of Italy and therefore just as much of an outsider.

Gaia's reproduction of what my colleagues at Women United might call "old-fashioned" male attitudes toward women and female sexuality echoes Michael Herzfeld's story of Cretan women in the town of Rethemnos who were highly critical of a newly arrived woman who was unmarried and living with a male partner (Herzfeld 1991). What seemed at first to be a reproduction of male concerns with female chastity by the neighborhood women was actually suspicion and fear that a sexually free outsider would seduce their husbands and sons. Once the women were able to verbally express this fear directly to the newly arrived woman, what had been hostile interactions became friendly and warm. Herzfeld argues that in these types of situations "we encounter acts that *appear* to endorse an androcentric ideology while actually casting a critical perspective on the way in which men behave. What appears to the outsider's eye as an uncritical acceptance of hegemony becomes, from an internal perspective, the expression of defiance"

(Herzfeld 1991:93). In Gaia's case the hostility of her actions did not transform into friendly relations, but aspects of Herzfeld's argument still apply in that Gaia was clearly suspicious of women who came to Women United as outsiders, particularly those whose manner, dress, or past history could be interpreted as suggesting uncontrolled sexuality. By reproducing stereotypically male comments, Gaia inadvertently placed a barrier between herself, her family, and her community, and the women she classified as dangerous outsiders.

When I asked Rita why a woman like Gaia would want to be part of Women United, Rita suggested that for many women it is important to *apparire* (appear), cultivating an image of involvement with charity work and public service. Rita told me that Gaia was a woman "of little culture" who nonetheless tried to appear as though she were part of Parma's upper-class circles. Other colleagues at Women United had made similar comments about Gaia and had called her an embarrassment to the organization. They spoke of her lack of intellectual ability, especially her poor command of the subtleties of Italian grammar and her use of a mixture of Italian and dialect.[4] Gaia's lack of higher education, along with an occupation and family that placed her squarely in the *operaio* (worker) class or *piccola borghesia* (lower bourgeoisie), enabled the caseworkers to criticize and distance themselves from her on the basis of class.

When I asked Rita why she thought the caseworkers had never tried to change the situation within the organization, Rita told me it was because of hierarchy: "You grow up in the family knowing your place. At a certain point you also know there is no point in trying to contest. They don't rebel because there is no point, nothing will change." She went to say that their feeling of powerlessness was "a defect of the system" and that people with power have a "sacred circle" that protects them and shields them from criticism. Rita explained that in Italy, family counts for everything, and if you come from a powerful family you have many entitlements not granted to others. Rita's statements echo the statements of other friends and colleagues in Parma who complained about widespread corruption and the importance of the *raccomandazione* (recommendation) in everything from jobs to hospital visits. There is no simple English equivalent to *raccomandazione*—it means more than just "recommendation," as it encompasses clientelism, nepotism, and the proverbial pulling of strings. Knowing someone or having a relative in a particular position can help Italians on a daily basis to navigate bureaucratic intricacies and inefficiencies. The *raccomandazione* can be

key to avoiding daily hassles like waiting in lines to file papers or waiting months for an appointment for an X-ray or mammogram.[5] It is also
often the only way to land coveted university, civil-service, and political positions. Many of my colleagues within Women United expressed
resentment that the president might never be thrown out because of her
network of connections throughout the city, gained through her role in
local politics and her mother's connection to the film industry.

Parody and Play

Despite murmurings among caseworkers and a few board members
that the president was on her way out, during my first six months in
Parma no action was taken by the board to call for new elections. The
caseworkers developed various strategies of resistance that helped
them cope with their inability to change the situation at hand. They
began calling the president "piranha," and drawings of fish began ap-
pearing around the office. The caseworkers and interns began going
out for dinners together, and almost the entire evening would be spent
imitating the president's personality quirks. Each time we went to dinner, the same battery of impersonations and stories would be acted out.
Instead of being boring or repetitive, the performances grew funnier
with each reenactment. The caseworkers, interns, and I would laugh so
hard tears came to our eyes. There are many subtle and creative ways
for individuals to express frustration and resistance. As Dorinne Kondo
argues, resistance need not always take the form of "radical rupture
or apocalyptic change" (1990:259); the caseworkers were pushing back
through their parodies.

Another example of caseworker resistance occurred in December,
when the board decided to produce a calendar to sell at Christmastime
that would both publicize the organization and raise funds for its activities. After much discussion, the board decided the calendar would
be a collection of recipes from the women volunteering and working at
Women United. The caseworkers objected to the notion of producing a
calendar of recipes, but as with many of the decisions made at Women
United, they had no say in the decision-making process. It would be
one thing if the recipes were from the women who had lived in the
safe house, the caseworkers explained, but to have a calendar of Italian
recipes from the board and staff just put women in the same place they
had always been: the kitchen. Maura spoke to me at length about the
calendar project:

I don't agree, first of all because this year everyone is talking about the end of the millennium and everyone has to have a calendar. It seems to me that an organization like Women United should do anything but a calendar. I was in agreement with a calendar that depicted important women we've had, that we have, and thank God exist today in history. With their expressive faces, with faces that are significant. But to have women, once again with recipes, no. . . . I will only sell this calendar to men because they need to learn how to cook. . . . I will tell them, "learn Grazia's recipe, learn Sonja's recipe, learn my recipe, and then invite me over to eat."

Maura's refusal to sell the calendar to women and other caseworkers' refusal to sell the calendar to anyone was another push back against the board. But as with the nickname for the president and the dinners of joking and letting off steam, this resistance did not directly dismantle the structure of relations inside the organization. Throughout the fall of 1999 I wondered whether I would ever see the caseworkers exert their agency in any type of system-altering way. Then in the middle of January, Amalia, one of the younger board members, who had tried repeatedly to get people to take notice of the objectionable actions of the president, decided to resign. Amalia's resignation was the catalyst for a chain of events that eventually led to the ousting of the president.

I ran into Amalia in the center of town right after she had typed up her letter of resignation. She explained that she was tired of being insulted by the president and seeing her insult other people involved with Women United. In her letter she had written:

I want to make it known to the board that my decision to resign was caused by the strong incompatibility with the president of the association. I do not agree with her aggressive and offensive behavior, which is made even more serious by the fact that she represents an association that is dedicated to fighting violence. . . . I believe that in order to help women in difficulty there first needs to be respect between the volunteers and caseworkers of this organization, a value that unfortunately the current president does not understand.

Amalia's letter was the first powerful act of resistance I had seen since I arrived at Women United five months earlier. The very next day Isabella, a caseworker who had been with the organization since the crisis of 1997, announced that she too was disillusioned and disappointed in the organization and had decided to resign. Isabella's decision to leave Women United came on the tail not only of Amalia's resignation, but of another crucial event: the organization's decision to enter a local competition administered by the city government. Women United had been invited to apply, along with Parma's other women's organizations, for a large grant to administer a new temporary safe house for women and children.

At a meeting to discuss the organization's application, much of the discussion centered on complaints that the competition had been created to help a cooperative that had been founded by the women who left Women United during the 1997 crisis. Some of the members of the board had heard from outside sources (friends involved with local government) that the competition itself had been rigged and that the requirements stipulated by the rules of the competition could only be fulfilled by the women working at that cooperative. Both Veronica and Carlotta felt that the organization had to enter in order to be able to protest when the cooperative was awarded the contract. Isabella questioned the gossip circulating about the competition and disagreed with the idea of entering a competition with the sole purpose of challenging another organization; she left the meeting saying she had no time to help out.

When I spoke with Isabella later that evening, she listed the numerous reasons why she could not continue working at Women United. She explained that she disagreed with almost everything the organization was doing—the calendar, the way they were entering the competition, and the fact that none of the board members or volunteers was willing to assume responsibility within the organization.

How many times have we sat down and talked about all the problems. And nothing ever changes. You were here last year when we had the big meeting with the board, and nothing changed. . . . Martina told me if I had the desire and the dedication I would find time for the project. I've worked evenings, weekends, and vacations many, many times. We're always doing things at the last minute. And I would do it again if it were for something I believed in, we believed in, if it was for the women. So don't tell me I don't have dedication and just want things that are easy. The worst violence I have experienced in my life was at Women United. The way Carlotta has treated you, Amalia, Cinzia, me, it is very serious and everyone pretends it doesn't exist. . . . Someone gets called an asshole, stupid, and told to screw off in a women's organization? What do I tell the woman who comes in later saying her husband tells her to screw off; do I tell her to report him to the police?

I listened intently as Isabella let off steam. She voiced her frustration with Women United as well as her exasperation that the organization could be experiencing the same problems as those that occurred during the crisis period of 1997. In the days following Amalia and Isabella's resignations, the atmosphere within the organization grew increasingly morose. The caseworkers were saddened by the resignation of a co-worker and both caseworkers and board members alike lamented the fact that the safe house was sheltering only one woman and had not been full for close to a year. Despite the lucidity and bluntness of Amalia's resignation letter, no special meeting was called. If board members talked about the resignation, I was not privy to those conversations. I did, however, hear that Isabella's resignation was attributed to a lack of dedication and a desire to move on to a more lucrative career. A more pressing issue was the lack of referrals from Parma's social services and other women's organizations in the region. Without the income generated by the safe house, the organization would almost certainly run out of money and be forced to close. The caseworkers blamed the president for arguing with the head of Parma's social services and thereby damaging relations with the organization's primary source of referrals. The president, and some members of the board, blamed the caseworkers for not working hard enough and turning women away out of laziness. The president took me aside at one point to complain that there is a difference between her generation and the younger generation (referring implicitly to the caseworkers and specifically to Isabella): "I'm not saying we're better, I'm just saying we're different. The younger generation thinks of the work here as a job. When they find one that is less stressful, less difficult, they want to leave. They don't have the same commitment."

Throughout the week following Amalia's and Isabella's resignations, discussions continued to focus on whether Women United would be forced to close. Then, one afternoon in January, Martina announced that there would be a meeting the following week to discuss the future of Women United. Everyone was invited—all board members, volunteers, psychologists, lawyers, and caseworkers—to weigh in on whether Women United would close down for good. Martina still wielded great power within the organization despite no longer being president. As the principal founder of Women United (in the early days her office served as the organization's headquarters) she was widely respected within the organization, and though she rarely intervened in affairs outside of her role as board member, when she did everyone involved took it very seriously.

Martina opened the meeting by explaining that the competition sponsored by the local government represented a moment of crisis for Women United. After much discussion the board had decided not to enter the competition because they calculated that the organization did not have enough money or people to handle running a second shelter. Unless something changed, Martina explained, in a short time the organization would run out of funds. Martina characterized the problem as being threefold: first, there was an economic problem; second, there was a problem with the organization's external image; and third, there was a problem with the organization's relations with other groups and entities. The three problems Martina enumerated were closely interrelated. The organization had an economic problem because it no longer had a good reputation in local and regional circles, and the organization no longer had a good reputation because relations were strained between the organization and other groups. Martina expressed her deep personal connection to the organization and pointed out, "Women United has been very important for Parma, for women, and for us." She encouraged the group of board members, caseworkers, and volunteers to figure out how the organization's problems could be resolved.

As soon as Martina opened the meeting up for discussion, voices began to rise, as people began competing with one another for the opportunity to be heard. Some board members asked how the organization's reputation could have deteriorated so quickly. Others wondered why there were no women in the safe house. The vice president expressed concern over the running of the organization and the work ethic of the caseworkers.

We have few volunteers and we aren't capable of handling large projects. The other associations in town have many more paid people. I don't understand why we don't have any women in the safe house. If I worked for the organization and knew my paycheck was coming from the safe house, I would make sure we had a full house. I don't understand. The people who work here have a lack of interest, they turn women away.

At this point there were murmurings of disagreement, but no one came straight out and directly disagreed with the vice president to defend the caseworkers. As a volunteer, I knew that at times the shelter was forced to turn away women, not out of laziness but because of the organization's bylaws. The bylaws prohibit Women United from housing women with alcohol or drug addiction problems, women with male children over fourteen, women who are unwilling to stop seeing their abusive partners, and women with mental disorders.

Martina continually tried to steer the conversation toward the reputation of Women United and whether the organization could regain its credibility, while board members continued to question what had happened to cause strained relations with other organizations. Although it was impossible to find a single cause for the organization's loss of credibility, all of the caseworkers and many of the board members were aware that the president had argued with the head of social services on the streets of downtown Parma. I had heard the story of this public argument numerous times but I noticed that no one was willing to raise this incident or the president's aggressive personality as a contributing factor to the decline in credibility. Then, midway through the meeting, the president got up to leave. She had warned everyone as soon as the meeting started that she had another obligation that evening and would have to leave early. The president's departure gave Cinzia the opportunity to stand up for the other caseworkers and say what no other board member or caseworker was willing to say:

I don't want to hear that women don't come to Women United because the caseworkers are rude when they answer the phone. . . . I'm sorry I have to say this but it needs to be said. The reason we no longer have a relationship with social services and the local government is because Carlotta has argued with everyone, including the head of social services. She called her stupid and incapable. Everyone in Parma has heard the story.

After Cinzia finished speaking, the entire room erupted into a cacophony of voices. The vice president tried to defend Carlotta by refuting the validity of the story. Others said that, regardless of its validity, the story had indeed made its way around the city and the damage was clear. Martina eventually regained control of the meeting. Hours later, when the meeting finally came to a close, the board had decided that although they would not call for new elections, the president would not be allowed to hold external meetings on her own. Martina—one of few people able to keep Carlotta's aggression at bay—would accompany her on all official business. One week after the meeting, Carlotta tendered her resignation.

The president's resignation marked the end of a distinct phase of the history of Women United. Propelled by the resistance of the caseworkers, the board's decision to remove Carlotta from her position of absolute power within the organization allowed for the transformation of everyday relations between board members and caseworkers. Caseworkers were invited to attend board meetings on a rotating basis and, though they were still not entitled to vote, were able to express their opinions and perspectives to the board when various issues came up. Shortly after Carlotta's resignation, a new president was elected by the board, and at the time of this writing, daily life within the organization continued to be far more harmonious and productive. In fact, four years after her election, the new president was still in office, and the organization had expanded its sphere of operation by opening a second safe house and an information booth in the local hospital.

Transformation

The tensions surrounding Carlotta's presidency and the election of a new president reveal more than just the micropolitics of the organization. Despite the fact that men were not present within the group, internal relations and tensions at Women United took shape in ways that mirrored gender tensions in the larger society. In an organization founded *by* women *for* women as a place to find solidarity and support, the presence of hierarchy and the use of gendered oppositions reveal the connection between gender and power, and shed light on the difficulties women face when they try to challenge the system within which their identities as women, and activists, are based.

Within Women United, daily social life reproduced many of the same gender dynamics the women of the organization worked so hard to overturn. This reproduction underscores the way in which, as so many scholars have noted, gender emerges as a key site for the production and reproduction of power. What is interesting about Women United is that the hierarchical relationship between board members and caseworkers, and the caseworkers' strategic use of gender categories to make sense of their subordinate position, illustrates the reproduction of gender relations and gendered hierarchies within an environment composed solely of women. Through their everyday resistance, particularly the parodies of some board members and attributions of "maleness," the caseworkers reproduced the organization's ideological precept to provide solidarity and support for all women, while at the same time revealing the organization's disjuncture between theory and practice.

As the "women" of the group, the caseworkers of Women United saw themselves as providers of the type of support and assistance the organization was founded to provide. They saw the president and particular board members as "men" who wielded power and influence within the organization, controlled the daily decisions and movements of caseworkers, and disrupted their efforts to provide services to women. When I asked caseworkers (and even some board members) why there was such conflict and tension within the organization, their response was invariably linked to the pursuit of power and influence. They explained that women in Italy had to work much harder to achieve powerful positions in society, and in the process became increasingly like men.

Such rhetoric resonates not only within Italian society but within a Western cultural context more generally. Within the United States we often hear debates in the popular press about women in positions of power and discussions of whether women become more "like men" during their rise through the ranks of corporate America, academia, and politics. As Billing and Alvesson (2000) point out in their discussion of the gender labeling of leadership, for many years the traits associated with successful business and management skills were those deemed "masculine" by societal interpretations of gender. Such traits include quantitative and analytic skills, competitiveness, rationality, and an ability to filter out "feelings, vulnerabilities, and dependencies" (144). In recent years, "feminine leadership" has gained increased attention in the business world as something that can make organizations less hierarchical and more flexible and participatory. At the same time, the stay-at-home dad is beginning to emerge as a more acceptable alternative role for men. As women exhibit both "masculine" and "feminine" leadership styles and men exhibit "masculine" and "feminine" approaches to parenting, gendered signifiers begin to separate, ever so slightly, from their signifieds, and gender-bending signs begin to emerge, as evidenced by the discussion of *mammi* (male moms) in the Italian press.

Gutmann warns of the dangers that come from "attributing to masculinity anything and everything that men do" and asserting "that when women are courageous or violent or stoic, they are thereby surely acting like men" (1997b:839–840). Gutmann is of course right that as analysts we should refrain from viewing local cultures through the lens of our own sex/gender system, but when local people themselves use labels of "masculinity" and "femininity," they must be studied as such. Indeed, we must study the very process of naturalization, as it unfolds, and as it shifts according to time, place, and context. Just because the people we work with might declare aggressiveness to be a "male" quality does not mean that we as analysts, by studying or reporting such discussions, are guilty of reproducing essentialized understandings of gender. On the contrary, by exposing the ongoing construction and naturalization of gender we highlight the performance of masculinity and femininity in various cultural settings, and shed light on how such performances can reveal reproduction as well as change.

Daily life within Women United provides an example of the simultaneous reproduction and transformation of the hierarchical gender structure of Italian society. Board members and caseworkers at Women United performed and analyzed their roles within the organization in distinctly gendered ways. Although it may be argued that the case of Women United is evidence of the resilience of the hegemonic and hierarchical structures that shape so much of social life, such a viewpoint fails to account for the subtle but transformative acts of resistance on the part of caseworkers, and the perhaps unsavory but nonetheless transformative acts on the part of board members when they became "more male than men."

I noticed a similar process at work within Family Aid. Although the acts of resistance there were ultimately not as transformative as the sequence of events at Women United, the shelter supervisors at Family Aid, through their personal decisions to have children out of wedlock, or support abortion rights, or tell distinctly different "fairy tales of service," challenged the ideological underpinnings of their organization in their own way. Whether through the subtlety of individual choices, the performance of parody and play, or protest by resignation, the actions of the women working at Family Aid and Women United revealed the disruption of gender norms within Italian society and signaled the possibilities for resistance inside and outside the shelter walls.

CHAPTER 7

Gendered Divides

ILARIA SPENT YEARS FIGHTING against what she termed a "traditional" vision of women, in the realms both of politics and of her private life. Like so many of her friends and colleagues in Udi and other women's groups, Ilaria sought to distance herself and her society from particular understandings of gender relations. In an interview about her experiences as an Udi activist, Ilaria told me about the intensity of their group discussions, the achievements of their political campaigns, and their commitment to creating new forms of gender relations in Italian society.

One afternoon, in the early spring of 2000, we sat for several hours on a terrace that overlooked a vista of urban rooftops. We talked in depth about Ilaria's experiences as a daughter, wife, mother, and Udi activist. During our conversation, an incongruity began to emerge. While Ilaria spoke confidently about her commitment to move society toward new approaches to gender, at the same time she lamented the collapse of "tradition" and the end of an era when people looked out for one another. She spoke of the dissolution of community togetherness and the emergence of a more self-absorbed generation in which "I'm for me and everyone else will have to make do."

Ilaria's nostalgia for a particular understanding of the past, a time when people lived harmoniously and helped one another, emerged in our discussion of class, regional, and ethnic difference. Ilaria compared the migrants from southern Italy that she had grown up with in the 1940s and 1950s to the Albanian immigrants who began coming to Parma in the 1990s. She noted that although structurally the groups were very similar (in that they arrived in Parma with the hope of finding jobs and creating new lives for their families) and faced similar difficulties as outsiders, the opportunities for interaction in the 1950s were very different from the opportunities in the 1990s. She explained,

Today there are a series of status symbols that everyone has. From this perspective there has been a general social leveling. But, at the same time, whereas before there were moments of collective togetherness, in which people exchanged knowledge, cultural models, visions of life, and other things . . . now our worlds are more restricted and separate. There is less communication across different groups, groups themselves are more homogeneous. . . . If there is a group of Albanians, they will speak with other Albanians. . . . Before, it wasn't like this. When I was growing up I knew the southerners, I worked with their children because some of them came to the Pci headquarters . . . I knew everyone, I had tons of fun. . . . Perhaps the distance between groups was great even then, but at least there were opportunities to mix. Now there are very few. Now you won't see a foreign child unless you happen to have a grandchild some day who goes to nursery school. If I go out I see a bunch of well-dressed kids, if I go to work I see a group of colleagues, but I no longer have the feeling there is collective interaction.

Ilaria's simultaneous longing and disdain for particular aspects of the past exemplifies the way in which individuals of a variety of political orientations use the categories both of tradition and of modernity in strategic ways to articulate their visions of the way society ought to be. Just as a Catholic politician might promote the importance of tradition when it comes to marriage and family, and the importance of modernity when it comes to fiscal responsibility, so might an activist like Ilaria express structural nostalgia for community togetherness and structural disdain for patriarchal gender norms. In this book, I have argued for more flexible understandings of tradition and modernity in order to capture the subtleties of this perpetual pull between an imagined past and a future that the present never quite approximates.

Gender presents an interesting context within which to think about what a flexible approach to tradition and modernity can mean for the discipline of anthropology. Just as there have been numerous challenges in recent scholarship to the homogeneity of modernity, there have also been challenges to the uniformity of gender. In an effort to move away from the rigid and essentializing frameworks often based exclusively on Western understandings of gender, feminists are embracing new approaches that integrate gender with the study of politics, power, and difference.

At the beginning of this book, I discussed the response I often heard when I told people in Parma I had come to study intimate-partner violence. Many wondered why I would study partner violence in the north when the south is the place with "traditional" gender relations, the place where women are *sottomesse*, or subservient, to their husbands, the place where women experience intimate-partner violence. The desire to distance the Italian north from the Italian south—an Orientalist division that has been a strong force in Italian political and social life since the peninsula was unified in the 1860s—took on a gendered hue as people responded to my research.[1]

This displacement of partner violence, from the north to the south, is an example of what Jane Schneider argues that northern elites and intellectuals engage in to quell their "anxieties about belonging to Europe" (Schneider 1998:8). By creating a weaker, more traditional, and backward other, northerners are able to reinforce their own dominance and claim kinship with Europe, the very source of high culture and modernity. By separating, at the level of rhetoric, a traditional and inefficient south from a culturally and socially modern north, "the opposition North–South repositions Southern Italy as the territorial watershed between Italy as Europeanized (or Americanized) and Italy as African" (Pandolfi 1998:286–287).[2] This geographical displacement is accompanied by a temporal displacement of intimate-partner violence and patriarchal gender norms from the present to the past. By drawing on a perception of the past that paints gender relations as uniformly patriarchal, individuals can suppress some of their questions about whether contemporary gender relations satisfy the perceived requirements of modernity.

A rape case I read about while working with lawyers in Parma illustrates how the state, as well as local actors, can use such spatial and temporal displacements to defend their positions in local and global hierarchies.[3]

In 1999, a judge in Parma decided to reduce the sentence of a twenty-three-year-old man accused of kidnapping and raping his thirteen-year-old girlfriend. The judge made this decision not because the facts of the case were in doubt, but because both the young man and the girl hailed from a town in southern Italy. The judge explained in his ruling:

It appears uncontestable that the crimes indicated indeed occurred (in the case of the charge of sexual violence the accused admits there were sexual relations but denies having used force). Taking into account the socioeconomic conditions in which these facts took place, the evident immaturity of the boy—convinced, as is custom in many *zone meridionali* [areas of southern Italy], that following an escape with a sweetheart it is necessary to demonstrate virility—it appears just to concede *le attenuanti generiche* [extenuating circumstances].

Such a decision is a clear example of how the spatial displacement of gendered violence from the north to the south of Italy, as well as the temporal displacement from the present to the past, provides a convenient way to deny the violence that occurs in the north and excuse the violence that occurs in the south. The decision also reveals an implicit use of gender and gendered violence as a way of filling the categories of modernity and tradition. If northerners living in Parma can fill the category of "tradition" with particular proficiencies of gender—namely, subservient women and men who rule with an iron fist—it becomes easy to deny that intimate-partner violence is a problem in a "modern" city like Parma.

Yet the categories are not nearly so neat in the lived experiences of the people I knew in Parma. Residents I spoke with praised the city's modernity and at the same time worked hard to preserve many aspects of its tradition—the legacy of Maria Luigia, the *parmigiano* dialect, parmigiano-reggiano cheese, Verdi's operas, even the widespread practice of bicycle riding. Through my research I met individuals like Ilaria, who praised the achievements of Udi but lamented the loss of community togetherness; individuals like Veronica, who was proud of her decision not to become a mother but felt a surge of regret when she saw that her best friend had had a child; individuals like Nuccio, who acknowledged that his violence and infidelity were wrong but remained unsure of how to respond to his wife's new position in society; and individuals like Luisa, Allegra, and Pia, who faced multiple layers of shame while living in violent marital relationships. Many of the women and men I spoke with found themselves negotiating various aspects of their own identities and their relationships with each other in the years following the decline of nationally organized women's groups. The categories of tradition and modernity, old and new, Catholic and communist, and south and north became convenient modes for classifying perceptions of the way gender relations ought to be.

It may be tempting to align the many oppositions within Italian society, and within this very study, into parallel formation, but upon close examination it is clear that the oppositions are far less rigid than they initially appear. For some, Women United may align with communism and modernity, but the organization is also clearly shaped in many ways by its coexistence with Family Aid, Catholicism, and tradition. In fact, it is the dynamic interplay among these oppositions, and their strategic use, that gives meaning and substance to the categories themselves.[4]

Intimate-partner violence is one part of a continuum of gender relations, gender proficiencies, and gender hierarchies that individuals engage with on a daily basis. In a variety of settings—including organizations, marriages, and families—individuals shape such relations, proficiencies, and hierarchies in their own ways, through their own modes of reproduction and resistance. Giovanna and her husband let their potatoes sit in a pan until the potatoes grew into flowers; Franca decided that Saturdays were her day to resist by not cooking a standard multicourse meal. More forceful modes of resistance occurred with the resignations at Women United and when Luisa and Allegra decided that one marriage was enough for a lifetime. Even in a rigidly controlled environment like Family Aid, shelter workers engaged in resistance when they told the fairy tale of their service, and when Claudia explained that "pregnancy is not always a beautiful thing."

By beginning my fieldwork with three different networks of people in Parma—Women United, Family Aid, and the Rocco di Marco neighborhood group—and following various branches of these networks as they wended their way through the city, I was able to learn about daily life among different groups of friends, neighbors, and relatives. At the same time, I was able to see that although there were many divisions among these groups—Catholics and communists, members of Cif and members of Udi, caseworkers at Family Aid and caseworkers at Women United—there were many points of overlap in their stories about the daily negotiation of gender, gender relations, and violence.

Violence against loved ones will always be "defiant of sense-making" (Merry 1994:971), but by situating narratives of violence within a particular cultural context, and as one part of a continuum of hierarchy and subordination, we can draw connections between the negotiation of gender and other processes of meaning formation. Such attention to local processes can help inform new ways of addressing the nearly universal occurrence of intimate-partner violence and provide insight into the challenges, frustrations, and successes people experience as they continually add new meaning to the categories that structure their daily lives.

The cultural specificity of the layers of shame experienced by the women I interviewed in Parma—layers shaped by Catholic norms of family and sacrifice, state norms of marriage and mistreatment, and feminist norms of freedom and autonomy—points to the need for ethnographic work that contextualizes the experience of intimate-partner violence within particular social and political realities. What might these layers of shame look like in other parts of the world? What are the political and social discourses that shape the experience of intimate-partner violence? How do women and men negotiate the competing demands of local and global norms of gender proficiency?

As I mentioned at the very beginning of this book, our mandate, it seems, is twofold: first, we must endeavor to subject violence among intimates to the same theoretical and methodological rigor we use to assess other forms of global violence; and second, we must make our studies accessible to people who can apply the knowledge to locally formed and informed interventions. Just as ethnographies of war, ethnic conflict, and the state can "ask how people engage in the tasks of daily living" and "analyze not only the explicit acts of bodily harm that occur in violent conflict but also the more subtle forms of violence" (Das and Kleinman 2000:2), so can we study and question the violence that occurs in the home and draw links with other forms of culturally legitimate and illegitimate violence. The insight that "perpetrators, victims, and witnesses come from the same social space" (Das and Kleinman 2000:2) takes on heightened meaning when applied to intimate-partner violence. Anthropologists study many forms of violence all over the world; why not study the violence that occurs in the home? Why not study a form of violence in which perpetrators, victims, and witnesses live side by side, not only within the same city or neighborhood but within the very same household?

We would do well to begin by questioning what it means to be a woman and a man, and what it means to be a *good* woman and a *good* man in particular social contexts at particular points in time. If violence is seen as one part of a larger continuum of gender relations, then it makes sense to begin by examining that continuum. Works by Counts, Brown, and Campbell (1992), Merry (1994), Gutmann (1996), and McClusky (2001) have alerted anthropologists to the importance of studying violence among intimates. I hope that such works are only the beginning of growing anthropological attention to the ways in which women and men experience, perpetrate, and resist such violence in their daily lives.

Reference Matter

Notes

INTRODUCTION

1. According to Italian researcher Patrizia Romito (2000), the "Zero Tolerance" campaign was launched in 1997 by the city government of Bologna. This followed on the heels of the United Kingdom's "Zero Tolerance" campaign, which was started in Scotland in 1992. In Bologna, the campaign consisted of commercials, exhibits, meetings, an Internet site, and a national conference. In 1994 the WAVE (Women Against Violence Europe) Network was founded. The network united women's organizations across Europe that were working to put an end to violence against women and children. In 1997, WAVE first received funding from the newly established DAPHNE initiative, which was created by the European Commission to provide support for organizations dedicated to eliminating violence against women and children. Since that time, WAVE has continued to provide a database of organizations, services, articles, research, and other matters pertaining to violence against women, as well as to provide other services to the larger network of women's organizations across Europe (WAVE 2005).

2. During my first year of graduate school I decided that my doctoral research would focus on a Jewish community in northern Italy. I arrived in Bologna that very first summer with the goal of meeting members of Bologna's active Jewish community. On only the second or third day of my trip, I went to the *ghetto ebraico* (Jewish Ghetto) and knocked on the synagogue's main doors. I introduced myself as best I could with my limited Italian and explained that I was an anthropologist from the United States hoping to meet members of the local community. With a look of genuine recognition, the woman who had opened the door ushered me in and proclaimed, "Oh, of course, you're an anthropologist. We have one of our own! He's probably right upstairs eating lunch." I quickly learned that indeed, the Jewish community of Bologna had its own

anthropologist—another anthropology student who had already been working in the community for several summers! It was disconcerting to discover so soon that I would need to find a new project, but the initial disappointment turned into an exciting adventure. The anthropologist I met that day in Bologna is an accomplished scholar and someone I kept in touch with throughout my time in the field.

3. As part of Italy's "red belt," Parma maintained a leftist local government throughout the post–World War II period until 1998, when the city voted in a center-right mayor, Elvio Ubaldi, and thus joined the ranks of other formerly leftist cities in the Emilia-Romagna region. Throughout the post–World War II period, Italy's "red belt" stretched across much of the region of Emilia-Romagna, including cities such as Bologna, Parma, Modena, and Reggio Emilia. Emilia-Romagna was considered "red" because it consistently voted in high percentages for the Italian Communist Party (Partito Comunista Italiano, Pci). In November of 1947, the Pci had close to half a million members in the region, and in the elections of 1946 the Pci and Psi (Partito Socialista Italiano, Italian Socialist Party) together received more than 66 percent of the vote (Ginsborg 1990:201). The Pci and Psi maintained power in the region from the end of World War II through the end of the Cold War. During this period Bologna, the largest city in Emilia-Romagna, emerged as a model for the Communist Party (Kertzer 1980:18).

4. Residents of Parma pride themselves on their aristocratic connection to Maria Luigia (Empress Marie Louise). Maria Luigia was the daughter of Francis I of Austria and the second wife of Napoleon (see Marchesi 1994). In 1816 she was sent to rule the duchy of Parma, Piacenza, and chose Parma to be her capital city. She left a profound mark on the city that is still visible today in the many public works she commissioned (including the famous Teatro Reggio), the violet perfume that she made popular, and the feeling of aristocratic superiority among residents of Parma that many to this day link with her reign.

5. Parma is consistently rated one of the top places to live in Italy by the newspaper *Il Sole 24 Ore*. In 1999, it held the number-one post, with four other cities in Emilia-Romagna following closely behind—Piacenza, Reggio Emilia, and Bologna all placed in the top five (Berselli 1999:25). According to the president of the local *camera di commercio* (chamber of commerce), "Our success has long roots—Parma was the capital of a duchy and maintains an extremely strong cultural tradition . . . the small and medium-sized firms have demonstrated an extraordinary capacity to react to the new challenges of the global market" (Bonicelli 1999:25).

Often referred to as "food valley" because of its strong agricultural sector, Parma hosts one of Europe's most important annual international food expositions. The province of Parma—which includes the *comune* (municipality) of Parma as well as a number of small outlying communities—generates more than half of its annual income from food industries. Parma's parmigiano-reggiano, prosciutto, and tomato products are prized by and exported to restaurants and gourmet shops around the world.

In addition to economic success, another source of pride for residents of Parma is their passion for art, music, and theater. Mayor Elvio Ubaldi, elected in 1998, devoted much attention throughout his tenure to restoring historic aspects of the city center. As journalist Emilio Bonicelli points out, for Parma the model is Salzburg, the Austrian city that has become a European cultural center; and "if Salzburg has Mozart, Parma has Verdi" (1999:25). Parma lays claim to the operatic composer Giuseppe Verdi as well as the conductor Arturo Toscanini, both of whom were born in the province of Parma.

6. This is a study about heterosexual violence, gender relations, and sexuality. Throughout the book, when I speak of gender relations I am referring to heterosexual gender relations. In addition, the focus is on intimate-partner violence against women. Although violence against men certainly exists, I have chosen to focus on violence experienced by women and perpetrated by men.

CHAPTER 1. ENGAGING THE FIELD

1. During the day, automobile traffic in the city center is limited to taxis, buses, police vehicles, and people with resident permits.

See Del Negro (2004) for an extensive discussion of the Italian *passeggiata* and the negotiation of modernity in a small town in central Italy. *Passeggiata* can refer either to a casual walk or stroll, as in *voglio fare una passeggiata* (I want to take a walk), or to the communal promenade that takes place on a daily basis in towns and cities across Italy. Often occurring at dusk, right before or right after dinner, *la passeggiata*, with the definite article "the," usually refers to a stroll in a particular part of the city center where people walk to see and be seen by city residents. Although some form of the *passeggiata* takes place every evening in Parma, the weekend *passeggiata* has many more participants. Del Negro describes the arena for the *passeggiata* in Sasso, a small town in the region of Abruzzo, as consisting of a particular stretch of the city's main street that leads to the central piazza. In Parma there was a similar spatial boundary that primarily included Via Cavour and a stretch of Strada della Repubblica. And just as Del Negro discovered what she terms a "turning point" where strollers would stop and turn around in order to reenter the space of the *passeggiata* (2004:24), I too noticed a particular spot on Strada della Repubblica where people would stop and ever so casually turn around in order to reenter the line of people strolling through the center of town. Just as Del Negro points out, there was no need to disrupt conversation or make a conscious decision—residents intuitively knew the precise place when a turn back was in order.

2. Known as *la vasca* (the basin, or tub) in local jargon, Parma's Via Cavour fills with middle- and high-school students nearly every afternoon after school gets out. On Saturday afternoons the numbers soar, and it is often difficult to navigate a path through the many groups of teenagers who have gathered to socialize with their peers.

This area has many high-end brand-name shops, such as Max Mara, Furla, and Mandarina Duck, but there are also many family-owned stores. Window displays in Parma are works of art in which everything from clothing and shoes to whole legs of prosciutto and large wheels of parmigiano-reggiano are displayed with the utmost attention to design and form. The appearance of a store window is often just as important as what is inside.

3. Such comments resonate with what Del Negro found in her work on the *passeggiata* in the town of Sasso. Del Negro reports that "in the townsfolk's most negative representation, the passeggiata is described as a 'passerella' (fashion runway)—a shallow and self aggrandizing display of Sasso's recently acquired wealth" (2004:37). Del Negro underscores the theatrical and performative elements of the *passeggiata* and points to the care with which the younger women of Sasso dressed for the daily occasion. She notes that it was important to be *"presentabili* (presentable, suitably dressed) and *in ordine* (neat, tidy, well put together)," which often required changing from "inside wear" to "outside wear" (2004:25,27). I noticed a similar attention to clothing among residents of Parma and found that women and men of all ages were concerned with their presentation of self. My next-door neighbor was a tailor who catered almost exclusively to male clients who came to him for handcrafted suits of impeccable quality. Like Del Negro, I too noticed that people not only paid attention to clothing but actually cared for their clothing to a far greater extent than I was used to in the United States. And as Del Negro notes, it was far more important to have several high-quality outfits than to have a "large wardrobe of mediocre items" (2004:27). It was quite acceptable to wear the same outfit two days in a row; many people changed out of their more formal clothing as soon as they came into the house.

4. I am grateful to Professor Maria Minicuci for explaining the nuances of *bella* and *brutta figura.*

5. In Parma, one's financial troubles are ideally always hidden. I was told numerous times—always in generic terms—that there are people who walk through the streets in expensive brand-name clothing but do not have enough money to buy meat for dinner. A local newspaper article written to expose Parma's hidden poverty opens with the sentence *La povertà abita anche a Parma,* or "Poverty also exists in Parma" (Ginepri 1999). The article goes on to tell the stories of people living at the poverty level in Parma. Although there is much discussion about the problems faced by new immigrants—overcrowded apartments, lack of food and essentials, the difficulties involved in finding jobs and affordable apartments—the poverty of those who are native to Parma is rarely discussed.

6. There is a spirited rivalry between Parma and Reggio Emilia. Like other Italians, residents of Parma display a strong sense of *campanilismo* (parochial rivalry) when it comes to their home city (see Galt 1992; Counihan 2004; Del Negro 2004).

7. In Parma, as in much of Italy, class is largely dependent on family background. Occupation and education are important, but the most defining factor in determining class identity is family status. Although many families in Parma maintain their class status for generations, others are able to maneuver

their way into higher class levels, as evidenced by many of the new wealthy industrial families. In the span of two or three generations, these families have transformed local bakeries and butchers into large-scale multinational corporations. As Sylvia Yanagisako argues in her analysis of family-run silk firms in the northern Italian city of Como, embracing a static understanding of class can blind us to "the diverse historical trajectories of the people who constitute a class at a particular point in time." Only through a more dynamic understanding of class and class subjectivity, Yanagisako argues, can we understand how individual subjectivities change and transform (Yanagisako 2002:96). In Parma and much of Italy, class mobility often takes place on a family rather than individual basis. Del Negro found a similar emphasis on family, and notes that although "one can invoke class transcendence through fashion and style," such performances are often recognized as such, for "one is always someone's daughter or son with a collectively known past" (2004:40).

In his work on recent Italian history, Paul Ginsborg divides Italian society into several social classes (2003:39–62). At the top, he places the *grande borghesia*, a group that can be further divided into the families of old money, power, and stature, and the *nouveaux riches*. According to Ginsborg, the next level in the contemporary class hierarchy is that of the dominant "modern middle classes," comprising the upper middle classes (which include professionals, entrepreneurs, managers, politicians, and others) and the lower middle classes (which include shopkeepers, artisans, white-collar workers, and others). The working classes (industrial workers, workers in small firms, and service workers) make up the lower rungs of Ginsborg's hierarchy. At the very bottom are the roughly 10–15 percent who lived in poverty during the 1980s and 1990s.

Ginsborg's depiction of class is similar to what I discovered in the course of my fieldwork in Parma. I learned that the highest class in Parma is the noble class, which is made up of people who are present-day counts and countesses. Although I never personally met anyone of this class, my friend Amalia assured me that there are still quite a few of these noble families living in Parma who can trace their connection to nobility back for generations. A step below this noble class is the wealthy class, or *alta borghesia* (high bourgeoisie). This class may be divided into two groups: the *industriali* (industrialists) such as the Barilla, Tanzi, and Greci families (founders of the multinationals Barilla, Parmalat, and Greci respectively), and the *liberi professionisti* (free professionals) such as the families with generations of *notai* (notaries), lawyers, or other high-earning occupations. The next class, as described to me by my friend Amalia, is the *media borghesia* (middle bourgeoisie), which comprises people who have university degrees and work as professionals or high-level employees in the public or private sector.

When I asked Amalia what class our mutual friend Chiara would fall into, Amalia paused and said, "Well, her mother had a degree in pharmacy and her father was a doctor, so yes, she would be part of the *media borghesia*." For Amalia, it did not matter that Chiara herself had neither a university degree nor a high-paying job. She came from an intellectual and professional family, which was enough to secure her position in the *media borghesia*. Amalia, who also did not have a university degree or a professional position, classified herself as belonging to the *popolari* (popular) class. Others have termed this class the *piccola borghesia* (petite bourgeoisie). In Ginsborg's classification, this would correspond to the lower middle class. Amalia's mother was a housewife and her father owned a successful furniture repair business. Although Amalia lived in roughly the same economic bracket as Chiara, her family's more humble shopkeeping origins placed her a notch below in terms of Parma's class hierarchy. Amalia's class includes, among others, families with small businesses, teachers, lower-level employees, and government workers. The *classe operaia*, or working class, comes next in the class structure, and includes people who come from families of factory workers, construction workers, truck drivers, school custodians, and other manual laborers. The lower class in Parma is represented by poor families with parents who either are unemployed or have only part-time or seasonal work. In Parma, the lower class has been augmented throughout the past century by the migration of southerners searching for a better life in the north, and in recent years by the influx of immigrants, primarily from Africa, Eastern Europe, and the Balkans.

8. According to research conducted in the late 1990s in the northern Italian province of Trieste, among recipients of social services (women 18 to 92 years of age) 6 percent reported physical or sexual intimate-partner violence in the previous year. In a different study that involved a representative sample (women 25 to 60 years of age) the findings went up to 8 percent (Romito 2000:61). Patrizia Romito extrapolates that between 20 and 30 percent of women in Trieste have experienced either physical or sexual intimate-partner violence at some point in their life (61).

9. "Mentality" has been used throughout the twentieth century as a way to "characterise what is held to be distinctive about the thought processes or sets of beliefs of groups or of whole societies" (Lloyd 1990:1). As Lloyd points out, French sociologist Lucien Lévy-Bruhl (1923) used and popularized the term *mentalité* as an essentialist device to distinguish a primitive, "pre-logical mentality" from the "logical or scientific mentality" of Western civilizations (1990:1). Herzfeld (1997) takes up the question of social or cultural mentality by pointing out the spuriousness of applying any sort of division between logical and pre-logical mentalities to the study of nationalism and cultural intimacy. He does so by connecting the concept of mentality to the Greek word *noötropia* (a description of particular national stereotypes), which Greeks use to distinguish themselves from outsiders and construct a discourse of national pride. Herzfeld alerts us to the fact that anthropologists have largely ignored the construct of mentality despite its broad popular use. He argues that mentality should be treated not as an "analytical construct for studying national differences, but as an artifact used in the construction of those differences and as an important link in the relationship between nationalism and scholarship" (1997:79).

10. The reluctance to speak of an "Italian mentality" makes sense given the general lack of national unity and pride among Italians, except at national

sporting events such as the Olympics and World Cup soccer. One potential reason for this lack of national pride is Italy's relatively late formation as a political unit. As Denis Mack Smith notes, "Up to 1859–61 the regions were still politically divided, with different historical traditions of government and law. . . . Dozens of different customs barriers existed along the course of the River Po—a striking example of that municipalism or *campanalismo* which impeded national unification" (1997:3–4). Much of this *campanalismo*, or local pride, continues to this day.

11. These scholars include Lila Abu-Lughod (1998), Deniz Kandiyoti (1997, 2002), Lisa Rofel (1999), Aihwa Ong (1999), Dorothy Hodgson (2001), Heather Paxson (2004), and Elizabeth Krause (2005).

12. Care for the elderly is a significant addition to the household work and child care for which women are often responsible. Throughout my time in Parma I met numerous women, usually in their fifties and sixties, who cared for elderly relatives on a daily basis. Many of these women worked long days in the office and came home to face the demands of their own households as well as the demands of sick or elderly relatives. For women, care for the elderly (*la cura degli anziani*) involves not only caring for one's parents but also caring for one's in-laws (usually a husband's parents), and aunts and uncles who may not have children of their own.

13. My findings resonate with much of what Carole Counihan (2004) learned through her extensive research on food and gender in Florence in the 1980s and 1990s. According to Counihan, "Because Italian standards for neatness and meal complexity were demanding, household chores took a lot of time. In addition to all food preparation and cleanup, women reared children, did piles of laundry, ironed everything down to the underwear, swept and dusted every day, washed the bathroom and kitchen floor every day, and often mended clothes and darned socks as well" (2004:80).

14. When I spoke with Italian friends about the expression *lavoro di cura*, some were surprised I had heard it used to describe the caretaking work performed *by* family members *for* other family members. As my friend Carolotta explained, "I can say that a nurse, a social worker, or an immigrant employed inside the home practices *lavoro di cura*, but if I am talking about my mother and her elderly parents, I say that she takes care of them." When I asked Carolotta why she would not use the term to describe her mother's caretaking work, she told me that her mother does this work out of love, not out of obligation. To suggest otherwise could even be seen as offensive. Through additional research I discovered that although the term *lavoro di cura* was not as colloquial as I had originally thought, it had gained traction through the work of researchers and activists focused on alleviating the burden of household labor shouldered primarily by married women. In 2003, for example, the head of Parma's Council on Equal Opportunity (Assessorato alle Pari Opportunità) dedicated the year to the theme of *condivisione del lavoro di cura fra i generi e le generazioni*, or sharing the caretaking work among genders and generations. Activities included a regional conference, various research projects, and even a publicity campaign

to raise awareness of the message *lavori di cura a cura di ognuno,* or "caretaking work cared for by everyone" (Pari Opportunità 2004).

15. In 2002, Italy's highest appeals court ruled in favor of a thirty-year-old man who sued his father for cutting off his monthly allowance of US$675 (Riding 2002). The father was wealthy and could easily afford the allowance but argued that his son had a law degree and that it was time his son "stopped turning down job offers and claiming that a well-paid and fulfilling opening would eventually come along." Parental obligations have no legal age limit in Italy, and many parents are more than happy to have children remain at home through their thirties. The court reinforced the obligations of parenthood when it ruled that the son in question was not responsible for supporting himself "where labor conditions do not satisfy his specific qualifications, his attitudes and his real interests, so long as there is a reasonable possibility of satisfying his aspirations within a limited time, and support is compatible with the economic possibilities of the family" (Riding 2002).

16. The number of *stranieri* (foreigners) who reside in the province of Parma (which includes many smaller towns and villages as well as the city of Parma) increased from 5,944 in 1995 to 27,724 in 2005—almost a fivefold increase over the span of ten years. The greatest numbers have emigrated from Albania, Morocco, Tunisia, Moldavia, India, the Philippines, Romania, and Senegal. Within the city of Parma in 2005 there were 13,376 registered foreigners, which is approximately 7.7 percent of the city's overall population (Borani 2005). Although it is impossible to know precisely how many foreigners are living in Parma illegally, it is safe to assume there are at least as many unregistered as registered immigrants. The issue of immigration in Italy has been addressed by Carter (1997), Cole (1997), Lunghi (2003), and others. Although immigration is an important issue to explore in Parma, the topic is outside the bounds of this particular study.

17. *Mammo* is *mamma* with a masculine "o" ending. During my fieldwork I read the term in local and national media, but rarely heard it used in everyday conversation.

18. The stereotype of spoiled children is nothing new for Italy. In Luigi Barzini's dated but well-known book *The Italians,* he writes of the Italian family: "There must be children, of course, lots of children, especially sons who can carry on the name. Nothing should be spared to produce them. Everything is done for them in Italy. They are the protagonists of Italian life. Their smallest wishes are satisfied" (1964:193).

19. It is important to note that many of these generalizations, particularly those that come from media sources, do not take into account the tremendous variation among the different regions of Italy. A trend that is pronounced in northern regions such as Emilia-Romagna or Lombardia or Veneto may or may not be as prevalent in central and southern regions of Italy. Most of Italy (aside from Venice, Trieste, and Rome) was united as a country in 1861 (Smith 1997:7), ,but the country retains many linguistic and social differences to this day. Birthrates, family size, residence patterns, and cultural practices can vary greatly from region to region.

20. With the high percentage of unemployment, low entry-level salaries, and high housing prices, many young people live at home because they simply cannot afford to move out. There are others, of course, like the lawyers, consultants, and other highly paid professionals I met in Parma, who live with their parents because it is easier, because they do not want to hurt their parents, and because they would feel lonely living alone. In many families, children are encouraged to focus on their studies or their careers, and although some may contribute economically or otherwise to the household, many do not. One exception to the trend of Italian children remaining at home well into their thirties is the population of students who enroll in universities far away from their home towns and cities. Many of these students share apartments with other out-of-town students and return home on weekends to be with their families and friends from high school.

21. Some also leave the parental household to *convivere*, or live with a partner.

22. Anthropological scholarship has responded to the work of Butler (1990) and others by devoting attention to the historical and cultural malleability of gender through studies of the body, the performativity of gender, and issues of narrative and subjectivity, but the dilemma of how to contribute to a feminist project without reinforcing a static, reified, or natural conception of "women" or "gender" remains only partially resolved.

This problem of essentialism and reification was addressed in the 1970s and 1980s by scholars working on issues of race and ethnicity. The primordialist view, articulated by Edward Shils (1957), Clifford Geertz (1963), and others was displaced by the work of Frederick Barth (1969) and others. Part of the problem facing feminist studies is that, conceptually, the field has been stymied by the issue of binary biological essentialism. Whereas studies of ethnicity and race were able to distance themselves from primordial notions of ethnicity, naturalized ideas of sex and gender have proved much more difficult to think past.

Although the concept of strategic essentialism, as defined by Gayatri Spivak (1986), is an apt description for what marginalized groups do when they gloss intragroup differences by playing up standardized, essential characteristics to create realms of common strategic political interest, as a theory it does not help academic feminists find their way out of the quagmire of reification. Spivak herself notes that the phrase has been misinterpreted to mean that feminists can be both anti-essentialist and essentialist depending on the situation and what is politically at stake (Nicholson 1997).

The problem for academic feminists is that essentialism, no matter how strategic, perpetuates a universalized and reified understanding of "women." As Butler reminds us, "Strategies always have meanings that exceed the purposes for which they are intended" (1990:4). Linda Alcoff states the problem succinctly when she writes, "The dilemma facing feminist theorists today is that our very self-definition is grounded in a concept that we must deconstruct and de-essentialize in all of its aspects" (1997:330–331). Alcoff's solution is to argue for a positional definition of woman that "makes her identity relative to a continually shifting context, to a situation that includes a network of elements involving others" (1997:349). It would then be possible to use the content of such contexts as a platform for feminist political action.

23. See Belmonte (1979), Kertzer (1980), and Brenner (1998).

24. It may become clear from my portrayals of the three organizations that one is a richer account of the group's internal social life. This is due to the different positions I held within the three groups and the differences in the organizations themselves. Although I was involved in day-to-day life in both Women United and Family Aid, Women United was a smaller organization which provided me with more intimate and sustained contact with the caseworkers and board members. Because of my position within the organization and the close friendships I developed with caseworkers, board members, and volunteers, I often found myself spending a considerable amount of time (outside of business hours) with the women of Women United. As anthropologists in the field are always "in the field," the social events I attended with the women of Women United (dinners, parties, outings) provided further opportunities for me to understand intimate aspects of local daily life. My role within Family Aid, a much larger organization, was largely limited to my shifts as an evening and weekend shelter supervisor and weekly meetings at the organization's headquarters. Unlike Women United and Family Aid, the Rocco di Marco neighborhood group did not have a physical location and met several times a month at various neighborhood locations. As such, there was no institutional social life in which to participate.

25. There have been numerous ethnographic studies conducted in Italy by both native and foreign scholars—including Belmonte (1979), Blok (1974), Cornelisen (1969, 1976), Corriga (1977), Davis (1973), Douglass (1984), Galt (1991, 1992), Goddard (1996), Minicuci (1981, 1988, 1989), Papa (1985), Pardo (1996), Pitkin (1985), Schneider and Schneider (1976, 2003), Signorelli (1983), Siebert (1991, 1999), and Silverman (1975), among others—but until recently, ethnographic work in Italy has focused primarily on southern regions and on towns and villages as opposed to cities. Work by Kertzer (1980, 1996), Li Causi (1993), and Signorelli (1996) called attention to the importance of conducting fieldwork in urban settings within Italy, and in recent years, work by Carter (1997), Counihan (1988, 2004), Feldman (2001), Krause (2001, 2005) and others have responded to this call through their ethnographic focus on northern, urban areas.

26. I have chosen to use the Italian term *ragazza*, rather than the English translation "girl," which does not accurately capture the use or meaning of the term. *Ragazza* is a common term of address for young women through their thirties (as is the corresponding *ragazzo* for young men). It is neither offensive nor disrespectful, and the plural *ragazze* or *ragazzi* is even used by people in their fifties and sixties to refer to friends or a social group. More formal terms of address such as *signorina* or *signora* are used for business interactions and would not have been appropriate in this context.

27. In addition to the humorous interconnections between my various net-

works, there were a few occasions when my separate social spaces intersected in a less comfortable way. One such occasion came about when a woman I first met at Women United went to live in a shelter run by Family Aid. During the period of time when the woman's situation was of direct concern to both organizations, I found myself evading questions in order to preserve confidentiality.

Another uncomfortable situation occurred when I met with a group of women who used to be part of Women United but had left to open their own cooperative in town. Although I was not planning to become involved with the cooperative, I thought that taking one of their sewing classes could be a good way to meet more people and learn more about the organization. One day, shortly after I had signed up for the course, I received a call at Women United. The volunteer who answered the phone was surprised to receive a call from the cooperative and even more surprised to hear that they wanted to speak with me. After the call, I explained what I was doing and why I was interested in taking the course. The volunteer gave me a big smile and said she was great friends with the women at the cooperative and that she herself was interested in taking classes there. This reaction initially surprised me as I knew there was a great deal of tension between the two organizations. Then, almost as an afterthought, the volunteer told me that the particular class I had chosen seemed very boring and that although she would never take such a class, I was free to do what I wanted. For the next few hours I agonized about what to do. Would it be best to take her comments at face value, ignore the underlying message, and go ahead and take the class? Or was the risk of alienating the volunteer and perhaps all of Women United too great? In the end I decided that my contacts and friendships at Women United were far too valuable and important to take such a risk. Although a bit disappointed that I had decided to play along with town politics, I knew that in the end the conflict between the women and the organizations was too large for me to navigate on my own. I also could not help wondering whether the cooperative's decision to call me at Women United, rather than at home, was somehow an indication of a hope to use me as a pawn in the larger conflict.

28. The vast majority of my interviews were tape-recorded, but occasionally they were not. In addition to presenting a written form that explained my research and provided guarantees of confidentiality, I also gave each interviewee the option not to be tape-recorded. I myself made the decision not to use a tape-recorder when interviewing lawyers, judges, and reporters. In the chapters that follow, I draw freely from these interviews. Any statements or passages within quotes represent direct translations from interviews and conversations when I had either a tape recorder or a pen and notebook in hand. Any statements or passages without quotes represent reconstructions of conversations. Except where indicated, all translations are my own.

29. Psychologists who volunteered for Women United occasionally used the term "trauma" in talks and lectures, but the language of trauma and post-traumatic stress disorder (PTSD) was not part of everyday discourse within Women United and Family Aid.

CHAPTER 2. POSTFEMINIST UNCERTAINTIES

1. Much work has been done on gender, feminism, and the intersection of family, work, and women's lives in Italy. See Beccalli (1994), Bono and Kemp (1991), Birnbaum (1986), Cicioni and Prunster (1993), Hellman (1987), Kemp and Bono (1993), de Lauretis (1990), Rossi-Doria (1996), Marcuzzo and Rossi-Doria (1987), and Passerini (1991, 1993, 1996), among others, for detailed accounts of the Italian women's movement and feminism in Italy. See Minicuci (1981, 1988), Pandolfi (1991), Papa (1985), Saraceno (1980, 1987, 1998), Siebert (1991, 1999), Signorelli (2000), and Oppo et al. (2000), among others, for accounts of women's lives in various parts of Italy.

2. Judith Butler (1990) also speaks of a "postfeminist" period, but her use of the term refers to an intellectual theoretical positioning that followed the criticisms of theories of universal patriarchy and the collapse of universal understandings of the feminist project. Butler writes: "Perhaps there is an opportunity at this juncture of cultural politics, a period that some would call 'postfeminist,' to reflect from within a feminist perspective on the injunction to construct a subject of feminism" (1990:5).

3. In 1974 a referendum to overturn the divorce law was defeated by 20 million votes to 13 million (Birnbaum 1986:271). In 1981 two referendums to change the abortion law (one sponsored by the Catholic group Movimento per la Vita, the other sponsored by the Partito Radicale) were defeated by large margins (Passerini 1996:146).

4. The Foucaultian concept of surveillance (Foucault 1979) is helpful in understanding the way in which the women are controlled through the ideological discourse and methodology of the organizations. At Family Aid, there is also a physical component of surveillance in that some of the women living in the shelters are subject to twenty-four-hour supervision.

5. These women are popularly referred to locally, as elsewhere in Italy, as *ragazze madri* (girl mothers). The term "single mother" or "single parent" does not have an equivalent in colloquial Italian.

6. Throughout the post–World War II period in Italy, there were two dominant and competing ideological systems, and corresponding political parties—the Communists (Pci) and the Christian Democrats (Dc). Following the defeat of fascism in Europe, the coalition that had worked to pass a new constitution in the 1945–47 period divided into two camps during the 1948 election: the Communists and the Socialists on one side, and the Christian Democrats and their allies on the other (Ginsborg 1990:115; Pratt 1996:134). It was a bitter fight, as "the election was fought not just for control over the state but to determine the position Italy was to occupy within the emerging world order, and, it was said, for the heart and soul of the Italian people" (Pratt 1996:135). The Dc won the election of 1948, a victory that marked the beginning of nearly four decades of rule by the Dc (or a Dc coalition) and Pci opposition.

7. A good friend in Parma who worked for the supermarket chain Panorama explained that, being *di sinistra* (on the political left), she was ideologi-

cally more closely aligned with the management at the competing supermarket chain, COOP. Other leftist friends in Parma told me that they refused to shop at Standa (a department-store and supermarket chain) because it was owned by Silvio Berlusconi, the leader of the right-leaning party Forza Italia.

8. Kertzer was one of the first anthropologists to write an ethnography of urban life in northern Italy. His book *Comrades and Christians: Religion and Political Struggle in Communist Italy* (1980) paved the way for a new generation of Italian anthropology that moved away from a preoccupation with towns and villages in southern Italy. More than a decade after Kertzer did his fieldwork, Luciano Li Causi (1993) conducted a study of communist life in Siena, a central-Italian city known for its "red" history. The resulting book, *Il partito a noi ci ha dato!: Antropologia politica di una sezione comunista senese nel dopoguerra*, traces an ethnographic history of Pci members in a Siena neighborhood.

9. The Church and the Dc engaged in many forms of anticommunist propaganda, portraying communists as, among other things, devils, animals, and barbarians. The Church even went so far as to excommunicate all communists through an "Avviso Sacro" issued in 1949 (Kertzer 1980:106). Although the decree was interpreted in different ways by different parish priests and was ultimately revoked, the fact that it was passed illustrates the degree to which the Church was involved in the political battle over the future direction of the Italian state.

The Communist Party also fought vigorously against the Catholic Church and the Dc, but instead of demonizing Catholicism, the party sought to create a division between Catholicism and the Church in the minds of voters. As Kertzer explains, "The Pci fought its battle on two levels. On one, it sought to win over the masses to communism by discrediting the Church. On the other, it sought to erase any fears among the people that it was anti-Catholic" (Kertzer 1980:115). In fact, many card-carrying Italian communists continued to attend mass and participate in Catholic rituals. What would seem to be an irreconcilable ideological contradiction was managed quite adeptly by Italians who were able to integrate both the politics of communism and the religion of Catholicism into their daily lives.

10. Kertzer (1980) points out the "structural similarity" between the Church and the Pci when he explains that both "try to place themselves at the center of their adherents' social, political, ritual, and ideological life" (1980:249). Although historically the Pci and the Dc were diametrically opposed, it is through this opposition to one another that they are closely tied. Without the threat of communism, the Dc would not have been able to generate such enthusiastic support, just as without the threat of the Vatican's power, the Pci would never have been able to mobilize as many people. Kay B. Warren (1998) notes a similar process in her work on the Pan-Mayanists and grassroots popular Left activists of Guatemala. Warren suggests that although they were fundamentally opposed in their ideologies, it was through this opposition that each movement was forced to adjust its ideological positioning.

11. Although members of the Pci were clearly part of the political left, it is important to point out that as a political distinction, "Catholic" did not

necessarily correspond to the right of the political spectrum. The Dc was a centrist party with both left-leaning and right-leaning members. Following the collapse of Italy's first republic and the creation of a new political landscape, former Dc members went on to join a variety of political parties, both left and right of center.

12. There are two main branches within the leftist feminist movement in Italy. As Elisabetta Addis (1989) notes, the histories of leftist Italian feminism written in the late 1980s "read as if two parallel histories had unfolded." One tradition has its roots in the Italian political left, borrows from the Marxist principle of class struggle, and views political and legal change as key components of the feminist cause; the other "descends from a French philosophical and psychoanalytic tradition and holds that only that which a free woman is willing to say to other women is an advance for feminism" (Addis 1989:1).

13. Both Udi and Cif were financially and politically connected to the Communist and Christian Democratic parties, respectively.

14. Within Italian feminist discourse, a woman has *autorevolezza* (literally, "authority") when she is recognized within herself, outside of any existing hierarchy or structure of power within society.

15. See Nicholson (1997), Mitchell and Oakley (1986), and Cott (1987) for discussions of American feminism; see Moi (1987) and Fraser and Bartky (1992) for discussions of French feminism; and see Birnbaum (1986), Bono and Kemp (1991), Hellman (1987), and de Lauretis (1990) for discussions of Italian feminism.

16. In the United States, there were two women's movements in the 1960s: the women's rights movement and the women's liberation movement (Nicholson 1997). The women's rights movement united many working women in the fight against gender discrimination. This movement was focused on achieving practical results for the lives of everyday women. The women's liberation movement, on the other hand, developed out of the new left within the United States and has been the source of many of the theoretical works associated with second-wave feminism (Nicholson 1997). Women involved with the women's liberation movement focused on explaining the depths of women's oppression through history. Many engaged with Marxist and structuralist thought to come up with new theories that accounted for the subordination of women. In the late 1960s and 1970s, the women's liberation movement divided over the question of sameness versus difference (Nicholson 1997). Many liberation feminists supported the idea that "women and men were basically the same" (1997:3), and used this to argue for changes in the basic structures of society; other feminists, who became known as "radical" feminists, began to move away from this line of thinking. Radical feminism, exemplified by the work of Kate Millett (1970) and Shulamith Firestone (1970), and gynocentric feminism, exemplified by the work of Carol Gilligan (1982) and Nancy Chodorow (1978), focused on the differences between men and women. As Juliet Mitchell and Ann Oakley (1986) point out, early radical feminism is perhaps best represented by Firestone's *The Dialectic of Sex* (1970), in which Firestone argues that there are basic and fundamental biological facts that underlie women's subordination. According to

Firestone, it is the "biological family," the "sexual-reproductive organization of society," that forms the basis of cultural superstructure.

17. See Chodorow (1978) and Gilligan (1982).

18. *Grand Hotel* was a popular serial publication that used photographs of actors in comic-book style to recount soap-opera-genre plots.

The reference to comic books resonates with David Kertzer's (1982) interview of an Udi activist. While discussing the importance of the women's magazine *Noi Donne* (We Women), the activist, Evelina Zaghi, explained, "It's a magazine that many women find difficult to read, because it's a feminist magazine without any comics. It deals with serious problems women face, like the cottage industry and women working in the factories . . . All those who just read the comics, about Annabella and the princess and the queen, it's disgraceful; it doesn't solve anything" (Kertzer 1982:56).

19. *Sfigato* usually translates as "unlucky," but in this case Giovanna used the term to mean that men had lost their place in society.

20. Being a believer, *essere credente*, is often used in Italy to refer to someone who believes in God and the principles of Catholicism. This does not necessarily mean that the person supports the ecclesiastical hierarchy and the institution of the Church. Indeed, it can at times be used to distinguish those who do not follow Church doctrine from those who do.

21. These governments have been led by the following presidents of the Council of Ministers: Giuliano Amato (1992–93), Carlo Azeglio Ciampi (1993–94), Silvio Berlusconi (1994), Lamberto Dini (1995–96) Romano Prodi (1996–98), Massimo D'Alema (1998–2000), Giuliano Amato (2000–2001), and Silvio Berlusconi (2001–2006).

22. The "clean hands" investigation implicated numerous members of the Italian political establishment and resulted in a series of corruption charges and trials.

23. As of 2002, there were more than fifteen major political parties in Italy, including Alleanza Nazionale (National Alliance), Centro Cristiano Democratico (Christian Democratic Center), Cristiani Democratici Uniti (United Christian Democrats), Comunisti Unitari (Communist Party), Democratici di Sinistra (Democrats of the Left), Democrazia Europea (Democrats of Europe), Federazione dei Verdi (Green Federation), Fiamma Tricolore (Tricolored Flame), Forza Italia (Go Italy), Democratici (Democrats), Lega Nord (Northern League), Partito Liberale (Liberal Party), Partito Popolare Italiano (Italian People's Party), Partito della Rifondazione Comunista (Communist Refoundation Party), Socialisti Democratici (Socialist Democrats), Radicali (Radicals), and Unione Democratici per l'Europa (Democratic Union for Europe).

CHAPTER 3. POLITICS OF GENDER AND SHELTER

1. See Paxson (2004) for a discussion of the concept of gender proficiency.

2. Kertzer points out that despite a theoretical stance that advocated a change in gender relations, in practice scant attention was paid by the Pci to

the position of women in Italian society. Based on his work in Bologna, Kertzer argues, "There is certainly no expectation locally that a man, by joining the Party, will thereby change his traditional views of male superiority. Women are expected not only to earn money but also to take care of the children and the apartment and always to have meals ready for their husbands" (1980:60).

3. By "younger generation" I mean women in their early twenties to early thirties; with "older generation" I refer to the mothers of these women, who were in their fifties and sixties.

4. Caseworkers would often refer women to the volunteer lawyers and psychologists, who offered counseling free of charge. Although they could not provide professional services as part of their volunteer work with the center (lawyers could not provide legal representation and psychologists could not offer therapy), they could and did provide advice and guidance. The women were free, if they so chose, to seek out legal representation and/or therapy by visiting the lawyers and the psychologists in their respective offices. Although the professional advice was very helpful for the women, I noticed that from time to time the caseworkers grew frustrated when their own services, as caseworkers, were not fully utilized by the women coming to the center. In supervision meetings the caseworkers spoke of the importance of encouraging women to come back to the center not just for professional services, but to meet with caseworkers on a weekly or monthly basis.

5. According to women who had been involved with Parma's Biblioteca delle Donne (Women's Library)—a feminist collective in Parma with close ties to the French philosophical strand of leftist Italian feminism—in recent years many groups have adopted the idea of gender and sexual difference without understanding or practicing the theory of *il pensiero della differenza sessuale* (the thought of sexual difference). For the women once involved with Parma's Biblioteca delle Donne, sexual difference is a political project that recognizes that there is no such thing as a neutral body, and holds that only through relationships with other women (scholarly conversation, political dialogue and engagement) will women emerge as subjects.

6. Kroeber was interested in classification and how people arrive at different systems of classification. He did not, however, believe that one could a priori assume a link between systems of classification and social institutions. This is where he disagreed with Rivers, who argued that kinship terminology is a direct result of the social structure of society (Radcliffe-Brown 1952:60).

7. The list was a cooperative effort developed by a group of leftist women's centers in the Emilia-Romagna region. Although each center is administered and funded independently, there is a regional network that facilitates cooperation among them. The standardized checklist enables the centers to collaborate more easily on a variety of projects.

8. There are three different police forces in Italy: the military police, known as *carabinieri*, the state police, known as *polizia*, and the local police, known as *vigili urbani*. Nearly every town has *carabinieri* and *vigili urbani*, but only the larger cities and provincial capitals have *polizia*. As the capital of the province of Parma,

the city of Parma has all three. In rough terms the *vigili urbani* are responsible for directing traffic, issuing tickets, and doing street patrols, while the *polizia* are responsible for criminal investigations, responding to criminal emergencies, and overseeing the issuing of passports and work permits. The *carabinieri* are a part of the military and handle many of the same higher-level crimes as the *polizia*. In an emergency, the residents of Parma can call either 113, which rings at the headquarters of the *polizia*, or 112, which rings at the headquarters of the *carabinieri*. A *denuncia* (complaint/report) may be filed with either force. In theory, all three police forces work together and cooperate with one another, but in practice this is not always the case. Many of the *vigili urbani* I met often felt slighted by the *polizia* and disrespected by the general public. They complained that the community does not respect their authority and thinks of them as merely the people who write traffic tickets.

9. There are only a handful of founders who are still active with Parma's Family Aid organization. Many of the new volunteers do not have a history of Catholic feminist activism or involvement with Cif.

10. In 1999, Parma's Family Aid organization provided assistance (including food and clothing) to a total of 498 women, of which 393 were foreign and 105 were Italian. During my year of fieldwork, however, roughly one-third of the women living in Family Aid's first-stage (supervised) shelters at any given time were Italian.

11. Jeff Pratt explains that the importance of charity and working to help others is part of a "Christocentric shift within Catholicism" that emphasized the life of Jesus Christ—his teachings, charity, and sacrifice. This shift "involved also a reminder of his commandment to love one's neighbour (*il prossimo*) and that a Christian life is lived not just through private acts of devotion and the sacraments, but in acts of love, charity, and fellowship with other human beings" (1996:137).

12. The women of Women United, on the other hand, always referred to the women seeking help as "women" and addressed them with the formal *lei* during meetings. The women of Women United sought to minimize the power differential between the woman seeking help and the woman offering help by emphasizing their common identities as women.

13. This shift is due in part to the rise in immigration throughout the 1990s. Although the number of young Italian women seeking help has gone down, the increasing number of foreign women needing assistance means that the organization still serves large numbers of women.

14. According to statistics produced by the Italian statistics agency, ISTAT, the total number of voluntary abortions performed in Italy declined steadily during the eighties and nineties, from 231,008 in 1982 to 132,073 in 2001. Per 1,000 women aged 15–49, 16.7 had abortions in 1982, and only 9.1 had abortions in 2001. For the region of Emilia-Romagna, the numbers per 1,000 declined from 24.6 in 1982 to 10.4 in 2001 (ISTAT 2004).

CHAPTER 4. TWO SIDES OF SHAME

1. *Vergogna* can be linked to the notion of *brutta figura*, as feelings of shame are likely to accompany the cutting of a poor figure. The emotion or feeling of *vergogna* can stem from the actions one takes (or doesn't take) as well as from the way one is made to feel by others; it can encompass dishonor, disgrace, and embarrassment as well as guilt.

2. One pivotal incident that Luisa brought up many times in our discussions occurred at a point during their relationship when Luisa was extremely busy taking care of her father, who was sick in the hospital. Between work and going to the hospital, Luisa barely had time to eat. It was during this period that Davide decided to bring home a stray dog. Instead of caring for the dog himself, Davide just added the dog to the pile of household duties Luisa was already attending to. When she got home in the evening after a full day of work and many hours spent in the hospital, Luisa had to prepare dinner and then take the dog out for a walk. Reflecting back on this period she acknowledges that it was caring for the dog that pushed her beyond her breaking point.

3. For many of my friends and colleagues in Parma, the moral code of the Catholic Church had a presence in everyday life, regardless of whether they thought of themselves as religious. For example, friends who never attended church, and defined themselves as *laici* or non-religious, said they would probably still baptize their children so as not to deprive them of that particular rite of passage. In a similar way, regardless of one's own religious identity, local Catholic norms about marriage, motherhood, and family, as well as ideas of sin and sacrifice, combined with the masculinist norms of the state to shape the feelings of *vergogna* many women experienced.

4. In local discourse about violence against women, the phrase *subire violenza* is almost always used. Literally translated as "to endure violence," the phrase refers to the experience of violence on the part of the victim. In many instances, the phrase is somewhat ambiguous. For example, the sentence, "*Questa signora ha subito violenza per cinque anni*" (This woman has endured violence for five years) can mean both that she experienced violence for five years and that she put up with violence for five years. *Subire violenza* is also ambiguous in that *violenza* can be used to refer to physical, psychological, or sexual violence. The word "abuse" (*abuso, ingiuria*) is rarely used in local discourse to refer to violence against women, whereas "violence" (*violenza*) and "mistreatment" (*maltrattamento*) are often employed.

5. The Cretan sheep thieves Michael Herzfeld (1985) worked with saw priests as "antisocial beings" who were outside of the "normal reciprocities of social life" and distrusted them because of it. In spite of this distrust, talking about sheep theft in local coffee shops was likened to "confession." In Italy, I observed that priests were at times seen as trustworthy precisely because of their distance from ordinary social relations, but at other times were viewed with suspicion.

6. There are some priests who follow papal law to the letter, but there are

others who voice their disagreement with certain laws, particularly those prohibiting contraception and divorce, and make their own decisions regarding what does and does not qualify as a sin.

7. Prosciutto is used in Parma as an appetizer, a light second course, a filling for sandwiches, a topping for pizza, and as an ingredient in a wide variety of dishes. For many Parmigiani, the best way to eat prosciutto is with *torta fritta*, square pieces of dough that when fried in pig lard become rich, slightly sweet pockets of bread filled with air.

8. In one of her radio conversations at Radiotre (published in 1980), Chiara Saraceno spoke with Laura Balbo by telephone and together they discussed the *doppia presenza* (double presence) of women in Italian society. In their discussion Laura Balbo refers to the work of Ilona Kickbusch, who defined three dimensions of family labor: (1) the work of maintenance, (2) the work of consumption, and (3) the work of relationships. Balbo and Saraceno explain how these three aspects of family labor take shape in the Italian context and require work both inside and outside the home. The work of maintenance involves caring for and cleaning the home, maintaining appliances, and tending to other household possessions. The work of consumption includes shopping for food and other goods, choosing where and what to buy, and transporting the purchases back home. It also, however, includes the "work of bureaucracy," which means navigating the various levels of bureaucracy in Italian society, whether for school, a mortgage, the hospital, or any of the many institutions that provide services but require patient and skillful maneuvering. Finally, the work of relationships involves maintaining relationships within the nuclear family (husband and children) but also includes caring for the elderly and maintaining ties with members of the extended family (Saraceno 1980:161–167).

9. In another chapter of her radio conversations at Radiotre (1980), Chiara Saraceno suggests that certain aspects of household labor actually increased with the introduction of "timesaving" appliances such as washing machines, electric irons, and vacuum cleaners. According to Saraceno, tasks that were once done every six months became tasks that could be done on a regular basis. People began changing their clothes more often, which meant more washing and more ironing. When *il bucato* (the laundry) was done by hand and took two days, clothes were washed far less frequently, and the standards for cleanliness were far less stringent. Saraceno suggests that the same is true for other aspects of household labor. With the introduction of new appliances and the shift of paid labor out of the home and into the factories, the "standards of maintenance" intensified and the roles assigned to women increased. Saraceno's suggestion that the standards of "a 'beautiful house,' a house 'in order'" are far higher than those of fifty years earlier (1980:84) echoed much of what I heard from friends and colleagues in Parma.

10. Italy routinely ranks as one of the European countries that provides the least amount of support for families, and during the 1990s the amount of money spent on family support actually declined (*La Gazzetta di Parma*, Nov. 6, 1999:2).

11. According to data on Parma produced by ISTAT from the 1990 census, 60 percent of women and 97 percent of men worked outside the home. In 2000 there was an unemployment rate of 6.3 percent for women and 2.9 percent for men (Servizio Stampa e comunicazione della Giunta, Emilia-Romagna).

12. See Chapter 1 for statistics on grown children in Italy living in their parents' homes.

13. According to a paper presented in 1999 by a representative from ISTAT, the average age at which Italian women marry rose from 25.6 in 1990 to 27.1 in 1996 (statistics for first marriages only). The average age at which women give birth to their first child rose from 26.9 in 1990 to 28.1 in 1996 (Sabbadini 1999). Separate data have shown that in Italy, life expectancy at birth went from 69.0 for men and 74.9 for women in 1971 to 76.2 for men and 82.6 for women in 2000 (ISTAT 2001).

14. The desire to *fare bella figura* surely shapes the desire to provide an abundance of high-quality dishes and a variety of wines and other beverages, especially in cases of "official" meals for colleagues or other professional purposes. It is important to note, however, that the desire to provide good food and wine, particularly for family and close friends, also stems from the cultural understanding of food as means of expressing one's pleasure at being in the company of loved ones.

15. It is curious that the example of men pushing baby carriages often came up as an example of new understandings of manhood and masculinity. One reason might be that pushing a baby carriage is a public act. Some men may also be doing the laundry and cleaning the house, but such tasks are usually done in private, and men who do them may be reluctant to admit to this blurring of roles. Pushing a stroller, however, takes place outside and often during the daily *passeggiata*, when residents of Parma publicly perform various aspects of their identity. Clearly, for many men and women, pushing a baby carriage has emerged as part of what it means to be a modern father.

CHAPTER 5. GENDER PROFICIENCIES

1. Public competitions, or *concorsi*, are used as standard hiring procedure for positions in many areas of state and local government. Schoolteachers, office workers, state functionaries, police personnel, postal workers, and non-elected positions throughout government offices and agencies are all hired through the *concorso* process. Participants in *concorsi* are not only competing against the many other entrants, they are also competing against the strength of the *rac-comandazione* (a recommendation from someone with ties to the people making decisions). Many routinely complain it is impossible to win a position through a *concorso* without having connections or engaging in corruption.

2. The Italian legal system is based on the principle of civil law. Unlike common law, which developed in medieval England and derives from a system of precedents, civil law originated in ancient Rome and is defined by the presence of written codes. These codes are a form of social regulation and provide struc-

ture and guidance for many realms of individual and community life. They determine not only the legality or illegality of various actions but outline the rules for many aspects of social life, including the rights and responsibilities of marital and kin relations. As a unified nation since the 1860s, Italy has had two civil codes: the 1865 Civil Code, which closely resembled the Code Napoléon, and the 1942 Civil Code, which was instituted in the era of Mussolini (Cappelletti et al. 1967). Although there is a large volume of legislation that remains uncodified, the current civil code addresses many aspects of Italian society and includes books titled "Persons and the Family," "Succession," "Property Rights," "Obligations," "Labor," and "Protection of Rights." The 1942 Civil Code is still in use today, but there have been significant revisions, including substantial changes enacted in 1975 in the area of family law.

3. See de Grazia (1992) for a detailed account of the treatment and experiences of women under Italian fascism.

4. In 1961, the Constitutional Court upheld the discrepancy in punishment by arguing that differential treatment for adultery does not violate the principle of equality outlined in Article 3 of the Constitution. According to the court's ruling, when a wife has extramarital relations it causes more serious damage to family structure and unity. Although the court acknowledged that a husband's adultery can also damage family unity, it ultimately ruled that the conduct of an unfaithful wife represents a worse offense and can "affect the most delicate structure and the most vital interests of a family," particularly when there are young children who must "think of the mother in the arms of a stranger" (Corte Costituzionale, Sentenza 28, Nov. 1961, n. 64). In 1968, this judgment was overturned, and the court declared the disparity in punishments to be unconstitutional. The new judgment argued that "the law, by not attributing relevance to the adultery of the husband and punishing that of the wife, puts the latter in a state of inferiority where she is forced to endure infidelity and has no protection in criminal court" (Corte Costituzionale, Sentenza 19, Dec. 1968, n. 126).

5. Specifically, articles 144 and 145 of the Civil Code.

6. Cecilia asked me to use her real name rather than a pseudonym.

7. Lidia requested *patrocinio gratuito*, which enables those unable to afford legal fees to have free representation by young lawyers who are just beginning their careers.

8. A judicial separation, as opposed to a consensual separation, is when the judge hears both sides and issues a ruling on the terms of the separation.

9. For many years, abandoning the conjugal household without documented reason was a crime under Italian law. Although the specific crime no longer exists, abandoning the conjugal household without documented reason can still be cause for a *denuncia*, because a spouse who does so violates the marital duty of cohabitation. Whenever a married woman decided to leave her husband, and her home, to live with friends, relatives, or in a shelter, the lawyers at Women United always encouraged her to notify her husband by telegram in order to avoid the possibility of a police report.

10. Cecilia explained that at first Lidia's husband refused to pay anything at all, even though the judge had ordered him at the initial hearing to pay £1,500,000 a month. He had slowly begun paying £600,000 or £700,000 per month, but never the full £1,500,000. At the meeting to decide on the terms of the consensual separation, Cecilia decided to accept the £900,000 per month, reasoning that her client was more likely to receive the monthly alimony if it was a figure both parties had agreed upon.

11. Title XI of the Italian Penal Code of 1930, titled "Crimes Against the Family," contains the following four headers: Crimes Against Marriage, Crimes Against Family Morality, Crimes Against the State of Family, and Crimes Against Family Assistance (Padovani 1997).

12. Judgment no. 3032, Corte di Cassazione, Section 6 (March 13, 1987).

13. Judgment no. 4015, Corte di Cassazione, Section 6 (April 17, 1996).

14. According to Laura McClusky, some domestic-violence researchers have developed a theory of "status-inconsistency," which "suggests that in societies maintaining a gender hierarchy, men are likely to beat their wives if their wives reach a status higher than their own" (McClusky 2001:5).

15. The word *fidanzato/a* is a loose term that can refer to a boyfriend or girl-friend, a fiancé(e), or even an extramarital romantic partner.

16. A *casa* (house/home) for most people in Parma is an apartment. Couples often live their whole lives in the apartment they purchase and move into as newlyweds.

17. The English word "trauma" was used commonly in both its clinical and colloquial meanings.

18. Leonardo was referring to women who supposedly go to Greece to drink, party, and engage in sexual relations without worrying about the moral codes of their parents, neighbors, or society.

19. The father in the classic 1977 film *Padre Padrone* (a portrayal of pastoral life and father/son relationships in rural Sardinia, directed by Paolo and Vittorio Taviani and based on the autobiography of Gavino Ledda) is an archetype of the classic *padre padrone*, master of family and household. The power of husbands and fathers over wives and children was not only a cultural norm, it was explicitly part of the Italian Civil Code until the reform of family legislation in 1975.

20. Indeed, many individuals remember only certain aspects of the past while choosing to forget others. For instance, both critics and supporters of "traditional" gender roles may remember the explicit rules of behavior while conveniently forgetting the way in which individuals circumvented, resisted, or challenged such rules.

CHAPTER 6. ENGENDERING RESISTANCE

1. Each week the shelter supervisors, social workers, and president met with a psychologist to discuss daily life within the shelters. Discussions usually focused on issues and problems within the shelters and how best to help the

residents. The meetings enabled the women working in the shelters to communicate with the women in the main office and make sure everyone was on the same page regarding strategies to follow with particular residents and in the running of the shelters.

2. Every week the caseworkers participated in a supervision meeting (led by a psychologist who volunteered her time) to discuss the various women they had worked with during the previous week. It was a time for the caseworkers to share their experiences and emotions and to receive advice from their coworkers.

3. A vulgar word for "prostitute."

4. Gaia would frequently refer to the caseworkers as "náani," which means "honey" or "dear" in dialect. Although a perfectly acceptable term of endearment among family members and very close friends, Gaia's use of the term in a work setting confirmed her lack of sophistication in the eyes of the caseworkers.

Proper use of Italian grammar in non-intimate settings—outside the realm of family members and close friends—is an indication of class, as it can demonstrate the level of education one has received. Upon meeting a new person, my more intellectual and *borghese* (middle-class) friends in Parma would at times comment on how well the person spoke Italian, primarily focusing on whether he or she used the subjunctive tense in the proper manner. Colleagues at Women United would often infer the education level of a client by her command of language and grammar.

The local dialect, called *parmigiano*, is used by both lower and upper classes, but in distinctly different and marked ways. The use of dialect or a mix of dialect with standard Italian in everyday conversation—when buying groceries or meeting an acquaintance on the street—can immediately mark someone as being from the countryside and of a lower class. On the other hand, the use of dialect in poetry or theater or the use of certain expressions among relatives and close friends can signify a degree of intellectualism and connection to one's heritage. For example, some of my colleagues at Women United who had university degrees and had spent years of high school studying Latin and reading the classics of Italian literature would speak flawless Italian while conducting the business of the organization—meeting with social workers and local officials, working with other women's shelters in the region, and speaking with doctors, lawyers, and psychologists. At other times, while sipping a cocktail in the *piazza* or taking a cappuccino break during work, they would use phrases of *parmigiano* when telling stories or engaging in lighthearted discussions. Some of the more widely used phrases include: *co' díit?* instead of the Italian *cosa dici?* (what are you saying?) or *co' féet?* instead of the Italian *cosa fai?* (what are you doing?).

5. I myself learned of the benefits of the *raccomandazione* while getting a foreigner's permit of stay (*permesso di soggiorno*). After I got up early in the morning on multiple occasions to wait in long lines leading out of the foreigners' office (*ufficio stranieri*) of the local police station, only to be told I was lacking the proper documentation, a friend put me in touch with his brother, who worked

in the foreigners' office. I called the brother, and he told me to drop by any afternoon and he would take care of everything. A few days later I went to the office during off hours with all my papers, chatted with the people working in the office, and had my permit in a matter of minutes.

CHAPTER 7. GENDERED DIVIDES

1. Stereotypes within and outside Italy portray the Italian south as socially and culturally "backward" and "behind" the rest of Italy. Edward C. Banfield labeled southern Italians "amoral familists" in his 1958 book, *The Moral Basis of a Backward Society*, because of the "inability of the villagers to act together for their common good or, indeed, for any end transcending the immediate material interest of the nuclear family" (Banfield 1958:10). Other scholarly and popular works have reinforced this dualistic picture of a politically and economically modern north and a traditional, inefficient, and parasitic south (see Schneider 1998 for a full review of Italy's "Southern Question").

2. In fact, the depiction of southern Italy as closer, both socially and geographically, to Africa, was used by the separatist Lega Nord party during its rise to power in the 1990s.

3. See Herzfeld (2004) for a discussion of the "global hierarchy of value" and the "double-edged sword" of tradition. In Herzfeld's analysis, tradition is revealed to be both a pedestal and a tethering post for Cretan artisans who exist at the very margins of a global modernity and are assigned the task of reproducing tradition for the Greek nation-state.

4. David Kertzer begins his book *Comrades and Christians* (1980) by discussing the separate worlds of Catholicism and communism that divided Italian social and political life for decades, but ends it by talking about the overlaps and intersections that are covered up by the "two worlds" concept. On an analytic level it makes sense that both communism and Catholicism created separate social spheres with "comprehensive systems of beliefs and behavior, that are mutually exclusive" (Kertzer 1980:2). The problem with such an analysis, as Kertzer argues, is that it tells us very little about the commonalities between the two systems, and even less about what people really do in their everyday lives. There are intersections and similarities at the macro level of ideology as well as the micro level of individual practice.

Works Cited

Abu-Lughod, Lila, ed. 1998. *Remaking Women: Feminism and Modernity in the Middle East*. Princeton, NJ: Princeton University Press.

Addis, Elisabetta. 1989. *What Women Should Ask of the Law: Italian Feminist Debate on the Legal System and Sexual Violence*. Cambridge, MA: Minda de Gunzburg Center for European Studies, Harvard University.

Alcoff, Linda. 1997. "Cultural Feminism Versus Post-Structuralism: The Identity Crisis in Feminist Theory." In Nicholson, *The Second Wave*, 330–355.

Antolisei, Francesco. 1992. *Manuale di diritto penale*. Edited by Luigi Conti. Genoa: Giuffrè.

Antze, Paul, and Michael Lambek, eds. 1996. *Tense Past: Cultural Essays in Trauma and Memory*. New York: Routledge.

Appadurai, Arjun. 1996. *Modernity at Large: Cultural Dimensions of Globalization*. Minneapolis: University of Minnesota Press.

Aretxaga, Begoña. 1997. *Shattering Silence: Women, Nationalism and Political Subjectivity in Northern Ireland*. Princeton, NJ: Princeton University Press.

Argyrou, Vassos. 1996. *Tradition and Modernity in the Mediterranean: The Wedding as Symbolic Struggle*. New York: Cambridge University Press.

Arkell, Thomas. 1994. "Crisis of Confidence." *Geographical Magazine* 66:14–15.

Arosio, Enrico. 1999. "Mammone e me ne vanto." *L'Espresso* August 19:40–43.

Balbo, Laura, Maria Pia May, and Giuseppe A. Micheli. 1990. *Vincoli e strategie nella vita quotidiana: una ricerca in Emilia-Romagna*. Milan: F. Angeli.

Banfield, Edward C. 1958. *The Moral Basis of a Backward Society*. Glencoe, Il: Free Press.

Barbagli, Marzio, and Chiara Saraceno, eds. 1997. *Lo stato delle famiglie in Italia*. Bologna: Il Mulino.

Barth, Fredrik, ed. 1969. *Ethnic Groups and Boundaries: The Social Organization of Cultural Difference*. Boston: Little, Brown.

Barzini, Luigi. 1964. *The Italians*. New York: Atheneum.

Bassi, Tina Lagostena. 1993. "Violence Against Women and the Response of Italian Institutions." In Cicioni and Prunster, *Visions and Revisions*, 199–213.

Bassi, Tina Lagostena, Agata Alma Cappiello, and Giacomo F. Rech, eds. 1997. *Violenza sessuale: 20 anni per una legge*. Rome: Presidenza del consiglio dei ministri, Commissione nazionale per la parità e le pari opportunità tra uomo e donna.

Beccalli, Bianca. 1994. "The Modern Women's Movement in Italy." *New Left Review* 204:86–112.

Belmonte, Thomas. 1979. *The Broken Fountain*. New York: Columbia University Press.

Beltramo, Mario, Giovanni E. Longo, and John Henry Merryman, trans. 1969. *The Italian Civil Code*. Dobbs Ferry: Oceana.

———. 1996. *The Italian Civil Code and Complementary Legislation*. Dobbs Ferry, NY: Oceana.

Berdahl, Daphne. 1999. *Where the World Ended: Re-Unification and Identity in the German Borderland*. Berkeley: University of California Press.

Berselli, Edmondo. 1999. "Il benessere corre sulla via Emilia." *Il Sole 24 Ore* December 27:25.

Bhabha, Homi. 1994. *The Location of Culture*. London; New York: Routledge.

Billing, Yvonne Due, and Mats Alvesson. 2000. "Questioning the Notion of Feminine Leadership: A Critical Perspective on the Gender Labelling of Leadership." *Gender, Work, and Organization* 7(3):144–157.

Birnbaum, Lucia Chiavola. 1986. *Liberazione della Donna: Feminism in Italy*. Middletown, CT: Wesleyan University Press.

Blok, Anton. 1974. *The Mafia of a Sicilian Village, 1860–1960: A Study of Violent Peasant Entrepreneurs*. Oxford: Blackwell.

Bonicelli, Emilio. 1999. "Parma tra cultura e impresa." *Il Sole 24 Ore* December 27:25.

Bonilini, Giovanni. 1998. *Manuale di diritto di famiglia*. Turin: Unione Tipografico-Editrice Torinese.

Bono, Paola, and Sandra Kemp, eds. 1991. *Italian Feminist Thought: A Reader*. Oxford: Blackwell.

Borani, Paolo Camuti, et al. 2005. *La popolazione residente nei comuni della provincia di Parma—Struttura per età e sesso—famiglie—stranieri*. Parma: Provincia di Parma.

Bourdieu, Pierre. 1986. *Distinction: A Social Critique of the Judgement of Taste*. Trans. Richard Nice. London: Routledge and Kegan Paul.

Bourque, Susan C., and Kay B. Warren. 1981. *Women of the Andes*. Ann Arbor: University of Michigan Press.

Bozdoğan, Sibel, and Reşat Kasaba, eds. 1997. *Rethinking Modernity and National Identity in Turkey*. Seattle: University of Washington Press.

Brandes, Stanley. 1987. "Reflections on Honor and Shame in the Mediterranean." In Gilmore, *Honor and Shame and the Unity of the Mediterranean*, 121–134.

Brenner, Suzanne April. 1998. *The Domestication of Desire: Women, Wealth, and Modernity in Java*. Princeton, NJ: Princeton University Press.

Brown, Wendy. 1995. *States of Injury: Power and Freedom in Late Modernity*. Princeton, NJ: Princeton University Press.

Budgeon, Shelley. 2001. "Emergent Feminist (?) Identities: Young Women and the Practice of Micropolitics." *The European Journal of Women's Studies* 8(1):7–28.

Burke, Carolyn, Naomi Schor, and Margaret Whitford, eds. 1994. *Engaging with Irigaray: Feminist Philosophy and Modern European Thought*. New York: Columbia University Press.

Butler, Judith. 1990. *Gender Trouble: Feminism and the Subversion of Identity*. New York: Routledge.

Cappelletti, Mauro, John Henry Merryman, and Joseph M. Perillo. 1967. *The Italian Legal System: An Introduction*. Stanford, CA: Stanford University Press.

Carter, Donald Martin. 1997. *States of Grace: Senegalese in Italy and the New European Immigration*. Minneapolis: University of Minnesota Press.

Castellaneta, Domenico. 1999. "Portava i jeans, non fu stupro." *La Repubblica* February 11: Cronaca 10.

Chodorow, Nancy. 1978. *The Reproduction of Mothering: Psychoanalysis and the Sociology of Gender*. Berkeley: University of California Press.

Cicioni, Mirna, and Nicole Prunster, eds. 1993. *Visions and Revisions: Women in Italian Culture*. Providence, RI: Berg.

Cioni, Elisabetta. 1997. "Il sistema di parentela." In Barbagli and Saraceno, *Lo Stato delle Famiglie in Italia*, 214–223.

Cole, Jeffrey. 1997. *The New Racism in Europe: A Sicilian Ethnography*. Cambridge and New York: Cambridge University Press.

Collier, Jane Fishburne. 1997. *From Duty to Desire: Remaking Families in a Spanish Village*. Princeton, NJ: Princeton University Press.

Coontz, Stephanie. 1992. *The Way We Never Were: American Families and the Nostalgia Trap*. New York: Basic Books.

Cornelisen, Ann. 1969. *Torregreca: Life, Death, Miracles*. Boston: Little, Brown.

———. 1976. *Women of the Shadows*. Boston: Little, Brown.

Corriga, Giannetta Murru, ed. 1977. *Etnia, lingua, cultura: un dibattito aperto in Sardegna*. Cagliari: Edes.

Cott, Nancy F. 1987. *The Grounding of Modern Feminism*. New Haven, CT: Yale University Press.

Counihan, Carole. 1988. "Female Identity, Food, and Power in Contemporary Florence." *Anthropological Quarterly* 61(2):51–62.

———. 2004. *Around the Tuscan Table: Food, Family, and Gender in Twentieth-Century Florence*. New York: Routledge.

Counts, Dorothy Ayers, Judith K. Brown, and Jacquelyn C. Campbell, eds. 1992. *Sanctions and Sanctuary: Cultural Perspectives on the Beating of Wives*. Boulder, CO: Westview Press.

———. 1999. *To Have and to Hit: Cultural Perspectives on Wife Beating*. 2nd ed. Urbana and Chicago: University of Illinois Press.

Cowan, Jane. 1990. *Dance and the Body Politic in Northern Greece*. Princeton, NJ: Princeton University Press.

Daniel, E. Valentine. 1996. *Charred Lullabies: Chapters in an Anthropography of Violence*. Princeton, NJ: Princeton University Press.

Das, Veena, and Arthur Kleinman. 2000. "Introduction." In *Violence and Subjectivity*, ed. Veena Das et al., eds., 1–18. Berkeley: University of California Press.

Davis, J. 1973. *Land and Family in Pisticci*. New York: Humanities Press.

de Grazia, Victoria. 1992. *How Fascism Ruled Women: Italy, 1922–1945*. Berkeley: University of California Press.

Delaney, Carol. 1987. "Seeds of Honor, Fields of Shame." In Gilmore, *Honor and Shame and the Unity of the Mediterranean*, 35–48.

de Lauretis, Teresa. 1990. "The Practice of Sexual Difference and Feminist Thought in Italy." In Milan Women's Bookstore Collective, *Sexual Difference*, 1–21.

Del Negro, Giovanna P. 2004. *The Passeggiata and Popular Culture in an Italian Town: Folklore and the Performance of Modernity*. Montreal and Ithaca: McGill-Queen's University Press.

de Sandre, Paolo. 1997. "La formazione di nuove famiglie." In Barbagli and Saraceno, *Lo Stato delle Famiglie in Italia*, 65–75.

Desjarlais, Robert. 1997. *Shelter Blues: Sanity and Selfhood among the Homeless*. Philadelphia: University of Pennsylvania Press.

Desjarlais, Robert, et al. 1995. *World Mental Health: Problems and Priorities in Low Income Countries*. New York: Oxford University Press.

Di Leonardo, Micaela. 1984. *The Varieties of Ethnic Experience: Kinship, Class, and Gender Among California Italian-Americans*. Ithaca, NY: Cornell University Press.

Douglas, Mary. 1966. *Purity and Danger: An Analysis of Concepts of Pollution and Taboo*. London: Routledge and Kegan Paul.

Douglass, William A. 1984. *Emigration in a South Italian Town: An Anthropological History*. New Brunswick, N.J.: Rutgers University Press.

Firestone, Shulamith. 1970. *The Dialectic of Sex: The Case for Feminist Revolution*. New York: Morrow.

Feldman, Jeffrey. 2001. "Ghetto Association: Jewish Heritage, Heroin and Racism in Bologna." *Identities: Global Studies in Culture and Power* 8(2):247–282.

Fong, Vanessa. 2004. *Only Hope: Coming of Age under China's One-Child Policy*. Stanford, CA: Stanford University Press.

Forgacs, David, and Robert Lumley, eds. 1996. *Italian Cultural Studies: An Introduction*. Oxford and New York: Oxford University Press.

Foucault, Michel. 1965. *Madness and Civilization: A History of Insanity in the Age of Reason*. Trans. Richard Howard. New York: Pantheon.

———. 1979. *Discipline and Punish: The Birth of the Prison*. Trans. Alan Sheridan. New York: Pantheon.

Fraser, Nancy, and Sandra Lee Bartky, eds. 1992. *Revaluing French Feminism: Critical Essays on Difference, Agency and Culture*. Bloomington: Indiana University Press.

Galt, Anthony H. 1991. *Far from the Church Bells: Settlement and Society in an Apulian Town*. Cambridge and New York: Cambridge University Press.

———. 1992. *Town and Country in Locorotondo*. Fort Worth, TX: Harcourt Brace.

Gazzetta di Parma, La. 1999a. "Fra gli ultimi in Europa per gli aiuti alle famiglie." November 6:2.

———. 1999b. "I 'lavori forzati' delle donne occupate." December 16:1.

———. 1999c. "Il Vescovo: poche nascite." December 23:8.

Geertz, Clifford. 1963. "The Integrative Revolution: Primordial Sentiments and Civil Politics in the New States." In *Old Societies and New States: The Quest for Modernity in Asia and Africa*, University of Chicago Committee for the Comparative Study of New Nations, ed. Clifford Geertz, 105–157. New York: Free Press of Glencoe.

———. 1983. *Local Knowledge: Further Essays in Interpretive Anthropology*. New York: Basic Books.

George, Glynis. 1996. "Contested Meanings and Controversial Memories: Narratives of Sexual Abuse in Western Newfoundland." In Antze and Lambek, *Tense Past*, 45–63.

Gewertz, Deborah, and Frederick Errington. 1996. "On PepsiCo and Piety in a Papua New Guinea 'Modernity.'" *American Ethnologist* 23(3):476–493.

Giannessi, Belinda. 2004. "Voiceless Woman: Observe, But from the Centre." *European Journal of Women's Studies* 11(4):445–454.

Gilligan, Carol. 1982. *In a Different Voice: Psychological Theory and Women's Development*. Cambridge: Harvard University Press.

Gilmore, David, ed. 1987. *Honor and Shame and the Unity of the Mediterranean*. Washington, DC: American Anthropological Association.

Gilsenan, Michael. 2002. "On Conflict and Violence." In MacClancy, *Exotic No More*, 99–113.

Ginepri, Patrizia. 1999. "Quei poveri della porta accanto." *La Gazzetta di Parma* March 3:11.

Ginsborg, Paul. 1990. *A History of Contemporary Italy: Society and Politics, 1943–1988*. London and New York: Penguin.

———. 2003. *Italy and Its Discontents: Family, Civil Society, State, 1980–2001*. New York: Palgrave Macmillan.

Goddard, Victoria A. 1996. *Gender, Family, and Work in Naples*. Oxford and Washington, DC: Berg.

Golini, Antonio. 1999. "Six Billion and Beyond: Italy Perspectives," PBS. Electronic document, www.pbs.org/sixbillion/italy/it-golini.html, accessed August 28, 2002.

Golini, Antonio, Antonio Mussino, and Miria Savioli. 2000. *Il malessere demografico in Italia: una ricerca sui comuni italiani*. Bologna: Il Mulino.

Gordon, Linda. 1988. *Heroes of Their Own Lives: The Politics and History of Family Violence: Boston, 1880–1960*. New York: Penguin.

Guha, Ranajit, and Gayatri Chakravorty Spivak, eds. 1986. *Selected Subaltern Studies*. New York: Oxford University Press.

Gutmann, Matthew. 1996. *The Meanings of Macho: Being a Man in Mexico City*. Berkeley: University of California Press.

———. 1997a. "Trafficking in Men: The Anthropology of Masculinity." *Annual Review of Anthropology* 26:385–409.

———. 1997b. "The Ethnographic (G)ambit: Women and the Negotiation of Masculinity in Mexico City." *American Ethnologist* 24(4):833–855.

Hacking, Ian. 1996. "Memory Sciences, Memory Politics." In Antze and Lambek, *Tense Past*, 67–87.

Handler, Richard, and Jocelyn Linnekin. 1984. "Tradition, Genuine or Spurious." *Journal of American Folklore* 97(385):273–290.

Hautzinger, Sarah. 2003. Review of *Here, Our Culture Is Hard*, by Laura McClusky. *American Ethnologist* 30(3):470.

Hellman, Judith Adler. 1987. *Journeys Among Women: Feminism in Five Italian Cities*. New York: Oxford University Press.

Herman, Judith Lewis. 1992. *Trauma and Recovery*. New York: Basic Books.

Herzfeld, Michael. 1980. "Honour and Shame: Problems in the Comparative Analysis of Moral Systems." *Man* 15:339–51.

———. 1985. *The Poetics of Manhood: Contest and Identity in a Cretan Mountain Village*. Princeton, NJ: Princeton University Press.

———. 1991. "Silence, Submission, Subversion: Toward a Poetics of Womanhood." In Loizos and Papataxiarchis, *Contested Identities*, 79–97.

———. 1997. *Cultural Intimacy: Social Poetics in the Nation-State*. New York: Routledge.

———. 2004. *The Body Impolitic: Artisans and Artifice in the Global Hierarchy of Value*. Chicago: University of Chicago Press.

Hochschild, Arlie. 1989. *The Second Shift: Working Parents and the Revolution at Home*. New York: Viking.

Hodgson, Dorothy. 2001. "Of Modernity/Modernities, Gender, and Ethnography." In Hodgson, *Gendered Modernities*, 1–23.

Hodgson, Dorothy, ed. 2001. *Gendered Modernities: Ethnographic Perspectives*. New York: Palgrave.

Horn, David. 1994. *Social Bodies: Science, Reproduction, and Italian Modernity*. Princeton, NJ: Princeton University Press.

Irigaray, Luce. 1993. *Je, Tu, Nous: Toward a Culture of Difference*. Trans. Alison Martin. London: Routledge.

ISTAT (Istituto Nazionale di Statistica). 2001. *Parentela e reti di solidarietà: Indagine Multiscopo sulle famiglie "Familiga, soggetti sociali e condizione dell'infanzia,"* ed. Cristina Freguja and Maria Clelia Romano. Rome: ISTAT.

———. 2004. *L'interruzione volontaria della gravidanza in Italia: anni 2000–2001,* ed. Marzia Loghi. Rome: ISTAT.

———. 2005a. *Bilancio demografico nazionale, Anno 2004*. July 27, 2005. Rome: ISTAT.

———. 2005b. *Bilancio demografico regionale, Anno 2004*. July 28, 2005. Rome: ISTAT.

John Paul II (pope). 1995a. "Letter of Pope John Paul II to Women." Electronic document, www.vatican.va/holy_father/john_paul_ii/letters/documents/hf_jp-ii_let_29061995_women_en.html, accessed August 28, 2002.

———. 1995b. "Mary Sheds Light on Role of Women." Electronic document, http://www.cin.org/jp951206.html, accessed August 28, 2002.

Kandiyoti, Deniz. 1997. "Gendering the Modern: On Missing Dimensions in the Study of Turkish Modernity." In Bozdoğan and Kasaba, *Rethinking Modernity and National Identity in Turkey,* 113–132.

———. 2002. "Introduction: Reading the Fragments." In Kandiyoti and Saktanbar, *Fragments of Culture,* 1–21.

Kandiyoti, Deniz, and Ayşe Saktanber, eds. 2002. *Fragments of Culture: The Everyday of Modern Turkey.* New Brunswick, NJ: Rutgers University Press.

Kearney, Michael. 1996. *Reconceptualizing the Peasantry: Anthropology in Global Perspective.* Boulder, CO: Westview.

Kemp, Sandra, and Paola Bono, eds. 1993. *The Lonely Mirror: Italian Perspectives on Feminist Theory.* London; New York: Routledge.

Kertzer, David. 1980. *Comrades and Christians: Religion and Political Struggle in Communist Italy.* Cambridge and New York: Cambridge University Press.

———. 1982. "The Liberation of Evelina Zaghi: The Life of an Italian Communist." *Signs: Journal of Women in Culture and Society* 8(1):45–67.

———. 1996. *Politics & Symbols: The Italian Communist Party and the Fall of Communism.* New Haven: Yale University Press.

Kleinman, Arthur. 1995. *Writing at the Margin: Discourse Between Anthropology and Medicine.* Berkeley: University of California Press.

Kligman, Gail. 1998. *The Politics of Duplicity: Controlling Reproduction in Ceauşescu's Romania.* Berkeley: University of California Press.

Kondo, Dorinne. 1990. *Crafting Selves: Power, Gender, and Discourses of Identity in a Japanese Workplace.* Chicago: University of Chicago Press.

Krause, Elizabeth. 2001. "'Empty Cradles' and the Quiet Revolution: Demographic Discourse and Cultural Struggles of Gender, Race, and Class in Italy." *Cultural Anthropology* 16(4):576–611.

———. 2005. *A Crisis of Births: Population Politics and Family-Making in Italy.* Belmont, CA: Wadsworth.

Lancaster, Roger N. 1992. *Life Is Hard: Machismo, Danger, and the Intimacy of Power in Nicaragua.* Berkeley: University of California Press.

Lanza, L. 1991. "La violenza coniugale nel codice penale." In *Senza scampo. Una ricerca sulla violenza coniugale a Milano,* ed. S. Stefanizzi, *Società e violenza* series, Centro Nazionale di difesa e prevenzione sociale. Milan: Centro Stampa della Regione Lombardia.

Lévy-Bruhl, Lucien. 1923. *Primitive Mentality.* Trans. Lilian A. Clare. London: Allen and Unwin.

Li Causi, Luciano. 1993. *Il partito a noi ci ha dato!: antropologia politica di una sezione comunista senese nel dopoguerra.* Siena: Laboratorio EtnoAntropologico.

Lloyd, G. E. R. 1990. *Demystifying Mentalities.* Cambridge and New York: Cambridge University Press.

Loizos, Peter, and Evthymios Papataxiarchis, eds. 1991. *Contested Identities: Gender and Kinship in Modern Greece*. Princeton, NJ: Princeton University Press.

Lunghi, Carla. 2003. *Culture creole: imprenditrici straniere a Milano*. Milan: FrancoAngeli.

Luzi, Maria Pia. 1999. "I nuovi padri fanno i 'mammi.'" *La Gazzetta di Parma*, November 2:8.

Lyons, Harriet. 1999. "Foreword to the Second Edition." In Counts, Brown, and Campbell, *To Have and To Hit*, vii–xiii.

MacClancy, Jeremy, ed. 2002. *Exotic No More: Anthropology on the Front Lines*. Chicago: University of Chicago Press.

MacKinnon, Catharine. 1989. *Toward a Feminist Theory of the State*. Cambridge, MA: Harvard University Press.

Mack Smith, Denis. 1997. *Modern Italy: A Political History*. Ann Arbor: The University of Michigan Press.

Marchesi, Gustavo. 1994. *Storia di Parma*. Rome: Newton Compton.

Marcuzzo, Maria Cristina, and Anna Rossi-Doria. 1987. *La ricerca delle donne: studi femministi in Italia*. Turin: Rosenberg e Sellier.

Marino, Giovanni. 1999. "Lo stupro in jeans non c'è stato." *La Repubblica*. October 14: Cronaca 11.

McClusky, Laura. 2001. *Here, Our Culture Is Hard: Stories of Domestic Violence from a Mayan Community in Belize*. Austin: University of Texas Press.

Merry, Sally Engle. 1994. "Narrating Domestic Violence: Producing the 'Truth' of Violence in 19th and 20th Century Hawaiian Courts." *Law and Social Inquiry* 19(4): 967–993.

Milan Women's Bookstore Collective, The. 1990 [1987]. *Sexual Difference: A Theory of Social-Symbolic Practice*. Trans. Patricia Cicogna and Teresa de Lauretis. Bloomington: Indiana University Press.

Millett, Kate. 1970. *Sexual Politics*. Garden City, NY: Doubleday.

Minicuci, Maria. 1981. *Le strategie matrimoniali in una comunità calabrese: saggi demo-antropologici*. Soveria Mannelli, Italy: Rubbettino.

———. 1988. *Il segreto ovvero della verginità violata*. Soveria Mannelli, Italy: Rubbettino.

———. 1989. *Qui e altrove: famiglie di Calabria e di Argentina*. Milano: F. Angeli.

Mitchell, Juliet, and Ann Oakley, eds. 1986. *What Is Feminism?* Oxford: Blackwell.

Moi, Toril. 1987. *French Feminist Thought: A Reader*. Oxford: Blackwell.

Nardini, Gloria. 1999. *Che Bella Figura!: The Power of Performance in an Italian Ladies' Club in Chicago*. Albany: State University of New York Press.

Nicholson, Linda. 1997. *The Second Wave: A Reader in Feminist Theory*. New York: Routledge.

Ochberg, Richard L., and George C. Rosenwald, eds. 1992. *Storied Lives: The Cultural Politics of Self Understanding*. New Haven, CT: Yale University Press.

Ong, Aihwa. 1999. *Flexible Citizenship: The Cultural Logics of Transnationality*. Durham, NC: Duke University Press.

Oppo, Anna, Simonetta Piccone Stella, and Amalia Signorelli. 2000. *Maternità, identità, scelte: percorsi dell'emancipazione femminile nel Mezzogiorno*. Naples: Liguori.

Ortner, Sherry. 1996. *Making Gender: The Politics and Erotics of Culture*. Boston: Beacon Press.

Padovani, Tullio. 1997. *Codice Penale*. Milan: Giuffrè.

Paini, Anna. 1993. *Boundaries of Difference: Geographical and Social Mobility by Lifuan Women*. PhD diss., Research School of Pacific and Asian Studies, The Australian National University.

———. 1997. "From Parma to Drueulu and Back: Feminism, Anthropology and the Politics of Representation." *Canberra Anthropology* 20(1 and 2):125–146.

Palomba, Rossella. 1997. "I tempi in famiglia." In Barbagli and Saraceno, *Lo Stato delle Famiglie in Italia*, 163–172.

Pandolfi, Mariella. 1991. *Itinerari delle emozioni: Corpo e identità femminile nel Sannio campano*. Milan: F. Angeli.

———. 1998. "Two Italies: Rhetorical Figures of Failed Nationhood." In Schneider, *Italy's "Southern Question,"* 285–289.

Papa, Cristina. 1985. *Dove sono molte braccia è molto pane: famiglia mezzadrile tradizionale e divisione sessuale del lavoro in Umbria*. Foligno: Editoriale Umbra.

Pardo, Italo. 1996. *Managing Existence in Naples: Morality, Action, and Structure*. Cambridge and New York: Cambridge University Press.

Pari Opportunità. 2004. "Lavoro di cura: La condivisione del lavoro di cura fra i generi e le generazioni." Electronic document, www2.provincia.parma.it/page.asp?IDCategoria=1257&IDSezione=7441&IDOggetto=&Tipo=SERVIZIO, accessed April 6, 2006.

Passerini, Luisa. 1991. *Storie di donne e femministe*. Turin: Rosenberg e Sellier.

———. 1993. "The Women's Movement in Italy and the Events of 1968." In Cicioni and Prunster, *Visions and Revisions*, 167–182.

———. 1996. "Gender Relations." In Forgacs and Lumley, *Italian Cultural Studies*, 144–159.

Paxson, Heather. 2004. *Making Modern Mothers: Ethics and Family Planning in Urban Greece*. Berkeley: University of California Press.

Peristiany, John George, ed. 1966. *Honour and Shame: The Values of Mediterranean Society*. Chicago: University of Chicago Press.

Pitkin, Donald S. 1985. *The House that Giacomo Built: History of an Italian Family, 1898–1978*. Cambridge and New York: Cambridge University Press.

Pitt-Rivers, Julian. 1966. "Honour and Social Status." In Peristiany, *Honour and Shame*, 19–77.

Pleck, Elizabeth. 1987. *Domestic Tyranny: The Making of Social Policy against Family Violence from Colonial Times to the Present*. New York: Oxford University Press.

Pratt, Jeff. 1996. "Catholic Culture." In Forgacs and Lumley, *Italian Cultural Studies*, 129–143.

Provincia di Parma. 2001. "Parma." Parma: Ufficio statistica provincia di Parma.

Radcliffe-Brown, A. R. 1952. *Structure and Function in Primitive Society: Essays and Addresses*. Glencoe, IL: Free Press.

Riches, David. 1986. "The Phenomenon of Violence." In Riches, *Anthropology of Violence*, 1–27.

Riches, David, ed. 1986. *The Anthropology of Violence*. Oxford and New York: Blackwell.

Riding, Alan. 2002. "Italian Court Rules that Son Knows Best about Leaving Home." *New York Times* April 6:A3.

Righi, Alessandra. 1997. "La nuzialità." In Barbagli and Saraceno, *Lo Stato delle Famiglie in Italia*, 53–64.

Rizzo, Roberta, and Eugenia Romanelli. 1999. "Per forza o per amore." *L'Espresso* August 19:43–45.

Rofel, Lisa. 1999. *Other Modernities: Gendered Yearnings in China After Socialism*. Berkeley: University of California Press.

Romano, Beda. 1995. "Europa—esplode il problema demografico." *Il Sole 24 Ore* September 11:34.

Romito, Patrizia. 2000. *La violenza di genere su donne e minori: Un'introduzione*. Milan: FrancoAngeli.

Rosaldo, Michelle Zimbalist, and Louise Lamphere, eds. 1974. *Woman, Culture and Society*. Stanford, CA: Stanford University Press.

Rossi-Doria, Anna. 1996. *Diventare cittadine: Il voto delle donne in Italia*. Florence: Giunti.

Sabbadini, Linda Laura. 1999. "Modelli di formazione e organizzazione della famiglia." Paper presented at the conference of the Ministero Solidarietà Sociale, "Le Famiglie Interrogano le Politiche Sociali," Bologna, March 29.

Saraceno, Chiara. 1980. *Uguali e diverse: le trasformazioni dell'identità femminile: percorsi di storia sociale nelle conversazioni a Radiotre*. Bari: De Donato.

———. 1987. *Pluralità e mutamento: riflessioni sull'identità al femminile*, 2nd ed. Milan: FrancoAngeli.

———. 1998. *Mutamenti della famiglia e politiche sociali in Italia*. Bologna: Il Mulino.

Schneider, David. 1984. *A Critique of the Study of Kinship*. Ann Arbor: University of Michigan Press.

Schneider, Jane, ed. 1998. *Italy's "Southern Question": Orientalism in One Country*. Oxford and New York: Berg.

Schneider, Jane, and Peter Schneider. 1976. *Culture and Political Economy in Western Sicily*. New York: Academic Press.

———. 2003. *Reversible Destiny: Mafia, Antimafia, and the Struggle for Palermo*. Berkeley: University of California Press.

Schor, Naomi. 1994. "This Essentialism Which Is Not One: Coming to Grips With Irigaray." In Burke, Schor, and Whitford, *Engaging With Irigaray*, 57–73.

Scott, Joan Wallach. 1988a. "Deconstructing Equality-Versus-Difference: Or, the Uses of Post-structuralist Theory for Feminism." *Feminist Studies* 14(1):33–50.

———. 1988b. *Gender and the Politics of History*. New York: Columbia University Press.

Shils, Edward. 1957. "Primordial, Personal, Sacred and Civil Ties." *British Journal of Sociology* 8:130–145.

Siebert, Renate. 1991. *E femmina, però è bella: Tre generazioni di donne al sud*. Torino: Rosenberg e Sellier.

———. 1999. *Cenerentola non abita più qui: Uno sguardo di donna sulla realtà meridionale*. Torino: Rosenberg e Sellier.

Signorelli, Adriana. 2000. *Genere e generazioni*. Milan: FrancoAngeli.

Signorelli, Amalia. 1983. *Chi può e chi aspetta: giovani e clientelismo in un'area interna del Mezzogiorno*. Naples: Liguori.

———. 1996. *Antropologia urbana: introduzione alla ricerca in Italia*. Milan: Guerini.

Silverman, Sydel. 1975. *Three Bells of Civilization: The Life of an Italian Hill Town*. New York: Columbia University Press.

Simonetti, Maria. 2000. "Mammo, hai fatto carriera." *L'Espresso* January 13: 66–69.

Spivak, Gayatri Chakravorty. 1986. "Subaltern Studies: Deconstructing Historiography." In Guha and Spivak, *Selected Subaltern Studies*, 3–32.

Steedly, Mary Margaret. 1993. *Hanging Without a Rope: Narrative Experience in Colonial and Postcolonial Karoland*. Princeton, NJ: Princeton University Press.

———. 2000. "Modernity and the Memory Artist: The Work of Imagination in Highland Sumatra, 1947–1995." *Comparative Studies in Society and History* 42(4):811–846.

Stewart, Kathleen. 1996. *A Space on the Side of the Road: Cultural Poetics in an "Other" America*. Princeton, NJ: Princeton University Press.

Sutton, David. 1996. "Explosive Debates: Dynamite, Tradition, and the State." *Anthropological Quarterly* 69:66–78.

———. 1998. *Memories Cast in Stone: The Relevance of the Past in Everyday Life*. Oxford and New York: Berg.

Terragni, Laura. 1997a. *Su un corpo di donna: Una ricerca sulla violenza sessuale in Italia*. Milan: FrancoAngeli.

———. 1997b. "La violenza in famiglia." In Barbagli and Saraceno, *Lo stato delle famiglie in Italia*, 184–192.

Tonelli, Matteo. 2001. "È un parlamento sempre meno rosa." *La Repubblica* May 15, electronic document, www.repubblica.it/online/elezioni/donne/donne/donne.html, accessed October 14, 2005.

Trasforini, Maria Antonietta. 1996. "Microfisica della violenza: Una sintesi e un commento ai dati della Casa delle donne." In *Violenza alle donne: Cosa è cambiato?: Esperienze e saperi a confronto*, 118–130. Milan: FrancoAngeli.

Tsing, Anna. 1993. *In the Realm of the Diamond Queen: Marginality in an Out-of-the-Way Place*. Princeton, NJ: Princeton University Press.

United Nations. 2002. *Population Ageing 2002*. New York: United Nations Population Division, Department of Economic and Social Affairs.

University of Chicago, Committee for the Comparative Study of New Nations. 1963. *Old Societies and New States: The Quest for Modernity in Asia and Africa*. Ed. Clifford Geertz. New York: Free Press of Glencoe.

Ventimiglia, Carmine. 1988. *La differenza negata: Ricerca sulla violenza sessuale in Italia*. Milan: FrancoAngeli.

———. 1996. *Nelle segrete stanze: violenze alle donne tra silenzi e testimonianze.* Milan: FrancoAngeli.

———. 2002. *La fiducia tradita: storie dette e raccontate di partner violenti*. Milan: FrancoAngeli.

Visweswaran, Kamala. 1997. "Histories of Feminist Ethnography." *Annual Review of Anthropology* 26:591–621.

Warren, Kay B. 1998. *Indigenous Movements and Their Critics: Pan-Maya Activism in Guatemala*. Princeton, NJ: Princeton University Press.

Warren, Kay B., and Jean E. Jackson. 2003. *Indigenous Movements, Self-Representation, and the State in Latin America*. Austin: University of Texas Press.

WAVE (Women Against Violence Europe). 2005. Electronic document, www.wave-network.org/start.asp?b=5/, accessed September 2, 2005.

Wikan, Unni. 1984. "Shame and Honour: A Contestable Pair." *Man* 19:635–652.

World Resources Institute. 2003. EarthTrends: The Environmental Information Portal. Electronic document, http://earthtrends.wri.org/pdf_library/country_profiles/pop_cou_380.pdf, accessed March 30, 2006.

Yanagisako, Sylvia Junko. 2002. *Producing Culture and Capital: Family Firms in Italy*. Princeton, NJ: Princeton University Press.

Young, Allan. 1995. *The Harmony of Illusions: Inventing Post-Traumatic Stress Disorder*. Princeton, NJ: Princeton University Press.

Index

abandoning conjugal household, 225n9
abortion: Centro Italiano Femminile on,
   51; communist women in campaign
   for, 77; decline in number of, 100,
   221n14; Family Aid and, 95–96, 98, 100,
   173–174; fight for changing women's
   thinking on, 66; leftist and Catholic
   feminism opposed regarding, 69, 71;
   legalization of, 45, 63; referendums of
   1981 on, 216n3; Unione Donne Italiane
   on, 51, 54; younger feminists turning
   their attention to, 53
Abu-Lughod, Lila, 211n11
Addis, Elisabetta, 218n12
adultery, 140, 225n4
affidamento (entrustment), 59, 60
Alcoff, Linda, 213n22
alimony, 90, 146
Alleanza Nazionale, 72, 219n23
Alvesson, Mats, 195
Amoretti, Manuela, 73
antiviolence centers (centri anti-violenza),
   17, 19
Antolisei, Francesco, 139
apathy, political, 73–74
Appadurai, Arjun, 33
appliances: dishwashers, 122, 130; dryers,
   121; household labor increased by,
   223n9; washing machines, 121, 122,
   223n9
Aretxaga, Begoña, 154

Argyrou, Vassos, 16, 36, 152
Arosio, Enrico, 31, 32
autocoscienza (consciousness-raising; self-
   consciousness), 52, 61, 63

Balbo, Laura, 33, 223n8
Banfield, Edward C., 228n1
Barth, Frederick, 35, 213n22
Barzini, Luigi, 212n18
Bassi, Tina Lagostena, 17, 151
Beauvoir, Simone de, 57, 58
Beccalli, Bianca, 46–47, 54
bella figura, 10–13, 24, 119, 122, 127, 156,
   224n14
Beltramo, Mario, 140, 141
Berdahl, Daphne, 35
Berlusconi, Silvio, 127, 219n21
Biblioteca delle Donne (Women's Library),
   61, 220n5
Billing, Yvonne Due, 195
Birnbaum, Lucia, 50, 51–52, 53
birthrate, decline in Italian, 24–29
Bologna, 1, 13, 19, 71, 205n1, 206n3, 206n5
Bonicelli, Emilio, 206n5
Bono, Paola, 53, 55, 56, 57, 60–61
Bottai, Marco, 26
Bourdieu, Pierre, 12
Brandes, Stanley, 109
Brown, Judith K., 13, 15, 202
Brown, Wendy, 162–164
brutta figura, 11, 12, 222n1